The Pearl of Babel

Sacred Etymology

Observations of Ancient Language Development

"Unlocking the secrets origins of sacred writings"

Darrell J. Comte

www.sacredetymology.com | www.darrelljcomte.com

Contents

Preface

The Journey

It's been three decades since the younger version of myself began the path that led to this moment. As I reflect on my younger years, I recall being intensely frustrated by most of my life experiences, a common experience among young people in any generation. My approach to the subject matter differed significantly from today; it began as an emotionally driven endeavor, which led to many frustrations.

One such frustration came from experiencing multiple debates between "Creationism and Evolution." [I felt] the statements and arguments were endless loops of each side's point of view, with some facts to support their positions. Ultimately, I realized it was just about "what team to join" rather than seeking a meaningful understanding between one another. My frustration directed my perception of the arguments as a series of verbal exchanges between ignorance and arrogance. There was an underlying sense that both sides knew something was missing or were avoiding weaker positioning, making the focus about winning for their team.

I wanted better answers, ideally some idea of an "Absolute Truth" or something closer to it — as I said, "I was young," but I did realize this wasn't going to happen from these debates and decided to find answers on my own.

As with many things in life, the way it was being presented: If one was true, the other must be false. To be clear, I rejected the idea of a choice, but instead wondered: "If science is about finding the truth of things (and assuming it's correct) and God's word (the scriptures) has to be true, then both should be the same." So, the question was: Why aren't they the same?

Then my thoughts went to... Perhaps both are true, and maybe it's man's interpretation of the scripture that is flawed.

The first step

When I started, I had many questions: What am I trying to understand? Where should I begin? Why does any of it matter?

I realized the obvious starting point came down to two "seemingly" simple questions:

1- In what language was the Bible originally written?
2- How was biblical translation done?

One of the first things I became aware of is that such questions are not simple to answer, especially when digging deeper.

The rabbit hole(s)

When I first began, I obsessively researched and compiled a mountain of information. As part of this endeavor, I learned about religious **history**, **scripture**, **language**(s), and even **mythology.** The broader my research went, the more I noticed some common elements. The most commonly noticed aspects are the similar *Motifs (recurrent thematic elements)*, *Character types (Archetypes)*, and *Events*, in addition to the fact that other people throughout history have noticed many of the same things.

Specifically, the further I got into biblical scripture, the archetypal connections became apparent with other objects and things. I began to get the sense that everything was connected, like puzzle pieces of a larger, more complex reality. This realization, along with the overwhelming scope of the task brought me to the conclusion this was going to be a lifetime project. I also realized I needed to "live [survive] in the present" — this meant working, making an income, so I could eat, have shelter, etc.

After many years of personal life experiences and exposure to a vast array of topics and fields, particularly as technology has advanced, my understanding has evolved from what initially seemed like a two-dimensional puzzle coming together to something much more complex and dimensional.

One relevant factor is the effect of layering over time, including the interactions of people, as well as the fact that it has a pattern(s) to it.

As time went on, I was exposed to more *"rabbit hole"* topics in the **sciences**, one of which was about the human **mind** and its ability to recognize patterns. The more I expanded into other topics of knowledge, the more I began to realize that *everything* is about *perspective* and *personal interest.* More accurately, I began to understand that *everything* is *connected,* yet *separated* by *perspective and personal interest.*

Creating a Perspective

Regarding the vast amount of information I was getting exposed to. I began to understand "the idea of *perspective*" and how complexity is perceived. The fact is, there are many ways to view anything, and numerous factors that influence what a person thinks they are seeing. In its simplest form, we refer to this as a person's *point of view,* which is also influenced to a varying degree by personal *biases.*

Finding Balance

If everything is a *perception of truth* and all things have meaning, then **finding balance** is the only way to navigate through people's perspectives, like *a raft on water.*

To achieve this, a person needs to be **open-minded** [which is also an idea of *"Being humble before God"*], and includes **compromise** [which is the *sacrificing* of something].

> **Note:** The problem of **compromise** is the *"how this is done."* It can lead to *"Concept of a Greater Good"* [which is to pick a person(s) to be the *loser* or a *"Win-Lose Scenario"* versus finding a *"Win-Win"* version].

One of the better ways is to find *common ground* and build from there. The challenge here is that both sides must be willing and have honest intentions.

Becoming Observationally Aware

The idea of *being objective* is defined as: *not influenced by feelings* or *opinions* in considering and representing facts.

Note: My idea of *being objective* is looking at the *"big picture"* [or a *bird's eye view*].

The idea of being observationally aware is not just with one's own surroundings or time, but also the vastness of time.

Reflection

Understanding history is key to improving our future, but how we use what we can learn will be a *true test of our wisdom.*

After decades of examining various religious groups, scriptures and mythologies, ancient histories and cultures (traditions and practices), I noticed common motifs and narratives [As well as the many others who have referenced it]. There are many conclusions and ideas about why and how this is, which include the conflicting opinions [which is also a *Pattern*).

So, I decided to go back to the initial questions:

#1 — In what language was the Bible originally written?
#2 — How was biblical translation was done?

Section One
The Introduction

Let's begin...
or should I say "In the beginning"

I wanted to understand the Bible's creation narrative — specifically the 6 days [Genesis 1]. To do this, I needed to answer the two original questions I asked myself when I began this "journey," which were:

#1 — In what language was the Bible originally written?

*The answer is both **complicated** and **"not just one"***

The simplest way to answer this is that the older books were written in Hebrew [in its older versions]. Later books were in Aramaic [a sister language to Hebrew], and the latest books were in Koine Greek (the historical version of Greek).

The older versions of Hebrew are often referred to as "Biblical" Hebrew. — Note: Also called **Classical Hebrew.**

What is Biblical Hebrew?

For the sake of some sense of clarity, I will use the basic definition of: *A blanket term applied to much **earlier variants** of Mesopotamian languages — associated with writings which are now part of what is now referred to as "the Bible."*

Note: These **earlier variants** of languages are classified as archaic forms of languages and are labeled as terms like: Paleo-Phoenician / Paleo-Hebrew scripts.

  – Paleo-Phoenician → branched into many others: Greek, Latin (the romance languages: Italian, French, and Spanish, etc), and eventually influenced modern English.

  – Paleo-Hebrew → branched into many others as well: As

1

the ancestor languages to modern Hebrew and Aramaic (which was also used with other books in the Bible).

When it comes down to it, I would say there's no good way to actually get an answer to the question of: *What is "Biblical Hebrew."* The most notable fact is that the numerous variables make this even more complicated. Therefore, [for now], I am going to address the visual aspects of the language(s).

Example of the visual representation of the Paleo-style of writing

There are actually discovered texts written in this form of writing style, which include some of the oldest found. The most notable are known as the Dead Sea Scrolls.

#2 — How was biblical translation done?

The answer is again **complicated** *[I would state:* **"very much so!"** — which is still debated and ongoing in present time.

Personally, I would make the statement that translation begins with *the perspective a person takes* or the *biases they have* — this includes both the time period and culture of those doing the translations, which also leads to a layering effect.

What makes this complicated...

Translation via *Interpretation*

It's important to note that when it comes to translating "ancient" texts, it's not as simple as an *actual "word-for-word"* rendering. The reality is that *translation* [for the most part] is an *interpretation* of *the concept* [of what is being communicated] and as the presumed **intent of the person** *doing the communication (aka: the* **author***).*

What this really means is making a guess based on probability and calculating it using a specific methodology [of which there are many types].

Note: A vast array of interpretations and translations of the ancient words has been developed over thousands of years by many cultures and religious groups.

Another factor beyond methodology that influences interpretation is **time**, specifically the time [time period] when the *original, oldest,* or *older words* were reinterpreted to fit the later timeline of culture and language.

The result of these factors has not only led to the branching of religious organizations into various factions but has also produced hundreds of versions of translations.

How to un-complicate this?

My initial thought was that I would go to the source material: [the *"original"* text] to verify what others have interpreted.

I soon discovered the central issue with the concept of *"original"* text, especially when searching for the oldest writings. In fact, even the oldest writings are copies of an alleged *"original"* version — In other words, there are no longer the actual *"originals."*

So, the idea of finding the oldest version is the key reason for archaeology and discovery. Which is why the discovery and analysis of the Dead Sea Scrolls are and were important, as they are some of the oldest and largest collection of writings we have to date.

In summary: There are not originals – only copies. Although it appears the coping practice has been very well done, it doesn't effectively convey the timeline of the *"original"* [source] material. There's also the question of *"who"* wrote them.

The authorship crediting practice also generates an issue because sometimes texts were *"credited"* to older writers or prophets and their writings).

Note: It's understood to have been done to elevate the "authority" of the additional text.

How have people in the past tried to un-complicate this?

*The simple answer is **they didn't.***

This is where things get really complicated. In fact, the ideas of how to interpret biblical scripture have become so complex that new words and categories have been created to define the nuances of this complexity.

Terms like: ***Theology, Hermeneutics,*** and ***Exegesis***

The What, Why, and Hows of...

Hermeneutics is the *methodology* (and theory) of interpretation, and is considered the branch of knowledge that deals with interpretation. Also, described as the "Art of Interpretation and the study of exegesis."

There are many subcategories of methods or types of Hermeneutics:

> Allegorical... / Literal... / Moral... / Anagogical (Mystical) / Genre Hermeneutics / Spiritualized Interpretation / Historical-Grammatical / Historical-Critical (Higher Criticism) /
> *[There are probably more terms and types]*

Essentially, it's the **perspective** one takes, which will lead to the result(s) one is looking towards.

> *– The concept of the **path** one goes down, is the direction one is aiming at — as the idea of trying to hit a target.*
>
> **Note:** The concept of **Sin** is *to miss the mark."*

The Outcome(s), Conclusion(s) and Justification(s) of...

The discovery from the results of the perspective taken is basically labeled in two different ways/terms:

Exegesis -versus- Eisegesis

Exegesis is a *critical explanation* or *analysis* that includes the actual interpretation of a text. Although this sounds like a positive definition and concept, the term is generally used in a derogatory sense and has often been associated with having a negative reputation.

Whereas, **Eisegesis**, where one reads one's own meaning *into* the text, is much more prone to risk of falseness and influence of personal biases and emotions (especially *ego*).

Theology is the study of religious belief from a religious *(spiritual)* perspective, with a focus on the nature of divinity. It's taught as an academic discipline, typically in universities and seminaries.

In summary, there are various approaches to understanding the scriptures, including the authors' intent, meaning, truth, belief, and the nature of God or gods.

The fact is, there has always been a diversity of perspectives.

> *What all these perspectives have in common*
> *is their own version of "meaning!"*

This brings me back to the first question of the *"original" language,* and I thought: *If I am going to understand the interpretation and translations, perhaps first understanding the language from its origins and development is a good starting point.*

> **Note:** None of the biblical text discovered [at least to date] was written in the Glyph form, but the real question is: *was it ever?*

Origins of the Biblical Hebrew

Many (if not all) ancient human cultures developed a variety of stylized glyphs for recording information (but also as a *visual imagery of an aspect of meaning).* This process may have begun with a smaller number of glyphs, which then grew over time into thousands of them. So many that it was probably only a select few, highly educated individuals that could have the knowledge of this complexity.

Eventually, in Mesopotamia, a consolidated and limited set of glyphs was chosen. This set of glyphs is sometimes referred to as the "First" Alphabet. There are very few artifacts found in the glyph form, but more common archaeological discoveries are in the later writing versions. Examples of this later alphabet are classified as terms like: the Paleo-Phoenician and the Paleo-Hebrew scripts – *(Also called the Canaanite/Semitic languages).*

> **Note:** As the name implies, it evolved into the Hebrew and other sister languages, including Aramaic *(used in the books of Daniel and Ezra).*
> Through the Phoenicians *(sea-faring merchants)*, it evolved or influenced the development of what became the later Greek language, which influenced what became Latin, which influenced the Romance languages: Italian, French, Spanish — but also had influenced German and English.

Glyphs to Letters
The Visual Evolution

However, even these "Paleo" versions of writing had predecessors, classified as Proto-Sinaitic or Proto-Canaanite. These are named in relation to the location of their discoveries, in either the southern or northern regions of the Ancient Near East lands. The artifacts found are described as inscriptions in stone (sometimes also called *Pictograms* or the *Pictographic script*), and are what is known in simple terms as *"Glyphs."*

Many groups of people in the ancient Near East developed glyphs. The images represented seem influenced by their demographics, religious beliefs, and livelihoods. The graphic depictions were diverse, numbering in the thousands, and used by many cultures, from the Hieroglyphs of the Egyptians to the early Sumerian writings. The complexity of the visual representations eventually evolved into streamlined versions within each culture.

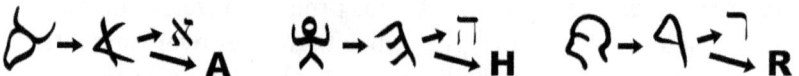

Dia. A Evolution of Glyphs to Letters (Proto- -> Paleo- -> modern)

> **Note:** The *"Glyph"* Alphabet was the proverbial "seed" for the development of a vast array of our modern languages.

There have been many changes in these evolving languages throughout history, both visually and functionally. However, the Hebrew language continued using the names of the original Glyphs to the letters they represent.

> **Note:** As a standard practice, Linguistic scholars study Ancient languages from the perspective of the sounds (pronunciations) associated with the corresponding Glyphs, and they generally categorize the method of interpretation based on the symbolic attributes or meanings, as mystical or metaphysical.
>
> The Hebrew language maintained the balance of the visual image and meaning through what is called: *Kabbalah*.

Letters and Meaning

The method of reapplying *"meaning"* to these letters has created different results, leading to religious, spiritual, and even mystical outcomes. The variety of these outcomes stems from the focus of a particular lens or perspective.

This aspect of Hebrew letters and analyzing *meaning* through a metaphysical lens isolates *"thought"* as a concept of truth, which led to the Jewish, esoteric method called **Kabbalah** (described as *"received wisdom"* and defined as *hidden or secret knowledge.*

> **Note: *Esoteric*** *definition:* Intended for or understood by only a small group, especially one with specialized knowledge or interests.

Over time, this has become associated with the term *"mysticism"* and branched to other types of mysticism practices, including many of the new age beliefs.

> **Note:** For many people, the idea of *Mysticism* is viewed to be a *magical* or *"woo-woo"* practice.

This idea of some *deeper or hidden* connection of *meaning* is **not** from some random association applied to the letters or words. The connection to these *meanings* is actually related to the attributes of the original glyphs from which the letters evolved.

Quick referencing tools

There are two referencing tags that will be attached to most of the Hebrew words:

1) The very commonly used numbering code from the Strong's Concordance, written as *<H###>*. While it is widely used, it has limitations and can lead to misunderstandings. Some consider it outdated and simplified, and recommend using modern, academic-standard resources instead.

2) A Hebrew to English letter code, which functions has a quick, visual "letter to letter" from Hebrew to English as the words are written, rather than how they sound.

Note: The Hebrew words are written from Right to Left, and the English word is written from Left to Right.

An example of these is the English translation of the name, **Adam** from the Hebrew spelling אדם *<H121>* which are the Hebrew letters: *Aleph + Dalet + Mem* generates the Hebrew/English letter code of **(ADM)**. This provides a visual understanding of the Ancient language in it's written form, and not just as an oral translation.

<u>Here is a quick reference to the Hebrew/English letter code</u>

א *Aleph* = **(A)**	ל *Lam* = **(L)**
ב *Bet* = **(B)**	מ *Mem* = **(M)**
ג *Gimal* = **(G)**	נ *Nun* = **(N)**
ד *Dalet* = **(D)**	ס *Samekh* = **(S)**
ה *Hey* = **(H)**	ע *Ayin* = **(a)**
ו *Vav* = **(V)**	פ *Pey* = **(P)**
ז *Zayin* = **(Z)**	צ *Tsadi* = **(Ts)**
ח *Chet* = **(Ch)**	ק *Quph* = **(Q)**
ט *Thet* = **(Th)**	ר *Rosh* = **(R)**
י *Yud* = **(Y)**	ש *Shin* = **(Sh)**
כ *Kaph* = **(K)**	ת *Tav* = **(T)**

Section Two

Glyphs

When trying to find information on an actual understanding of the Glyphs connected to the Hebrew letters, there are all types of speculation and assertions. The fact of the matter is that the amount of archaeological discoveries or "evidence" of the ancient Mesopotamian Glyphs, a.k.a. "Proto-languages" are rare and few.

Image: Proto-Sinaitic inscription #346

Below are representations of images of Ancient Glyphs, specifically the 22 letter Alphabet which eventually became the Hebrew Alphabet.

Note: And through the Phoenicians evolved or influenced the development of the later Greek — and making its way to influencing Latin, romance languages (Italian, French and Spanish) and eventually influencing English.

ል

The **Head of Ox**

"Traditional" Meanings: ***Strength, Power, Leader***

In ancient times, and still used by many people in today's time, the ox was simply the ***power*** animal, or the forerunner of the tractor. Due to the ***strength*** of these hardy beasts, nomadic and farming cultures used them to pull carts by tying ropes around their horns. Later, with the invention of the yoke, which bound two oxen together. Additionally, the farming community used them to pull a plowshare, the upgraded process of tilling the soil compared to doing it by hand. This cooperation brings forth the plants needed for farmers' survival, while oxen are cared for in return.

Its positioning as the first letter in the Alphabet represents the **leadership** position. The conceptual imagery of the relationship between putting the oxen up in front, as the source of ***power*** *(pulling forward)*, and the farmer stabilizing *(side to side motion)* the plowshare *(tilting in and pulling back)* as they till the soil "together".

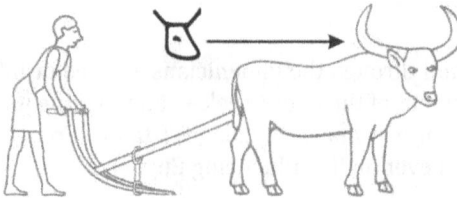

Fig. 1-1 Tiller of Soil, Plowshare, and Ox

The next component represents *perception*. In this case, it's the relationship a Farmer *[Tiller of the Soil]* has with the Ox. Symbolizing Mankind's *expression of...* and *relationship with* "God."

> **Note:** The visual imagery as the **Head** of the Alphabet can then infer the collection of letters after it symbolizes the rest of the body of the **Ox** — *[which may have some connection to the "Golden calf" story (with Moses and Aaron) - as a failure (or sin) of it | as well as, the generalized "Bull worship" of many ancient cultures]*.

The symbolic nature of the "Head" also seems to suggest the concept of location, as the *"place where the spirit resides."* Symbolically, the concept of *Spirit, Mind,* and *Thought* are interchangeable. When applying the *concept of thought* to God, it represents the idea of **"First Cause"** or the "Primordial Origins."

Thus, the "Head of __" can also be understood conceptually as the "Spirit of __" or "Mind of __." At its core, the "Head of Ox" glyph represents the **Mind of God**, and as the concept of the *"All knowing"* or *absolute knowledge.*

א

The Hebrew letter is written as א, pronounced as *Aleph* or *Alef* אלפ (ALP), which is also the word for Oxen.

A

In English, it's the letter "A". Additionally, it can be translated as the letter "E" (based on Hebrew pronunciation within specific words).

> **Note:** The use of the A versus E appears to function as a symbolic aspect of relating the (A) to a grounded or earthly connection (the ox) versus the (E) as an *elevated* or sky/ heavenly connection (the winged Ox, or other winged creatures — like Eagles (birds), Angels, etc.).

Examples of this pronunciation function:

אלהימ (ALHYM) *"Elohim"* [the plural version] or אל (AL) *"El"* [the singular version] as, **God** *(concept of Sky God/Father)*

אדמ (ADM) *"Adam"* translated as: *"Man or Mankind"*

* symbolically as (concept of God's Creation in His Image [on Earth] – also as the concept of God's Offspring/Son [as Earthly and the Grounded Father]. Later, **Abram**, as *Exalted Father* [the idea of the Mountain Father = as up high, but not winged], versus the "God Most High."

Note: This concept of two levels, as higher and lower, also relates to the idea of the *"Greater* and *Lesser"* or even as the *Heavenly* and *Earthly.*

Comprehensive "Conceptual" Meanings
Summary of Symbolic representation:

[God *"Greater"* level]

Mind of God *(aka: Spirit of God)*
[God's] Thought(s), as the ***"First Cause"***

[Man *"Lesser"* level]

*Begins with [God], then reflected to the image of Mankind [aka: ...in the image of God] – as that which gives us **Power, Strength,** and **Leadership.***

The Tent

"Traditional" Meanings: **House, Family**

For nomadic cultures, a **tent** is the **"family home,"** a portable shelter that provides protection from the elements and serves as a place to eat meals or sleep. Additionally, tents served various other purposes, including meetings and worship. Another term associated with this Glyph is the fixed version of shelter, called a **"hut."**

In modern terms, the word is understood as a **"house."** Although there are various cultural descriptions and types of shelters, they fundamentally represent the concept of *structures used by the community.*

> **Note:** When any type of structure [tent or building] is used for worship, terminology is changed and referred to as: *Places of Worship, Temples, Churches, etc.,* but still implies "God's House" or "House of God."

The extracted and generalized concept is that of **structure**, but this is the state that results from the *effort* being brought forward. However, if the Glyph is viewed from a bird's-eye view, it can be understood as a *floor plan* or *blueprint* — it conveys the concept of **initial planning**.

> **Note:** The (Hut/House/Home) is a place where plans are conceived and given birth. Traditionally, men made the plans [the masculine aspect], but conceptually [the feminine aspect], like the Mother's womb, or where incubation occurs.
> The generalized concept *[as a trope]* is also the idea "from darkness comes light" — as the starting place is dark (nothing) and then is brought into the light (understanding/ thoughts/ideas).

Note: The extracted concepts of אב (AB) <*H1*> translated as: *"Father"* = *"Strength of the family", "Leader of the house,"* but also as: *"God's Plan"* or *"God's Blueprint."*

When the letter is used as a prefix, it's most commonly translated as *"In,"* as in "to go into" or even "to be within" an object or event.

ב

The Hebrew letter is written as ב, pronounced as *Bet* בית (BYT), which is also the word for *Tent/House*.

B

In English, it is the letter, B. but translations based on Hebrew pronunciation are written either a **B** or **Bh**. Additionally, can be translated as the letter (V) [based on Hebrew pronunciation].

Comprehensive "Conceptual" Meanings
Summary of Symbolic representation:

[God *"Greater"* level]

[God's] Blueprint / Plan

[Man *"Lesser"* level]

*Begins with [God], then reflected to the image of Mankind as that which gives us **Family** and a **Home**.*

L **Ḷ**

The **Throwing Stick** *"Boomerang"*

[Also known as, the **Foot**]

"Traditional" Meanings: ***to Hunt | Gather, Walk***

The relationship of the two glyphs is a direct correlation to the term "hunter-gatherers." These communities used ***hunting*** tools, such as *throwing sticks*, to kill (catch) agile prey. Whereas the gatherers ***walked*** around to ***gather*** fruits, nuts, and more.

In addition, the early farmers ***walked*** behind a plowshare that an ox or oxen was pulling. The common link between both glyphs is the concept, "To go (out) and return with." Additionally, this can be taken further by considering the connection to survival—to obtain (***hunt*** or **gather**) food, which is part of the process of farming the food (nourishment).

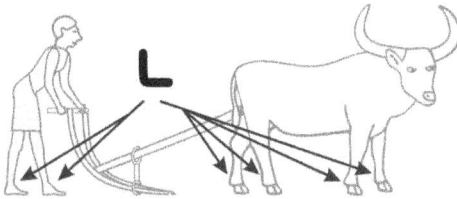

Fig. 1-2 Tiller of Soil, Plowshare, and Ox

In relation to the nomadic culture, they **walked** with the flock, as shepherds, to move, watch over, and **gather** their flock when there was a need to do so.

All of these actions can be generalized as completing a circular pattern, or making a loop, as well as the concept of preparation (as the earlier, or basic gathering "getting" of food/resources).

The glyph conveys the "*effort*" of the feet (G), as a relationship to "*Balance*" versus the glyph of the bent arm (Y), which conveys the "*effort*" of the hands/arm, as it relates to the "*Effect*" (with "*Cause* and *Effect*").

ג

The Hebrew letter is written as ג, pronounced as
Gimel/Gamal גמל (GML)

G

In English, it's the G, but it is also the origin of what branched or evolved into the letter C.

> **Note:** The *Gamal* גמל (GML) in biblical translations as *<H1581>* "Camel," but also as *<H1580>* translating as "*to wean, or ripen, or to deal fully.*"

The common thread between each of these descriptions is the concept of completing a circle.

– The camel was a merchant transport to travel back and forth on the trade route.
– Newborn Life is weaned when the infancy cycle is complete, fruit ripens to complete its growing process to provide nourishment, and to deal fully, or complete a full circle.

Symbolically, as completion (or cycle) of the journey (trade route), but also as a concept of preparation [completion of the stage as the first step of a larger purpose].

The first two letters as root, גמ (GM) *<H1571>* translated as: "*also | even, indeed, moreover*" [also is connected to a meaning of *assemblage*]

The Glyph meanings as "*Gathering/Preparation + <brings forth> Life/Truth,*" represent the "Balance of Nature." The idea of the preparation needed prior to planting the seeds of Life is the *"finding the balance"* (within the soil - nutrients, water, and sun) – but this is not just the bringing of life, it's also the relationship of prey and hunter (as death comes – in order to bring Life).

The concept of a duality to balance and how this comes with some sort of sacrifice (as a *give and take* -or- *the ebb and flow*).

Comprehensive "Conceptual" Meanings
Summary of Symbolic representation:

[God *"Greater"* level]

[God's] Preparation

[Man *"Lesser"* level]

Begins with [God], then reflected to the image of Mankind as the ability to **Hunt** *and* **Gather** *(Navigate/Survive the environment).*

17

The **Door** [*related*, the **Fish**]

"Traditional" Meanings: ***Entrance, Hang | Move***

The farming and nomadic cultures share this connection from the tent/house to a door as the ***entrance***. The Door is the symbolic image of a ***movement*** [as in passing *"through a door"* to enter the tent].

> **Note:** The use of a fish symbolizes this same concept of ***movement***, but within the water. The origin of this glyph would most likely have been (demographically) near the water among fishing communities.

The related imagery between both glyphs represents the concept of *"Moving toward, into, around, or within,"* and can be generalized as *"A **pathway** from, within, or to [something]."*

ד

The Hebrew letter is written as ד, pronounced as *Dalet* דלת (DLT) *<H1817>* translated as: *"Door"* (and the Fish is the דג (DG) *Digg/Dag* *<H1709>* translated as: *"Fish"*).

D

In English, it is the D.

Comprehensive "Conceptual" Meanings
Summary of Symbolic representation:

[God *"Greater"* level]

[God's] Path - [as the "Way"]
(representing Direction or Process)

[Man *"Lesser"* level]

*Begins with [God], then reflected to the image of Mankind (representing our choice(s), as the how [or way] we **move** through the environment/life: Individual Freewill, Belief, Careers, etc...)*

The point of a transition from one to another:

door *or* **doorway**

– or-

just **"the Way"**

(**Note:** The way one goes about [a thing] is a type of **methodology**, but influenced by **biases**]

The **Man with arms raised**

"Traditional" Meanings: ***Reveal, Look, Breath***

Putting our hands up and waving them to get someone's attention is an instinctual form of communication. This action is to get someone to ***look*** at you and ***reveal*** your location. In addition, when a person realizes something that should have been obvious, they will throw their hands up in the air. The association meaning as ***"breath"*** likely originates from the idea that God's Revelation to man is to ***breathe*** life into him.

It's the "Aha" moment, which is the encapsulation of the Revealing (H) *with the mind of God* (A).

In addition, when this letter is used as a prefix to many root words used in the Ancient Hebrew scripture, it's commonly translated as *"The."* This may be a functional translation on the surface, but it lacks the emphasis of ***"revealing"*** or ***"revelation."*** In addition to being the stage of the realization [of what to do next], it can also be viewed as a connection to a *"Call to Action."*

ה

The Hebrew letter is written as: ה, pronounced as: *Hey/Hay,* הא (HA).

H

In English, it's the letter H.

Note: An example of the symbolic use of this letter meaning function is in Genesis 17 when God makes a covenant with Abram; he's given the new name *Abraham* אברהמ (ABRHM) *<H85>*. This name was changed by adding the letter *Hey* (H), meaning *"to reveal,"* which directly implies an act of embedding (or receiving) *Revelation, gaining wisdom,* or *becoming more enlightened.* This descriptive storytelling within the letters is a common practice. If we break down the name *Abram* אברמ (ABRM) *<H87>* into its root words, something interesting happens. The אב (AB) *<H1>*, as noted earlier, translates as: *"Father,"* plus the רמ (RM) *<H7410>*, which translates as: *"high"* or *"exalted."* Abram, described as the *"Exalted Father,"* is the actual meaning embedded in the name itself. Interestingly, the (H) is added in the middle of the (RM), which presents the visual aspect of ascending up the mountaintop (as being *"exalted"*) to receive God's Revelation *[describing what Moses did to receive God's Revelations].*

Comprehensive "Conceptual" Meanings
Summary of Symbolic representation:

[God *"Greater"* level]

[God's] Revelation
(things that are revealed along the path or come out of the process)

[Man *"Lesser"* level]

*Begins with [God], then reflected to the image of Mankind as our **inspirations***
*Also represented as "The **Breath** of Life," and "Giving" Purpose to one's Life*

- represented as Concept, like: Gifts of the Holy Spirit (God)
The Breath of Life - a "Giving" Purpose to one's life.

Y

The **Tent peg**

"Traditional" Meanings: ***Secure, Add, Hook***

The meaning of this glyph is directly associated with the function of a tent peg, which is used to **hook** and provides the ability to **secure** the tent. The process of staking one peg after the other to **secure** the tent is the process of **adding** one after another.

When this letter is used as a prefix to many root words, it's commonly translated as *"And."* Although this may be linguistically functional, it only implies the concept of *addition*, which does not account for the direct relationship of the glyph that represents connection — the idea of ***anchoring*** or ***tethering***.

These concepts of *providing support (as tethering)* can also be related to the function of the umbilical cord, the physical ***tethering** of mother and child,* which will bring about the ***addition*** of an offspring to the tent (family).

The other characteristics of the *umbilical cord concept* are that it serves as a *"gateway"* (or *transition*) object of ***interaction*** between them, and the ***holding back*** of the child until they are ready to come into the world.

> **Note:** Other related concepts of this meaning are its similarity to what we observe with Gravity, both holding back objects from floating off the Earth's surface and causing the river waters to flow down the mountain, and its relationship to the giving birth process, as the stage of conception, as well as a symbolic umbilical cord.

Note: Other aspects of meaning are the initial stages of *conception, fertilization*, as well as the **attachment device/object** of tools used to aid in planting the seeds (during/after tilling the soil).

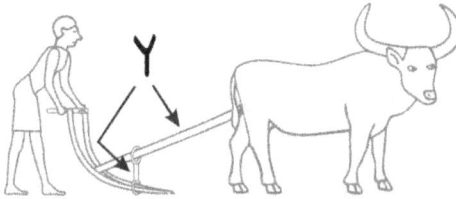

Fig. 1-3 Tiller of Soil, tethering/anchoring Plowshare to Ox

ו

The Hebrew letter is written as ו, pronounced as *Vav* וו (VV)

V

In English, it's translated based on pronunciation as either a V, W, O, or U.

Comprehensive "Conceptual" Meanings
Summary of Symbolic representation:

[God *"Greater"* level]

[God's] Connection <Restraint>
(All things are connected — the linking interactions)

[Man *"Lesser"* level]

Begins with [God], then reflected to the image of Mankind as our **connection, linking to,** *and* **interactions** *with all things.*

⌐⊏

The **Mattock** (Hoe/Spade/Farming tool)

"Traditional" Meanings: ***Food, Nourish, Cut***

This glyph is called the mattock (used in the hand of man), but it can also be seen as the plowshare (used in the hands of a man, while walking behind and being pulled by an ox). Both are ancient farming tools that serve the same function and are still in use today in various adaptations.

The mattock and plowshare evolved from a single-function tool to a two-tool combination. The first is a knife or pick that ***cuts*** the hardened topsoil, while the other is designed to widen the opening in the soil to drop in the seed. The purpose of processing the soil to plant seeds is to prepare the land for the next stage, or action, to achieve the harvest. The direct connection the tool has to farming and the harvest is to grow ***food*** for ***nourishing*** the community.

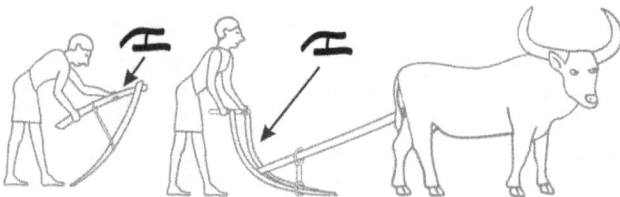

Fig. 1-4 Tiller of Soil (Singular - Mattock vs. Plural - Plowshare and Ox)

ז

The Hebrew letter is written as ז, pronounced as
Zayin זֵיִן (ZYN)

Z

In English, it's the Z.

Note: When comparing the relationship of the Gimal (G) as to gathering, or getting food(resources), to the Zayin (Z) as farming food(resources), there is a potential to have a similar meaning associated with words. The Gimal (G) can imply an earlier or first condition, whereas the Zayin (Z) represents a later or more developed one.

An example of this idea of earlier/later concept is the use of the word גֵּה (GH) *<H1454> used only once in* Ezekiel 47:13 [it's notes as probably *a scribal error* from זֵה (ZH) *<H2088>* which translated as: "*this*"}, but the (GH) infers the use of the [*shall be*] after the "*This*" in the translation. It shows a connection to its position or state [in time], (as concepts of past/present/future tense).

Comprehensive "Conceptual" Meanings
Summary of Symbolic representation:

[God *"Greater"* level]

[God's] Tool(s)
{representing device(s) that aid in progress}

[Man *"Lesser"* level]

*Begins with [God], then reflected to image of Mankind as our **devices**, not just as **physical tools** – but "**aspect of awareness** - as improving upon" – and as the critical development (and importance) of **opportunity**.*

*This may also represent the **motives** (and **coping mechanisms**) this is where the positive & negative aspects of choice come in.*

*(Mattock as, Weapon vs. Hoe) (Sword vs. Plowshare)
(as the two aspects of Creation: Destruction vs. Creation)*

25

ᗤ

The **Tent Wall** (Fence)

"Traditional" Meanings: ***Divide, Half, Outside***

Again, the relationship between the description of the tent wall and a fence can be compared to the Nomad/Farmer relationship, but serves a related function in keeping others ***outside*** of an area.

目

Fig. # Another version is described as a courtyard

In ancient times, courtyards (used as a private outdoor area) were often used as gathering spaces for the elite, as a symbol of power and wealth. They would be adorned with elaborate fountains, lush gardens, and intricate designs.

ח

The Hebrew letter is written as ח, pronounced as *Chet* חית (ChYT)

Ch

In English, it's translated based on pronunciation as either a (Ch) or (Hh).

Note: As a word, it is used in Genesis 1:30 | חית (ChYT) <H2416>, translated as, *beast [of the earth]* — then in the same line the (T) is replaced by the (H) which is the word , חיה (ChYH) <H2416>, translated as, *life*

Additionally, there is the related idea of branching off [concept of the branches of a tree or of a river] — *diversity [of family]*

In Hebrew, this is represented as חא (ACh), translated as: "*Brother*." The concept of the *branching of the family* symbolically represents the tree [aka: Family Tree]. In general, this connects to any branching off.

Note: This can also be symbolically, as a different relationship to an *external* branching of a *"brother."* As an *internal* branching — used in Genesis 2:22 "the creation of woman" from the *rib or side,* symbolizing *the partnership* of man(kind).

Firstly, man*(Adam)* is represented as alone like the exterior view or shell of the tent [probably, symbol of the protector/protection [like the skin of the family unit = body], and the creation of woman as the separation of the interior of the tent (as the *rib* - both as a protection to the heart and something that was removed from it) – as well as, a symbol of the protector/protection of the heart of the family unit = body].

Symbolic of a Man and Woman, when they unite, it's the actual reuniting of the original one, symbolizing the return to "*Oneness*" (the concept of a soul mate).

The name *Eve* is actually spelled in Hebrew with the *Chet,* as חוה (ChVH) <H2332>

Additionally, The *Nomadic* **tent wall** divides the outside from the inside, and divides the interior living area in half. [the common are from the private area -the veil]

Within the Ancient nomadic culture, the entryway or common area to the tent was known as the man's area, and the private area was known as the woman's area. The woman's area was designated for mothers to care for the children, and was also the "bedding" area. This privacy barrier concept is further represented, by the veil that women wear [as a mobile (personal) "tent wall"].

Comprehensive "Conceptual" Meanings
Summary of Symbolic representation:

[God *"Greater"* level]

[God's] Diversity
as a Branching Off <like branch(es) on a tree, maybe from "Tree of Life">

[Man *"Lesser"* level]

Begins with [God], then reflected to the image of Mankind
*as both **evolving** and **separating***

The **Basket**

"Traditional" Meanings: ***Surround, Contain, Mud/Clay***

When relating the word ***Basket*** there is a disconnect of importance from the perspective of time. In ancient times, it was not just the idea of making a basket, but the complexity of *weaving reed* to create products. A common and robust industry throughout Mesopotamia from the Sumerians to the Egyptians.

The method of reed weaving *(or reed craftsmanship)* expanded from the concept of a basket as a storage and transportation vessel to the reed boat as a water transportation vessel.

The general concept of *"products that have been produced by weaving together."*

Note: In a similar process, items such as *nets* and *eel pots* [the double basket trap] are made for catching fish.

The functional aspect of a **basket**, as *"to hold or **contain** [something or items],"* is also related to **clay** pottery.

The reed grass, as a material resource, was also used to make musical instruments and papyrus *(used as a source for Ancient Egyptian writing material versus the Sumerian writing material, which was the* clay tablets).

The idea of the process of weaving together the same material to make a functional product is expanded to the mixing of two different products *(grass and clay/mud)* used in the construction of *"mud brick"* to *"grass reinforced mud-brick."*

Note: The functional similarity to fiber-reinforced cement we use today (as well as *fiberglass* & *carbon-fiber* products).

> Other creation stories of the ancient Mesopotamia people included ideas of *wicker baskets* as *"the offspring of the gods"* floating on a great body of water, which dirt was then placed on the floating basket to make the land.

ט

The Hebrew letter is written as ט, pronounced as
Thet טית (ThYT)

Th

In English, it's translated based on pronunciation as
either a T or Th.

Note: The Hebrew word, טב (ThB) *<H2869>* defined as: *"good, pleases, fine* (used to describe the purity of [gold])

Symbolically, the *"Basket + brings forth -> Blueprint/Plan."* As a concept of "contained" or a portion of the *Plan,* which could infer: the part(s) of *"God's Plan"* and as *"being what is pure or the purity like gold."*

Additionally, the notion of *weaving a basket* or *shaping of clay into a bowl* is akin to the *molding or linking of people* [as a *Tribe*]. By extension, this could be the idea of *God's plan* for a group or tribe of people.

Other words with the letter association:
* טיח (ThYCh) *<H2915>* translated as: *mortar, plaster*
* טיט (ThYTh) *<H2916>* translated as: *mud, clay, calamity*
* טין (ThYN) *<H2917>* translated as: *clay.*

Comprehensive "Conceptual" Meanings
Summary of Symbolic representation:

[God *"Greater"* level]

[God's] Container(s) (or Clay)
{representing both that which can be or is developed into something}

[Man *"Lesser"* level]

*Begins with [God], then reflected to the image of Mankind as both our **limitation**, and **what we limit** (as **surrounded** and **containing**).*

The **bent Arm**

"Traditional" Meanings: ***Work, Throw, Labor, Worship***

The connection of a glyph of a bent arm is an easy leap to symbolic meanings representing things like work, labor, and throwing. The word worship means to labor or work for God. It's been described as the visual imagery of making a gripping action such as holding a tool [like a Mattock (the glyph, Zayin) or the Ox Goad (the glyph, Lam)].

This relationship to farming presents the action/effort of the hand and arm [as the tilling of the soil], whether using the mattock to hand dig or the ox goad to direct the oxen pulling the plowshare. Also, holding a weapon in the hand, like the Throwing Stick (the glyph, Gimal), which is also the action/effort of throwing.

> **Note:** Here is an example of the Ancient word building: The Hebrew word, יגב (YGB) *<H3009>*, defined as *"to dig or plow,"* starts withe the letter meaning *"action/effort"* and continues with a two letter root word, גב (GB) *<H3540>*, defined as *"back [of man]."* Symbolically, like the phrase *"Put your back into it,"* this represents hard work, and from a farmer's perspective, as to the action of *tilling the soil.*

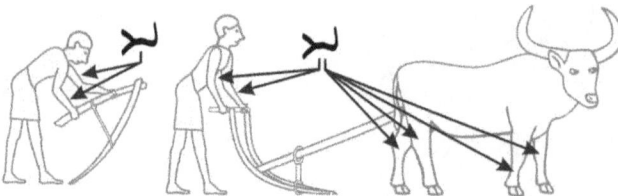

1-5 *Efforts* of the Tiller of the Soil and Ox

The relationship the *Yud* (Y) has to the *Vav* (V) = These concepts of providing support can also be related to the function of the umbilical cord, the physical tethering (of mother and child), which will bring about the addition of an offspring to the tent (family).

The *Yud* (Y) represents the ***effort*** brought forth from after the tethering/anchoring (V). Like what a person accomplishes after birth, or being held back (by outside forces or even oneself), the balloon floating away after the string is cut, the baby bird leaving the nest, etc...

Note: The image of the glyph of the *Yud* (Y) is as the *Vav* (V), but it's presented as fallen or laying down (the efforts of mankind after the fall as mankind re-birth after the gaining of the knowing of good and evil or the fruit of the tree of...) | and seeming represents the umbilical cord attached as the birth of is after = birthed from!

י

The Hebrew letter is written as י, pronounced as *Yud* יוד (YVD)

E

In English it is translated based on pronunciation as either a Y or I.

Note: This letter has evolved from the Hebrew *Yud* (Y) to Greek/Latin as (I), to Germanic (J), which is still pronounced as the "yo" sound, then to English, pronounced as the "jay" sound. As a result, we get transliterated words from *Yahweh* יהוה (YHVH) to *Jehovah*, *Iyov* איוב (AYVB) to *Job*, and *Yeshua* ישוע (YShVa) to *Iesous* to *Jesus*.

Comprehensive "Conceptual" Meanings
Summary of Symbolic representation:

<u>[God *"Greater"* level]</u>

[God's] Process
*{representing the effort, movement, or action as representing
the act of giving birth or bringing forth}*

Example: As the passage [of time/life] = יַם *(YM) Effort brings forth Life}*

<u>[Man *"Lesser"* level]</u>

Begins with [God], then reflected to the image of Mankind's **effort**, **work
(worship)**, *or* **action** *as representing the act of giving birth or bringing forth.*

Example: As the continuing [of lineages/generations] = יַנ *(YN)*

ᴜᴜ

The **Open Palm** (Sling)

"Traditional" Meanings: ***Bend, Open, Allow, Tame***

This glyph is known as the open palm or the upturned palm, and the symbolic imagery of the open palm stems back to a primal instinct of submission. A vast range of animals exhibit a related response of submission, which can range from lowering the body or head, and bending the spine and arms to protect head and neck from larger animals, to a pet dog turning up its belly. More advanced creatures, such as primates use these types of instinctual gestures as basic forms of communication. The upturned palm is still used as a form of submission, as in asking for help or food, which is employed by both humans and other primates, such as chimpanzees, apes, and monkeys. The use of gestures as a form of language is still evident in modern times, as seen in the instinctual movement of our hands while talking, as well as the use of a handshake, which serves as both a greeting and a symbol of sealing an agreement or bond of trust. Many of these types of gestures represent a primal openness or the submission-dominance relationship, allowing oneself to be tamed, or a bending of one's will.

כ

The Hebrew letter is written as כ, pronounced as
Kaph or *Kaf* ףכ (KP)

K

In English, it's either a K or Kh.

Hebrew words using this letter have a connection to man, often as a relationship to the hand, as with כתב (KTB) <H3789>, defined as *"to write down."*

In a generalized concept, this letter represents the idea of the *"primal"* nature of things as the driving source of intent, which can be viewed as *the flesh or body* [versus *the mind or thoughts*].

> **Note:** The relationship to the *bending of the spline* to become **upright** [walking upright on 2 legs] — as a *challenge* or *suffering* event [to fight the primitive nature of the body]
> -*versus*- The nature's (or the wild) default to be on all fours.
> The physical reflection of the **Spirit of Human "will,"** which is also the [reflecting God's "Will"]
> * Related to the (Ch): *the stage after the clay (the molding of...)*
> — the (K): the *human body (flesh is that which contains us),*
> [like a puppet, to our own will (controlling the strings)]
>
> [Similar to the phrase: "*Mind over Matter*"]

Comprehensive "Conceptual" Meanings
Summary of Symbolic representation:

[God *"Greater"* level]

[God's] Flesh (Body)

{representing being surrounded by God's presence or being cupped in the hands of God — it is what holds mankind together, like the protective flesh of humans — concepts of God becoming flesh}

[Man *"Lesser"* level]

Begins with [God], then reflected to the image of Mankind as [been given] flesh (body) – also the limitations of the physical existence.

The **Ox Goad** (Shepherd Staff)

"Traditional" Meanings: ***Teach, Yoke, Bind, Toward***

The ox goad was an implement used to spur or guide the livestock while they pulled plowshares, wagons, and even boats. It was a long stick (rod) with a pointed end, and at times had a metal object attached to strengthen the tip. The modern extension of the word "goad" reflects a type of pain associated with being pricked.

The other description, as the *Shepherd staff*, also known as a *crook*, was a gentler version of guiding, used with sheep. The latter meaning of a shepherd's staff is a less painful tool with a similar function, but it exchanges the strong ox with the passive sheep.

The function of this tool gives the person wielding it the ability to direct the movement of the animal, thus extending the meaning to symbolize the concept of "Authority," as it represents an extension of influence from something or someone other than itself.

Also defined as a part of something that is hook-shaped, curved, or bent, which represents the negative side of this, which also leads to another definition meaning, *crook*, a person who engages in fraudulent or criminal practices — the warning here is that things learned can have a negative (false [prophets]) side to them.

Overall, the idea is to educate through the ***teaching*** process, assisting in moving ***towards*** a path or direction. The concept of ***binding*** is related to the function of the ***yoke***, which was used to ***bind*** two oxen together to increase their power to pull. It was also a way to train a younger ox by pairing it with an older, seasoned one.

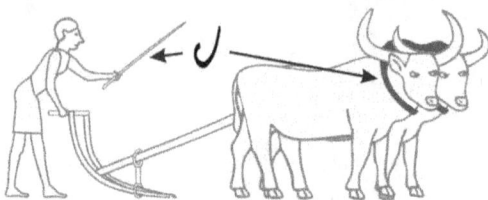

Fig. 1-6 Tiller of Soil, Plowshare, and Ox using Ox goad

Note: (Also, when 2 oxen are used, the **yoke** binds them together)

ל

The Hebrew letter is written as ל, pronounced as Lam or Lamed
למד (LMD)

L

In English, it's the L.

Comprehensive "Conceptual" Meanings
Summary of Symbolic representation:

[God _"Greater"_ level]

[God's] Teaching/Lessons

[Man _"Lesser"_ level]

*Begins with [God], then reflected to the image of
Mankind's **learning** and **teaching**.*

ᴧᴧ

The **Water**

"Traditional" Meanings: ***Chaos, Might, Blood***

The water glyph is an image of a wavy line, and variations of this imagery are still used today. Chaos describes the disorder of the surface of the water, as waves. Might represents the force of the movement of water, as tides.

The generalized understanding of water encompasses both a physical and a fluid nature [symbolically, the Lifeblood of all creation], and the metaphysical counterpart, Truth. The direct connection to life is the [red] water of life, or Blood; symbolically flowing through man, like a river.

> **Note:** The concept of Water representing *"Life"* appears to have been the initial meaning and, at some point, expanded to include the connection to *"Truth."*

The Hebrew word דם (DM) *<H1818>* translated as: *"Blood."* The glyph of the Door, meaning Pathway, and the glyph of Water, meaning Life and Truth, generate the phrase "the Path/Way brings forth Life/Truth."

> **Note:** A New Testament example of this is John 14:6 | Jesus answered, "I am the way and the truth and the life." Is the Hebrew letter, the *Dalet*, ד (D), and the *Mem*, מ (M). Furthermore, by adding the א (A), as a prefix to דם (DM) it generates the word, אדם (ADM) *<H120>*. Thus, by understanding the meanings, one could read as the "Strength(A) of the Blood(DM)," as well as, "Mind of God" (A) brings forth the "Path" (D) of "Life and Truth" (M).

39

מ

The Hebrew letter is written as מ, pronounced as Mem מֵם (MM)

M

In English, it's the M.

Note: אֵם (AM) <H517> translated as: *"Mother,"* which is the *Head of the Ox* (A) and the *Water* (M).

The glyph concept of *God*, as the *"Mind of God"* (A) = <brings forth> *"Life"* (M) = from the *"Mind of God"* comes the *"Life"* = connecting making **life** to the "Mother" terminology.

Comprehensive "Conceptual" Meanings
Summary of Symbolic representation:

[God *"Greater"* level]

[God's] Might
{representing the chaos brings forth order = Life}

[Man *"Lesser"* level]

*Begins with [God], then reflected to the image of Mankind's **Blood**
{representing the order brings forth chaos = perception of Truth}*

* Humans seek the Spirit/"Divine/God" which is seeking Truth

The ebb and flow of water "sea/ocean" as the Life to Truth [represents ebb and flow of chaos to order and back to chaos, repeating...]

The **Seed** (Sprout), **Snake**
"Traditional" Meanings: *Continue, Heir, Son*

The glyph is known as the *seed* [also, the *snake*]. Visually, the glyph resembles the appearance of a seed as it begins to sprout. It's the beginning state and the growth thereafter that defines the meaning as **Continue**, **Heir**, and **Son**.

The basic concept of meaning suggests the idea of *"it is to be"* or *"so it is"* and its function is used to infer a connection to the **generation(s)** to come as well as the **generation(s)** themselves.

The use of the letter [as a suffix] can infer both the singular and the plural, which is usually connected with the use of the *Yud* (Y). This would imply the *"efforts of or leading to that which is to be."*

Note: The general idea of the Seed Glyph is as a representation of bringing forth a [something] that will grow into another [something], or simply the concept of evolving.

נ

The Hebrew letter is written as נ, pronounced as Nun נונ (NVN)

N

In English, it's the N.

Note: In the English language, the influence and use of the "N" to represent generations is seen as a plural ending to groupings of people, like *America* to *Americans* and *Child* to *Children.*

Comprehensive "Conceptual" Meanings
Summary of Symbolic representation:

[God *"Greater"* level]

[God's] Snake/Serpent

{representing the concepts of setting in motion as planning for the future — of outcome of the moment <God's wrath is like the snake bite — of the clever, faster (a free) moving is the vantage point of God level}

[Man *"Lesser"* level]

*Begins with [God], then reflected to the image of Mankind's **Sprouting Seed** {the potential(sprouting) growth as outcome — the now is a sprout but will become a plan/tree | representing the generations of offspring | concept of planting and growing ideas as planning for the future}*

Concepts of the adaptive, slower (restricted, as planted seed) moving (as sprouting) is the vantage point of the mankind level (grounded, locked in time)

The **Thorn**

"Traditional" Meanings: ***Grab, Protect, Hate***

The connection of **grabbing**, as the meaning of the Thorn glyph, is an obvious one, but the others are not. The function of thorns on a plant is for **protection**, serving as a natural deterrent to keep animals from eating or reaching the fruit of the plant. The result of getting cut by the thorns may be a connection to the notion of **hate**.

There is an ancient Sumerian myth involving Gilgamesh. It describes a plant deep in the sea covered in thorns. While touching it would cause severe cuts, but eating it would make old men young again. The plant is dubbed the special plant of resurrection, and also implies the concept of being "Born Again." Visually, this presents the experiencing of life as harsh, but if they (the plant and experiencing life) are overcome, along with the act of taking them in (eating them), which leads to the path to wisdom and enlightenment. There are also other ancient Mesopotamian references to "thorned" plants, and with a connection to medicines and healing.

> **Note:** Another use of the letter is with the word יסד (YSD) <H3245>, defined as *"to set, establish,"* which has the Glyph/ Letter meaning of the *Effort of the Grabbing a Path*. The basic concept is to make the base of an object permanent, as with affixing a house to a foundation versus the flexibility of movement provided by a tent and pegs.

The aspect of the thorn infers that a rigid stance or way of thinking has the potential to cause *"pain"* or *"hate,"* whereas being *"flexible"* is to be open-minded.

The duality of the thorn can also be seen in the comparison to the *red rose*, where the rigid/hard thorn relates the red flower color to blood, and the *white lily*, where the soft thorn relates the white flower to protection and purity.

> **Note:** Like the idea of the (Ch) letter, as the *branching* (or splitting of...) "brother(s)" — the (S), as the *duality* of the thorn (representing the **negative** and the **positive**).

ס

The Hebrew letter is written as ס, pronounced as
Samekh סמכ (SMK)

S

In English, it's the S.

> **Note:** The Hebrew word סוכ (SVK) *<H5480>* defined as *"anoint,"* and is the Glyphs of the Thorn + Tent Peg + Open Palm *[duality/choice of good/bad + interaction + flesh/body].*

Comprehensive "Conceptual" Meanings
Summary of Symbolic representation:

[God *"Greater"* level]

[God's] Lotus Flower
{representing the dual nature of type thorned stems of flower —

As, a way to Protect}

[Man *"Lesser"* level]

Begins with [God], then reflected to the image of Mankind's **Thorn**

{representing the dualities (good and bad outcomes of... basis, ignorance & arrogance — the idea of the "potential to go either way".}

The **Eye**

"Traditional" Meanings: ***Watch, Know, Shade***

The glyph of the *Eye* has a direct connection to the function of the eye as the visual sensory device that transmits observable data to the mind. Observation is the direct connection to the meaning of **watching**, and it is the initial process of gaining **knowledge** of something. The eye is a device, a tool, and a symbolic image of the observation from the edge of darkness (the unknown) to the peak of light (the **known**). The ability of the eye to function is dependent on the existence of light, which objects in the line of sight cast **shadows,** obstructing the light of the sun. The use of describing the various degrees of colors, starting from the primary colors, is called shades of a color, which refers to the relationship between dark and light when it reacts to a particular color.

The ancient use of this symbolism is deeply connected to Egyptian culture and beliefs, including the sky gods, ruling or chief deities, and a later connection to the god of writing, wisdom, and learning.

Mankind's interaction with creation begins with the act of witnessing, which involves taking in data through the eye. Then the observations enter the mind as thoughts and then exit back out through the mouth as speech. This generalized concept of the eye as an input device and the mouth as an output device generates the visual cycle, which forms a continuous loop that can symbolically represent the eye from another eye's perspective.

ע

The Hebrew letter is written as ע, pronounced as *Ayin* עין (aYN)

(a)

In English, it's also pronounced as an A (a) sound.

Note: The letter/glyph, the *Eye*, and its connection to observing the physical attributes of creation, The letter ע is used in this way of connection with many Hebrew words in Genesis 1, such as רקיע (RQYa) *<H7545>*, which translated as: *an extended surface, expanse, firmament*; עשב (aShB) *<H6212>*, which translated as: *plant, grass, the herb*; מזריע (MZRYa) *<H2232>*, which translated as: *yielding, to sow, scatter seed*; זרע (ZRa) *<H2233>*, which translated as: *seed, a sowing, seed, offspring, descendants* to name a few.

Another Hebrew word with this interrelationship is *Yada,* ידע (YDa) *<H1843>* defined as: *"to know."*

Comprehensive "Conceptual" Meanings
Summary of Symbolic representation:

[God *"Greater"* level]

[God's] All-seeing Eye
{representing the What God's sees is clearer <Absolute Truth> than Man <Perceived or Perception of Truth>}

[Man *"Lesser"* level]

Begins with [God], then reflected to the image of Mankind's Third Eye {representing the Observations, Physically Seeing with eyes; and how the mind sees: Perceptions} <Perceived or Perception of Truth(s)>

The **Mouth** / (Corner?)

"Traditional" Meanings: ***Blow, Scatter, Edge, Open***

The glyph known as the mouth is presented as the *mouth* [of man]. There is also another glyph associated with this meaning that is the image of the double line, questionably thought to represent "corner". Even though it relates to the other glyph, it could represent the edges of a riverbank at the point it transitions into the sea or the *mouth* of the river.

Regardless, the meanings associated with it are connected to the mouth, such as the ability to ***blow*** air from the mouth. The definition of ***scatter*** is to go in various random directions and dispersed amounts of something, which is the visual of the way a river cuts through the land, and the connection to speech, as opinions or beliefs. It can also represent the general direction or path of thoughts seeking truth, not as a straight line, but branching in different directions.

Additional connection to a mouth is to the lips, which are the ***edges*** of the mouth, and in comparison to a river having two banks or edges, which transition to the ***opening*** of the mouth of both (man and sea/river).

> **Note:** The concept of the eye as input and the mouth as output is to represent the mouth as speech or to be spoken, and an aspect of what we *"to take in"* to ourselves, like food, or to be nourished, versus an observation.

An example of the connection of meaning as ***scatter*** can be seen with the Hebrew word, פָּאָה (PAH) *<H6284>*, defined as: *scatter/cleave/into pieces* (into the corners).

פ

The Hebrew letter is written as פ,
pronounced as *Pe* or *Pey* פֵא (PA)

P

In English, it's the P and Ph.

Comprehensive "Conceptual" Meanings
Summary of Symbolic representation:

[God *"Greater"* level]

[God's] Mouth
{representing the breath of life (as creating life) and speaking creation, etc.. }

[Man *"Lesser"* level]

Begins with [God], then reflected to the image of Mankind's mouth

{representing the breath of life (in order to life), and speaking words represents the reflection of creation , and eating to sustain life, etc..}

⌒∿

The **Man on his side** (Also, the fish hook)

"Traditional" Meanings: ***Wait, Snare, Chase, Hunt***

The glyph is depicted as a man lying on his side, and its meanings are associated with aspects related to **hunting** and **fishing**. **Waiting** is what is done before the arrival of something (The patience of **waiting** "stalking" for prey); the **snare** is set to trap the animal for food; the **chase** is what is done before the target is caught; hunting is to search for prey (the thrill of the **hunt**). Also, as the generalized connection to *"laying down"* – as to *overcoming or death to a foe*. Also, as *the submission of* (*to bow down* or *submit to*) – the idea of *"on bended knee."*

> **Note:** Other observations of the Glyph/Letter's function and use in words — displays a relationship to a type of incubation process: to fertilize (or water) the crops, or a visual imagery of the fetal position. The relationship to *Farming* as the transition from seed to the initial spouting (into plants/trees/crops).
>
> צאה (TsAH) <*H6627*> translated as: *excrement, dung* [which is nature's fertilizer] — used only twice (Deut. 23:13, Ezek. 4:12), but the actual letters used are צאת (TsAT). Also has a root connection to the word, יצא (YTsA) <*H3318*> translated as: *to go out, to come out, to bring forth, to flow [as a river], went out [flew as a bird], etc...* – used many times in Genesis

49

Note: The general concept is part of a process as a stage prior to the outcome. In addition, as possible connections to other Glyphs: the Seed (*Nun*) drawn as a solid head with a tail, which has a similar look but as a hollow head or circle, like concepts of an egg cracking open or an eye opening. This imagery could represent the concept of what emerges from or results from the growth of the seed.

The first use of the letter in Genesis 1 is with the Hebrew word הארץ (HARTs), which has the prefix letter ה (H). This is usually translated as *"the"* in conjunction with the root word: ארץ(ARTs) *<H776>*, which is defined as *"earth, land."*

Note: Furthermore, there is a symbolic relationship of the letter as the *"Fall of Man"* — this represents the "Location" where God placed Man to dwell and connects to an incubation of man = as the *Earth.*

Other examples of Hebrew words using the Tsade, and the connection of being part to the stage prior to the outcome, which is the word צלעת (TsLaT) *<H6763>*, which translated as *side* or *"rib"* from the Genesis 2 story [The creation of woman from the rib of man].

Note: The letter meanings read as the stage prior, or the incubation. The ribs form a shelter for the vital organs of the body as part of the incubation of life [as the egg is the shell to life].

The connection to the use of the *Tsade* [to the woman] within the word: rib, and the woman/Eve relationship to *motherhood.* In addition to the relationship to different words using the *Tsade*, such as the translated word *"Earth"* (ARTs), which represents a much larger shelter and part of the incubation of life [a connection to the term *"Mother Earth"*].

Note: other words relate to *Army, warfare* and make reference to this as: *making the belly swell* [which also is a attribute of *being pregnant*]. There is an interrelationship of aspects of *war and motherhood,* which seems to connect to the aspects of Creation and Destruction [also, like the function of the Glyph: *Mattock – used as a weapon of war or as a tool to grow crops*].

צ

The Hebrew letter is written as צ, pronounced as
Tsade or *sade* צדי (TsDY)

Ts

In English, it's the Ts, as well as the C.

The word closely associated with this letter is צדיק (TsDYQ) *tzadik,* which means *"a righteous person."*

> **Note:** *As from after the* (Ts) *or the "Fall" is the* (DY) = as (D) *the path (or way) that brings forth the* (Y) *effort*
>
> *– versus –*
>
> *The reflective order* (YD) = as *an effort* (Y) *bringing forth a path (or way).*

...which is represented by the word: ציד (TsYD) *<H6718>* translated as: *hunter, game (venison)* | meaning: *hunting, provisions, the chase, to catch food.*

> *The idea of "How one lives or behaves after the "Fall" or even from hardships or sufferings — also, as a behavior to the treatment of others: symbolically, as a hunter who preys on others = "predator" -or- the bringer of food to others as a hunter-hero of the people = "savior ."*

Comprehensive "Conceptual" Meanings
Summary of Symbolic representation:

[God *"Greater"* level]

[God's] Snare/Fish hook
{representing the "laying things out and waiting for action" as the way God interacts with life/creation}

[Man *"Lesser"* level]

Begins with [God], then reflected to the image of Mankind's Hunt

{representing the stalking action and dangers of the hunt, as the way Man interacts with life/creation}

The **Sun on the horizon**

"Traditional" Meanings: ***Time, Circle, Condense***

The specifics of what this glyph represents (as well as the other glyphs connecting to it) are noted as being of uncertain representation. The commonly accepted description is that of the sun on the horizon, with the imagery representing the cycle of the sun setting, rising, and setting. This cycle generates the concept of a circle and indicates a measurement of time.

> **Note:** Additionally, it's suggested to be a depiction of *the eye of a [sewing] needle* | (Hebrew קוף *quf* and Aramaic קופא *qopa* both refer to *the eye of a needle*), or *the back of a head and neck* (*qāf* in Arabic meant *"nape"*).

> Also, connected to the Greek letter Φ *Phi,* which is often called the *golden ratio* (because it's related to many patterns and proportions in nature, art, and architecture) – described as an irrational number, meaning that it has an **infinite** number of digits after the decimal point that never repeat. In addition, there is a relationship to the Fibonacci sequence and Π *Pi (a mathematical constant that is the ratio of a circle's circumference to its diameter).*

The generalized concept is the idea of how things begin and end, or as the connection to the process of existing within the light. The process is measured in terms of time and represents how the physical world interacts with itself through the motion of events. This motion or movement encompasses the expansion of the universe, the evolution of life, and the interaction of mankind with one another and their surroundings. It's the "what" to nature of existence, and the fountain that supports everything; without this motion our experiences would have no meaning. It's the pattern of this motion [as a circle, or recycling] which is key to understand the process and meaning of the glyph.

The relationship to **condense** [as it relates to time] may be connected to how the passage of time can affect (bring change) as well as the breaking down physical (organic) things as they age into rot, ruin, and eventually as dust. It is the ultimate recycle or re-circle.

Another glyph related to the *Quph* is known as a Proto-Sinaitic version, which is drawn as two circles ╄ and described as *a monkey*.

The description of a monkey and its tail has been associated with this glyph as well. ⏀

The concept of the dual circles and re-cycling is represented by a similar image, the infinity symbol. ∞

The Hebrew word for this letter, קוף (QVP), but it is also the word <H6971> which translates as: "*ape.*"
— used in 1 Kings 10:22 "*... and **apes** =* וקפים (VQPYM)
— used in 2 Chronicles 9:21 "*... and **apes** =* וקופים (VQVPYM)

ק

The Hebrew letter is written as ק, pronounced as
Quph, Quf or *Qof* קוף (QVP)

Q

In English, it's the Q.

* The (QP) with the (V) as interaction but holding back the past and bringing forth the spoken — representing time as that which will become the past, and is the present, and becomes the future. (QP) symbolized a process of building up, as gathering or stacking up, but in density or thickening [like a mountain or a stalagmite].

Comprehensive "Conceptual" Meanings
Summary of Symbolic representation:

[God *"Greater"* level]

[God's] as Infinite
{{representing the position beyond Time / as the continual "looping" circle}}
within (and throughout) time, the past <ancient> concept is the garden
story, the cycling/factual repeat process is the motion of time

[Man *"Lesser"* level]

Begins with [God], then reflected to the image of Mankind's as **Finite**
{representing the position in Time / placement within or along the circle}

Simply understand it as the ***"Past"*** *or as "Past Ways"*

The **Head of man**

"Traditional" Meanings: ***First, Top, Beginning***

The glyph is the Head of man. The Head is the external location of the input locations of the senses: Mouth, Eyes, Ears, and Nose. The meanings of **first** and **beginning** can represent the initial input of the senses, which is then transmitted to the brain and processed as "thought." The head of man is the imagery used to relate the interaction of the physical devices of input, but it is the non-physical essence of mankind's "thought" that is at the core of this glyph's meaning.

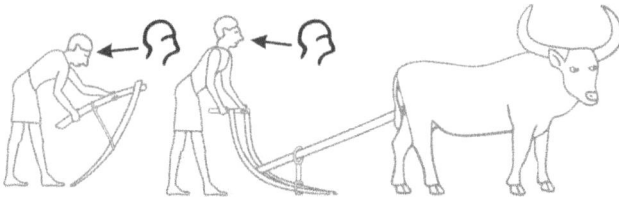

Fig. 1-7 The Head of Man [Tiller of Soil]

The connection of the letter meaning, **top**, is the location of the head to the body and it is also known as the crown, which represents the ruler or authority. The basic concept of a ruler is that of a leader of the people, as our thoughts are what rules [governs] our body.   A modern example of this would be the way we use the word ***perception***, which is defined as the ability to see, hear, or become aware of something through the senses.

As with the Head of the Ox, associated with the concept of a vantage point or perception of the Supreme Father (God), the Head of Man is a concept of representation from mankind's vantage point or perceptions. It's the concept of origin of what guides our actions, or as a ruling point of *"thought,"* and symbolized as the crown [the head piece of the ruler].

Another related concept is found in Jewish Kabbalah where the ten *Sephirot* associated with the process of creation, the **top** of which is known as the *Keter* [the *"Crown"*].

> The symbolic nature of the glyph is the ***first cause*** (the Head) of ***perception*** (of man.), and is the primordial aspect of ***creativity*** – or simply the concept of the ***Mind of Man***.

> **Note:** When words are combined with the two heads, Head of Ox (Aleph) and Head of Man (Rosh) which represents an interrelationship between a point of view of the Supreme (aspect of God) and perceptions of mankind. This can be seen in the first line of Genesis 1, which uses the combination of the two letters in the words that translate as *"In the beginning"*, *"creates,"* and *"Earth"*, as well as the third line of Genesis, which uses it with the word that translates as *"Light."*

ר

The Hebrew letter is written as ר, pronounced as
Rosh or *Resh* ריש (RYSh)

R

In English, it's the R.

Comprehensive "Conceptual" Meanings
Summary of Symbolic representation:

[God *"Greater"* level]

[God's] as [son] | Mind of Man
{representing the relationship to god's mind to man's mind}

[Man *"Lesser"* level]

Begins with [God], then reflected to the image of Mankind's Mind (thoughts)
{representing the } [Spirit of Man]

⊔⊔

The **Two front teeth**

"Traditional" Meanings: ***Sharp, Press, Eat, (Two)***

The glyph represents the *two* front teeth and serves the function of cutting food or taking the first bite. They are narrow-edged or **sharper** than other teeth for the function of **pressing** down and tearing into for the purpose of **eating**. It is also associated with both the **Sun** and **God**, or *the Sun god*, which in many cultures is *"creator god."* The relationship to creation is both bringing forth and destruction, and as both the light (brought forth) and fire (warmth and destruction).

> **Note:** The aspect of the two front teeth as a creation god symbology is in Central American myth, representing the creator god as a **Beaver**.

Another less-direct connection to this is in the use of swords, a narrow-edged tool/weapon with a function similar to that teeth, which represents a connection of creation and destruction. The concept of ***creation*** must be born from ***destruction*** can be seen with the Hebrew words described as *"destruction"* are שׁד (ShD) *<H7701>* and שׁדד (ShDD) *<H7703>*. Even further, by using a descriptive name of God, translated as *"God Almighty,"* אל שׁדי (AL ShDY) *<H7706>* actually translates better as: *God whom brings Destruction and Creation through His Efforts* — used in Genesis 17:1 as said to Abram, *"I am the God Almighty; Walk before Me..."*

The attribute of destruction is the breaking down or breaking apart of one thing and reassembling the parts into something new. It's this basic understanding that connects the ancient glyph and its meaning, and represents the *concept "to penetrate or something to take in."*

The connection of mankind's *"something to take in"* as a part of the creation process in in the Hebrew word, שֵׁד (ShD) <H7699>, translated as *breast,* the physical link to feeding or nourishing (to what was giving birth to). This link can be one of the reasons that the letter *Shin* is presented as the word ending with the N (Nun), the *seed/offspring (potential),* as a part of the process of creation. The idea of: *from that which was from broken down parts and born (or re-born in a continuous cycle).* It's this process that is translated as: "*Mighty."*

> **Note:** I have to mention the hand gesture the character *Spock* used in Star Trek. The formation of the hand is the letter *Shin.*
> The use of this gesture dates back to Jewish Priests holding up both arms with hands forming this letter in front of the congregation. An interesting observation is the Priest's stance is forming the glyph, *Hey (or the revealing/revelation).* The visual and symbolic nature of the stance of the Priest represents man's perceptions (the *Kaph*) and the *Hey,* extending out through the *Shin,* representing that which penetrates and reveals, and what we are open to. Symbolically, this can read as *"To take in, the revealing nature of the Creator."*

שׁ

The Hebrew letter is written as שׁ, pronounced as *Shin* שִׁין (ShYN)

Sh

In English, it's the Sh.

Note: The letter (Sh) is also very connected to the words/function/ symbolic = ***lamb*** (as with prepping to be slaughtered for the future survival) = the concept of *"prey animals"* to *"predator animals",* as the functioning of *Aspects of Creation*

Comprehensive "Conceptual" Meanings
Summary of Symbolic representation:

[God *"Greater"* level]

[God's] Duality
{representing the Father/son, Father/mother , etc...}

[Man *"Lesser"* level]

Begins with [God], then reflected to the image of Mankind's duality

{representing the positive and negative, good and evil, group and individual}

✝

The **Crossed Sticks**

"Traditional" Meanings: ***Mark, Sign, Monument***

There are many symbolic uses of crossed sticks, as well as the obvious use of the concept of *"X"* **marks** *the spot,* by to putting up crossed sticks to mark graves. The function of a **monument** is defined as something erected in memory of a person, event, or other significant occurrence. A sign serves both as a physical representation to **mark** the spot and as a non-physical representation, such as visions. The basic concept is to link together a fixed location to a fixed time. The other two glyphs/ letters that use the "T" sound are 1) the Basket glyph (*Thet,* ט), which is the completed weaving together of the reeds. The process of fastening together by twisting two strands at a time to reinforce and strengthen lesser things to create a greater one: This is the idea of "One-ness" and "Re-birth"; 2) The glyph of the Man on his side and also, the Fish hook (*Tsade,* צ), which is also represented as a "TS".

ת

The Hebrew letter is written as t, pronounced as *Tav* תו (TV)

T

in English, it's the Th.

Note: The Hebrew word, אמת (AMT) meaning *'Truth"*

The symbolic representation from the Glyph meanings: (A) =
The *First Cause*, or the *All-knowledge* | + → (M) = *Life/Truth* | + → (T)
= *Weaved together* = "Matrix" (as the *divine* process of weaving to
make a *universe* basket containing a life (Creation).

Comprehensive "Conceptual" Meanings
Summary of Symbolic representation:

[God *"Greater"* level]

[God's] Matrix

*Symbolically (or visually) things like: a [fishing] net, [vines] lattice,
weaving [of baskets], {representing the completion <complexity> of the
whole of creation, as one [interconnected] structure}*

[Man *"Lesser"* level]

*Begins with [God], then reflected to the image of Mankind's **Signs** <from God>
which is the Weaving together, or to see aspects of the matrix (seeing the patterns, as
well as making and working with them).*
** The use of a Monument is to mark the crossroads of an intersection (the
intersection between life and death is marked the crossed sticks <cross>, tombstone,
mausoleum as the monument)*

Section Three

Grammar

Language/Word Development

Currently, we understand and define the idea of **Grammar** as the **system** and **structure** of language.

— The idea of **Language** | *is understood as how **words** are used to communicate.*
— The idea of **Words** | *are made up of a combination of **letters** which produce a reference to a particular **meaning**.*

Construct of Words

To verify and clarify the meaning of a particular word, we also have dictionaries to look up definitions. Additionally, there are etymology dictionaries to look up the history and cultural influence of a word.

When researching the **etymologies of words**, one common occurrence that can be observed is the ***concept of a figure of speech*** and how it relates to explanation of *meaning*.

Example: The "Etymology" of the English word: ***Grammar***
— *from* late 14c Latin, *Grammar* – meaning: *Rules of [letters/language]*
— *from* 12c. French, *Grammaire* – meaning: *Magic of [letters/language]*

Note: Also, from here – into: *Grimoire* – meaning *"Book of Magic"*
— *from older* Greek, *Grammatike* – meaning: *Art of [letters/language]*

One feature of reviewing how words were understood is noticing the fluid nature of the *perception of meaning* and its relationship to *time* and the influence of *culture(s)*.

The shift in perception and understanding of words [or the variants of them] appears to have a direct correlation to the *time period and the people's way of life (culture)*. When researching word origins, there is a noticeable *layering effect*, like the geography of the layers of rock in canyon walls tells their story of development, or in archaeology, excavating down unearths layers of time and cultures that had built settlements upon settlements.

The idea of using the concept of *figure of speech* to assist (or guide) in generating visual imagery that compares one thing to another as a method to transmit and understand a concept (idea), and as a method to bring clarity to a *perspective of thought.*

As language developed over time, words shifted and expanded in an attempt to improve the precision of thought and communication. The development of words narrowed to more individual and specific associations to objects or concepts, but traces of the original, figurative relationship can still be found.

The linguistic attempt to develop a degree of precision in words and meaning *has been **layering*** (and *evolving*) *over time* and has created a feature of perception [of *"what was once the past understanding is a **hidden** perspective of meaning."*]

> **Note:** As a method of describing this process of a single starting point, layering over time and being hidden, an appropriate figurative comparison would be to link it to development of a *"pearl",* which begins as a single grain of sand *and ironically begins as an irritation of a foreign body, but grows and develops into something which is eventually viewed as both valuable and beautiful.* — by extension, to understand the growth of the *pearl "of words"* is to know their *"Etymology."*

Perception of Language

As an understanding of the concept of *"figure of speech"* in the **culture of farming**, which is also noticeable in the imagery of the Glyphs, another similar relationship and connection to meaning is found within Kabbalah, where they are described as the *Seeds of Creation.*

> **Note:** The "Etymology" of the English word: **Culture**
> *from* mid-15c., *"the tilling of land, act of preparing the earth for crops,"* from Latin *cultura* – meaning: *"a cultivating, agriculture,"* figuratively *"care, culture, an honoring,"*

The fact that the *farming motif* is the dominant function, with some overlapping connections to *nomadic (shepherding), fishing,* and *hunter-gatherer* activities and attributes. These motifs represent the nature of human living as the *"Life they Live."*

> **Note:** The correlation to the *farmer motifs,* as over-taking the *nomadic or shepherding motifs,* is reflected in the story of Cain *(Tiller of Soil)* killing and burying his brother, Abel *(the Shepherd).* — Symbolically, the *"killing aspect"* refers to a greater focus on *farming motifs,* in relation to the language structuring, and the *"burying* aspect" implies the intentional shift and may have happened slowly over time.

Development of Language

Expanding on the idea of the *farming motif* relationship to language development.

Format perspective as:

The process of the tiller of the soil is the preparation of the soil for the planting of the seeds, which will become the crops.

> The *crops* | the *outcome* or the idea of an *end product* = as symbolic of the concept of *Language.*
>
> The *seeds* [the *raw materials*] = as the Glyphs/*Letters.*

As a method of *word building*, aligning with the symbolic process of *seed* development would be a logical structural formatting choice.

Seed Construct

The current description of the Hebrew language is described as *primarily* based on a function of *trilateral* roots, or 3-letter root words [based on *consonants,* which correlate to the letters of the Hebrew Alphabet (as *consonants,* not *vowels*)]. Although most roots in Hebrew seem to be *trilateral,* many of them are *bilateral* (2-letter roots).

The concept of root words may describe an observed pattern regarding *how* the language is structured, but this does not explain *why* the roots were developed. As a premise of the developing structure, a link to the *pattern* of a seed transitioning into a seedling can be observed in a three-stage format.

The key stages are:

— The first stage: the "**Dry Seed**"

["Seed Dormancy" or the "Dormant Seed" = Dehydrated Seed | the plant-life version of hibernation of the seed].

— The second step: the "**Watered Seed**"

[Re-hydrated Seed] or the watering as an "external" influence to initiate seed growth — the "what sparked it into life" — to motivate it to fulfill its potential – [maybe even the concept of re-birth or renewed awakening!] as the "Watered Seed."

— The third stage: the "**Sprouting Seed**"

[is the sprouting of life that comes from the seed.]

The basic three-step **process** can be described as reflection of the *Path of the Seed* = **The Seed's Journey**, and also correlates to the word development structure as a **construct** of word building:

as **Structure**

1 - "**Dry Seed**" — directly relates to a 1-letter (or glyph)
2 - "**Watered Seed**" — directly relates to a 2-letter roots
3 - "**Sprouting Seed**" — directly relates to a 3 letter roots

Also, as reflecting the *Concept of "Cause and Effect"* – [as coming from the *"First Cause"* – the concept of the *Mind of God* (Aleph)]

as **Concept**

1 - "**Dry Seed**" — Concept of *Potential*
2 - "**Watered Seed**" — Concept of *Inspiration*
3 - "**Sprouting Seed**" — Concept of *Outcome*

If this pattern is continued and repeated as a layered process of time, it can be expanded to another level of a correlated (or reflected) structure. Following the process of the development of a seed into a plant.

As the second cycle of the 3-stage model

The Flower's Journey,
as *"The Flower to Fruit Path"*

as **Structure**

4 - "**Flower**" — relates to 4-letter words
5 - "**Pollinating Flower**" — relates to 5-letter words
6 - "**Fruit**" — relates to 6-letter words

Also, as reflecting the *Concept of Life*:

as **Concept**

4 - "**Flower**" — Concept of *Plant-life*
5 - "**Pollinating Flower**" — Concept of *Reproduction* [Birth/Rebirth]
6 - "**Fruit**" — Concept of *Animal/Human-life*

As the third cycle of the 3-stage model

The Adam's Journey
as *"The Path of Life"*
[In regard to "Animal/Human Life" versus "Plant-life"]

as **Structure**

7 - "**Adam**" — relates to 7-letter words

Note: The first 7-letter word used in Genesis 1:16 is הכוכמים
(HKVKMYM) translated as: *stars* — which are also structured as the
12 constellations.

8 - "**Adam & Eve**" — relates to 8-letter words

Note: The first 8-letter word used in Genesis 1:14 is ולמוערדים
(VLMVaDYM) translated as: *seasons* — which in Ancient Mesopotamia
conceptualized two seasons: *summer* and *winter*. (The Babylonian
calendar, used in Mesopotamia, was based on a year of 12 synodic
months.)

9 - "**Offspring**" — relates to 9-letter words

Note: It's noted that there are no 9-letter words in Biblical Hebrew. Although, it's interesting that human pregnancy = 9 months.

as **Concept**

7 - "**Adam**" — Concept of *Oneness*

[as Mankind/Humans = *Dry Seed* or *Full of Potential*]

8 - "**Adam & Eve**" — Concept of *Union/Re-Union*

[Male-Female] = Adam/Eve *[When Humans come together, we become Inspired].* Also, this connects to *the triggering of Pollination, when pollen from a male anther is transferred to the female stigma of a flower.*

9 - "**Offspring**" — Concept of *Family*

[When Humans take action, it's born from Potential + Inspiration - or when the two come together, action is born)

Note: The Result is the pattern of three (3) and layering of the pattern of 3 on top of 3 on top of 3, or the pattern or concept of 3-6-9.

There is a basic relationship between the *two* aspects of **structure** and **concept** that functions like the idea of a *shape* having the boundary line that contains it and the pattern it presents.

In other words, it's the stagnant, *internal* reflective nature of a thing, but when the movement [growing or flowing aspects] gets introduced, it will group [as an interaction of a set] in aspects of *three*.

Note: This pattern also functions similarly to the idea of *spirit* or *mind* aspect and the relationship to the *flesh* or *body* aspect – the concept of the *flesh* as the boundary line containing a *spirit* [of a person].

The "Glyph" Grammar

As of now, the focus has been on the concept of structure, specifically the constructs of seeds and journeys (*paths*), which are formatted in pattern sets of three (3) or "constructs of three."

There is another attribute connected to a **structure,** which is related to its function and actions (*efforts*), and this is referred to as the **system.**

When analyzing *Biblical Hebrew* writing in Genesis, another set of patterns was observed. These were functioning in what I break down as a set of four processes or a "Construct of Four."

Note: Additionally, they're layered and build upon themselves.

The idea is that when both groups of these patterns are combined or interwoven, they become the *system and structure* we define as *Grammar,* or in this case, what I referred to as the **Glyph Grammar.**

> **Note:** The primary reason I refer to it this way is because of the *Figure of Speech* of *Alliteration,* not because of the actual functioning of the time period of the use of the Glyph type language format.

The following explanation of patterns and the breakdown into 4 segments of a process format is only a portion of the complexity of usage and function.

Process 1 = The Reflective Nature [the reflection of One]

Process 2 = The "Effort" of [coming from] One becoming Two

Process 3 = The "Offspring(s)" [the Born from(s)] | "The Tethering"

Process 4 = The "Interaction" with One becoming Two — "The Union" of "The Tethering" and "The Effort"

Process 1

The Reflective Nature

The first process of the *Glyph Grammar's function* is the *concept of reflection*. Overall, I consider this aspect to be the most utilized and embedded in regard to both ancient word-building and scripture.

The idea of reflection can be understood in various ways. At its core, it represents the relationship of duality, *"two,"* yet connected to a singular, *"one"* source. This is easily understood as *seeing one's own reflection,* for example: *"in a mirror"* or *"on the surface of the water."*

The **One**, as the **One's reflection** concept.

Described as the observable result of *seeing one's own reflection,* also an explanation of a *degree of clarity* in defining what is being reflected.

The idea is that this relationship between the *"source object"* and its *reflective result* compares conceptually to that of a three-dimensional object (which is being reflected as the two-dimensional representation of it).

There is some variability in this attribute. The first is that the reflection is similar but not exactly the same. There are differences, such as being flipped versus reversed or two-dimensional versus three-dimensional, but also the state of *seeing one's own reflection,* which requires a *light source* versus *no light source (darkness).*

> **Note:** This aspect is represented in Genesis 1:2 as:
> *Describing the Earth as formless, void, and that **darkness** over the face[surface] of the deep. And the Spirit of God was hovering over the face[surface] of the waters.* In Genesis 1:3, *And God said, "Let there be **light** and there was **light.**"*
>
> Conceptually, and at the simplest level, this is representing being in front of a reflective surface, but *in the dark [unable to see or hidden in the dark],* then *turning on a light source,* which will make it possible to *see one's own reflection.*

This is an attribute of the **formula of reflection** *(and of "Creation")*, which is also repeated as a multiple **"dividing/ separating,"** but then leads to a **"gathering/collecting."**

> **Note:** from Genesis 1:4 – *describes a series of dividing/separating events... but 1:9 – the gathering of waters to let the land appear (again as if the lights turned on and one can see their reflection).* And again, the idea of a separate thing, but from within the first thing — *the waters and the land reflecting the other.* Then, it continues the *"dividing/separating" and "gathering/collecting" in 1:10 with the waters, as the Sea.*
>
> — But now 1:12 *on the Earth, there is the "dividing/separating" as stages of types of bringing forth(s) or as "gathering/collecting"* — of *the Grass yielding Herb "Seed" | The Tree yielding Fruit "Seed within"* [Symbolizing, a **Branching effect** of the *"dividing/separating"* — becoming *Greater* as it develops from the *Lesser*] The denotation of direction of reflection as, **The Lesser to Greater.**
>
> — and in Genesis 1:14 *the Sky aspect* [as the Above the Earth] is related in the same way. Denotes the direction (and position) of the reflected as **the Greater to the Lesser**, but with reference to the *Light*.
>
> The concept of reflection is: **The Greater & the Lesser |** or simply a *"Lesser"* version of the *"Greater"* one.
>
> **Note:** In Genesis 1:16, *This is used as The Greater Light and Lesser Light* (often understood as the Sun and the Moon - which are separate objects but has the common element of the **One**, which is the **light** = The Sun and the Light are directly connected and the Moon only reflects the Sun's light — *Sun=(producing it's Light) and Moon=(reflecting Light of the Sun).*

There is a generalized concept of everything as either coming from or branching from [as the *"Extension"* of] the *"One"* source but divided into a series of greater and lesser segments, like a Tree with various degrees of branches/branching — the idea that everything is related as a *"Oneness."*

****

Another attribute of a **light source,** or when adding **light** to anything, is the duality of **reflection:** *towards* ourselves, like the *mirror,* as either *external* or *internal.*

The idea of seeing one's own reflection is also a **concept of self-reflection** [the look at oneself, as an internal direction].

-versus-

Reflecting in the outward direction, as a **concept of *projection*** or the projected image of oneself. Symbolically, as the shadow. Although it's the same concept of separate but connected, it's the "lesser" way, or as a different reflective way.

The **One's shadow** concept

The shadow level reflection, as in seeing one's own shadow on the surface of the earth — described as the observable result of seeing one's own silhouette.

This could also be classified as the faded projection of oneself... [sometimes — as a degree of falseness that a person projects]

As a relationship of the Light and the Dark, this is a transitional state or attribute of the faded/shaded area. The idea that both are part of a darkness, but also as a consequence of the light. Additionally, it serves as a guide to indicate the direction of the light source's location [sometimes, as a *guiding to* or *from* reference].

Note: Maybe, even the idea of judgment of oneself, or symbolically the idea of one's conscience — and which way the shadow is cast, is how one justifies one's own actions — even the idea of one's own bias. [If we are in the light, we also have a shadow.]

Also, there is the idea of *"the full separation of it"* — is One becoming Two (or as two other Ones).

Note: This can be described as the relationship between *what was one* and *is now two*, but not as the same as the original. The concept is that this relationship of the Three-Dimensional object is **not** the same as (or the idea of an opposing version), versus the Two-dimensional representation of it. It's the concept of **"Other."**

This ends up being a spectrum of separations: from the **One**, as the **One's reflection** [as a representation of the original].

-to-

The idea of a clone (or copy) of the original — as the *same*, but also something *different*, like: *Eve from the rib/side of Adam -or- not the born of or from something, but different, like: "the concept of offspring."*

-to-

The idea of something completely opposite or opposing, like:

[God vs. Satan]

Variants of these concepts being used and described are:

God to Man | Heaven to Earth | Darkness to Light | Good to Evil | Meta or Non-Physical to Physical | Mind(Spirit) to Body(Flesh), etc....

The function of the **Reflective** process presents the concepts of the "Construct of Two" and coming from the "Construct of One."

The relationship to word building

The function of the process of reflection in word building is the development of the 2-letter combination or pairing together. The pairing of two letters then becomes a *"new* one unit" or 2-letter word *(but also just as a pairing unit of a concept).*

Example:

(A) + (B) = (AB) / אב <H1> as: *Father, Green[sprouts] and even, Fruit*

*Glyph meaning formula = **God's Plan** – the vastness of Creation*

(B) + (A) = (BA) / בא — not a word, but part of words inferring the concept of *narrowing down, reducing, or restricting aspects,* such as *entrance ways, to dig, engrave, making a declaration, or pits (tar or slime), a well [of water], and even a dungeon.*

*Glyph meaning formula = **Plan** <brings forth> [Mind of] **God***
– the focusing in on or limitations of the aspects of God and relates to mankind's attempt to do so [seems to be a connection to the commandment: *"Not taking the Lord's Name in Vain"]*

The connection to the *Seed Construct* and *Seed Glyph* with the word relationship.

(A) + (N) = (AN) / אנ – concept of the **Dry Seed** or *Potential*

*Glyph meaning formula = **God's Seed***
– As the primal aspect of *potential* from God

(M) + (N) = (MN) / מנ as of the **Watered Seed** or *Inspiration*

Glyph meaning formula = Watered Seed
מנ <H5408> translated as: *Manna [Food/Bread from Heaven]* – also inferring *inspiration* from God, as the nourishment given to mankind.

(Ch) + (N) = (ChN) / חנ – as the **Sprouting Seed** or *Outcome*

*Glyph meaning formula = **Branching Seed***

חנ (ChN) *<H2580>* translated as: *Grace, Pleasant, Precious* [diversity of *Outcome*] as: the vastness of plant-life from seeds.

— also, the reflection of this (NCh) translated as: **Noah** (as a *New Seed or New Outcome* from the *Potential* of Human Life after the *Flood [a Watering Seed concept]*).

The perception in something being *reflected* can be thought of as "*How it happens,*" specifically the "*effort*" behind it.

The idea of a function within or as part of the **reflective process,** rather than a separate process.

In other words, the action of the development of words or within words.

Process 2

The "Effort" of [coming from] One becoming Two

(The One's reflection parting from the One, or The One becoming Two)

Function of the *Yud* ` **[Y]** = "*The Effort*"

Later in NT or Gospels as: Christian concept of "Works"

The function aspect of the placement of the letter *Yud* ` (Y) as the "*Effort*" and how it effects the meaning.

The first example is the *Yud* ` (Y) "*Effort*" and the *Nun* נ (N) "*Seed/(Potential)*" — symbolizes (or reflects) the "*attempt to*" sprout (or the process to sprout the seed) = (NY) also, as the transition from "*watering of the seed*" to become the "*sprouting seed.*"

Although the (NY) is not technically a word, it's connected to a suggested root, ני (NY) *<H5204>* from the actual word used once in Ezekiel, בניהם (BNYHM) which translated as: *wailing.*

> **Note:** Also, symbolic of the *wailing* during *child birth.*

Other words, like: ניד (NYD) *<H5205>* translated as: *quivering [of lips]* | as meaning the *motion [of lips].*

> **Note:** Also, symbolic of the *vibration of an egg* before it hatches and the shaking, *unstable first steps* of a child [or other animals].

> ## Concept of *Direction (as a Cycle of Life)*
> ### "Seed to Plant" | "Offspring to Parent"

Note: But when the comparison shifts from the *Seed* to *Snake* — the symbolic perception shifts to an image of a *rattling of the tail* before the *strike/bite* (and the *wailing* that is cried out from it).

- versus -

The reflective nature *(the reversing order of the letters)*: (YN), as the *"Efforts* to *bring forth* the *Seed"* = as "the plant/tree produces the seed," versus the "seed which brings forth the plant/tree."

> ## Concept of *Direction (as a Cycle of Life)*
> ### "Plant to Seed" | "Parent to Offspring"

An example is בְּיָן (BYN) <H996> = translated as: *between, from, among* — used in Genesis 1:4 describing *separation/division* of *light* from *darkness*.

*Glyph meaning formula: Blueprint/**Plan** <brings forth> → **Effort** <brings forth> → Seed (the **Potential**) / Sprouting Seed (Generations) / Snake (concept of the "living" river of time - or as the changing/ evolving nature of things over time)*

> ## Generalized concept of *"How things will eventually grow apart (independent/individual) from its source"*

Biblical narrative examples like: *Adam to Eve* (from the Rib or side of Adam) — then later as their Offspring and their Generations: *Abel/Cain, Ishmael/Isaac, Esau/Jacob,* etc...

This concept can be understood in relation to both the *Bet* בּ (B) *"Blueprint/Plan"* and the *Nun* נ (N) *"Seed/Potential"*. These two glyphs/ letters reflect a common aspect of an earlier stage of something, such as the plan or potential to *be more* or to *become more.*

(B) + (N) = (BN) / בֵּן <H1121> translated as: *Son [Offspring]*

*Glyph meaning formula: Blueprint/**Plan** of the "Seed"(the **Potential**) / Sprouting Seed (Generations) / Snake (concept of the "living" river of time - or as the changing/evolving nature of things over time).*

> Generalized concept of *"How things will eventually grow apart (independent/individual) from their source"*

– as the moment of beginning the process to do so, as in the Child of [someone or something], but will grow up into becoming their own [thing], but still connected (or related) and potentially influenced by its parents.

Another concept is **Masculine** *and* **Feminine**

There is also a relationship to the concept of *Effort* presented in a masculine attribute of *"bringing forth"* versus a feminine attribute of *"giving birth."* In other words, the Father *seeds* in order to *bring forth* a child, but the Mother is that which *gives birth* to the child.

Introduction to **Suffixes**
(**Masculine** *and* **Feminine**)

The connection to masculine aspects and to the farming aspect of plowing and planting the seeds for crops which is also extended to the *"Effort to bring forth Life,"* in other words, linking to Glyph meanings of the *Yud,* ׳ (Y) as *"Effort"* and *Mem,* מ (M) as *"Life"* = ים (YM) as the masculine **suffix** or endings to words.

Whereas the ית (YT) is the feminine **suffix** to words, which is the glyph meaning of the *"Effort to bring forth the Weaving together."* The visual imagery of weaving together a basket is the interwoven assembly of parts to create a complex unified object. This symbolizes a relationship, the *"weaving of baskets -to- development of a baby [in the womb]."*

These represent the two basic branches (or differences) of the concept of *Being:* as *"created"* [the masculine, as *bringing forth*] versus *"begotten"* [the feminine, as *giving birth*].

Process 3

The "Offspring(s)" - *the Born from(s)*
(The New Ones or Newborns)

Function of the *Vav*, ו [V] = *"The Tethering"*

*Later in, NT or Gospels as: Christian concept of **"Faith"***

The function aspect of the placement of the letter *Vav*, ו (V) as the*"Tethering"* and how it effects the meaning.

This brings up another aspect of word building: the function of placement (location) letters in words, or what we now refer to as **Prefixes**, **Suffixes**, and **Infixes**.

A very common, but *"lost (or hidden) in translation"* function is the complexity of the letters as **prefixes,** especially with the *Vav*, ו (V).

Examples:

In English the translation outputs as multiple words → in Hebrew it's written as one word with the extra letters acting as a prefix to a root word:

– Gen. 1:2 *"And the earth..."* → וְהָאָרֶץ (VHARTs) = ו (V) *"And"*+ ה (H) *"the"*+ אָרֶץ (ARTs) <H776> *"earth"*

– Gen. 1:3 *"And said..."* → וַיֹּאמֶר (VYAMR) = ו (V) *"And"*+ י (Y) + אָמַר (AMR) <H559> *"to speak, say, utter"* | *"said"*

– Gen. 1:4 *"And the saw..."* → וַיַּרְא (VYRA) = ו (V) *"And"*+ י (Y) + רָאָה (RAH) <H7200> *"to see"* | *"saw"*

– Gen. 1:5 *"And the called..."* → וַיִּקְרָא (VYQRA) = ו (V) *"And"*+ י (Y) + קָרָא (QRA) <H7121> *"to call, proclaim, read, name"* | *"called"*

Note: Every line in Genesis 1 after the first line begins this way. In fact it's part of the ancient writing method.

Symbolically, the connection to the *Glyph of the Tent Peg* is the function of anchoring the base of the tent to the ground [as spaced apart, but functioning in a common purpose]. Also, like *hammering nails in a board* or *anchoring a net in the water.*

Note: This functions as, *the way something is "tethered"/ "connected" to the physical/"earthly" realm from the spiritual/divine/ "heavenly" realm.*

The use of the (V) as an **infix** ... the *interaction* of or with

Examples:

The Hebrew word, יָם (YM) <H3220>, defined as *Seas* [as the *"Body of Water"*] — generates a plural state or condition, like the plural yet fluid nature of it. The connection of the Glyph meaning as the *"Effort of the Water"* — symbolic of a *"Flowing River."*

The interaction of the ו (V) as an **infix** generates the Hebrew word, יומ (YVM) *<H3117>* translated as: *"Day",* *many days,* and an *"Age."* The visual representation of the (YM) *"Flowing River"* as the concept of *Time,* and of a *"Tent peg"* or a *stick poking out of the flowing river,* and the *disturbance* from it on the water as the *event in time.*

Note: The symbolic nature of a solid object interacting with the flowing water and the disturbance it creates implies this word to represent a reactionary moment of *life/truth* (M), not as a single unit of time, but as an interaction with the *flowing* (Y), plural nature of it.

The word, אור (AVR) *<H216>*, translated as: *"Light."*
Note: Symbolically, from the Glyphs represents the (A) *"Mind of God"* and the (R) *"Mind of Man"* and the (V) *interaction* = [*God interacting with Man*] is to be *"illuminated"* — *"is to bring the light"* and *"into the light"* from the *darkness.* [Also, represents the concept of the *Unknown to Known (or Knowable)* aspect of the *"Mind of Man"* from the *"All-Knowing"* aspect of the *"Mind of God."*]

The even more interesting use of the (V) as a **suffix** ... to *hold back* the nature of a word [it's attached to].

Example:

The word, תהו (THV) *<H8414>* translated as: *"formless."* – as (TH) is the concept of *"form,"* which is used in the word before this as היתה (HYTH) *<H1916>* as, *"was."* – used in Genesis 1:2 *"And the earth **was** (THV) **formless** (HYTH) ...* [the concept of *something exists* in a *form,* but also the *form* is *held back* — the concept of possibility of having *form* but not yet there.]

Process 4

The Interaction with One becoming Two

(The One's reflection reconnecting to the One or The Two connecting to One)

"The Union" of "The Tethering" and "The Effort"

Function of the *Vav,* ו [V] and *Yud,* י [Y]

*Later in NT or Gospels as: Christian concept of "**Faith & Works**"*

Additionally, when the *Vav,* ו (V), and *Yud,* י (Y) are used together = וי (VY) as a prefix, they function symbolically like: the concept of a *pregnancy.* The ו (V) as the *tethering of the umbilical cord* or *"conception,"* and the י (Y) is the *effort of giving "birth."*

> **Note:** The relationship of (VY) → now as, an *outcome* of *what is being reflected* = also, like a child attempts to reflect its parents. The concept of *born from* or the *"tethering" from* [the previous] thing.
>
> Additionally, the function of the **reflective** process, like a *mirror (or shadow)* = as the "**Greater** -to- **Lesser**" relationship of the reflecting versus reflected.

Example:

> The word, אמר (AMR) <*H559*> as *"to say, speak, utter"* – used 11 times in Genesis 1 as ויאמר (VYAMR) translated as: (V) as: "*And or Then* + (Y) [as the action of] + (AMR) [saying] as: *"said"*... [In this case, God speaking things into Creation.]
>
> > **The Glyph meaning:** *Mind of God <brings forth> + Life + <brings forth> + Mind of Man*

> **Note:** The interesting use of letters used to make this word is (AM) <*H517*> translated as: *"Mother"* — The (V) as *conception* + the (Y) as *giving birth* + (AM) as *Mother*

> Also, the relationship to the masculine *ox* to the feminine *cow* — and *speaking* as a method of creation and the similarity to the term [to *utter* = to *speak*] and the term *[udder]* to female cow <*to provide milk for its young*>.

Concept of וי (VY) as *"Conceived and Born"*

Symbolically, "being Born" or "Giving Birth."

The idea of *the initial moment of being inspired.*

The Reflection of ‏וי‎ (VY) to ‏יו‎ (YV)

Concept of (Y) *Effort* to *bring forth* the (V)
or the (YV) *"Effort to Conceive"*
(Tethering to the Effort) = The idea of *Sexual Intercourse*

Example:

The Hebrew Name: *Job*, ‏איוב‎ (AYVB) *<H347>* from the Book of Job: the patriarch famous for his patience.

Note: The (YV) as the concept of "*making the effort to conceive*" within the (AB) *<H1>* translated as: *"Father."*

The idea of a relationship to both concepts and to the *Union of a Father and Mother to bring forth Offspring.*

Additionally, going back to the Hebrew word, ‏יום‎ (YVM) *<H3117>* translated as: *"Day", many days,* and an *Age."* — through the perspective of ‏יו‎ (YV) as the moment of *conception and giving birth* + *<brings forth>* ‏מ‎ (M) as *"Life."*

The Process Concept

The overall concept of the **process** is based on the idea of **Reflection,** with its **function** being based on the (V) as *"Connection/Relationship/Tethering"* and the (Y) as *"Action/Movement/Effort"* within or how things interact with it.

The Overview

The complexity*(intertwining)* of the patterns

Reviewing the relationship of the pattern of the structures of the *[Dry Seed/Watered Seed/Sprouting Seed – Flower/Pollinated Flower/Fruit – Adam/Union(Adam-Eve)/Offspring]* and the pattern of the process aspects of *Reflection/Tethering/Effort)Action* as the transition between each stage.

There is a general idea of a *duality of things,* as something starting off as one thing then becoming another, but also with the *duality of direction,* as the placement of time and growth, versus creating something new.

The something *"Lesser"* becoming *"Greater"*

Seed to Sprout, Sprout to Plant (or Tree), Flower to Fruit, Offspring to Adult.

The something *"Greater"* becoming *"Lesser"*

Plant (or Tree) producing Seeds *[as an internal process],* Parents producing Offspring *[as a union of an external process].*

The idea of something *"Greater"* and *"Lesser"* in the duality format. [Also, descriptions of the *Sun* and the *Moon, as Day and Night.*]

Although with the idea of being paired in a duality relationship, there is also the Concept of being a *"Cycle"* or formatted in a sequenced format.

> **Note:** In the case of the cycle of the *Sun* (as the *"Greater Light"*) and the *Moon* (as the *"Lesser Light"*), which also generates a movement (as a passage of *Time*) and is expressed as the idea of marking the *"Seasons."*
>
> The *Sun (Day)* <bringer of *Light*> is connected to the warmth and life — also linked to **Summer**.
>
> The *Moon (Night)* <bringer of *Darkness*> is connected to cooling down and death — also linked to the **Winter**.

Another connection to this duality is the representation of the aspects of **Life** and **Creation,** and the cycle aspect is presented the *"Paths of..."*

The "Path" of **Life**

"Plant to Seed" | **"Parent to Offspring"**

- versus -

"Seed to Plant" | **"Offspring to Parent"**

The idea of the fully developed is the *"Greater" thing,* and the *"Lesser" thing* is what reflects it — The **growth** in its development *(direction)* process [in relation to *"Life"*, or *"Living"*].

Concept of *How things are expressed in the Earthly/Physical realm = Life = Living things*

The idea of being fully developed is also the end of life = "death."

The linguistic expression of this is linked to the Glyph/Letter: *Mem,* מ (M) – / *Glyph meaning: Life (and Truth)* and adding the cycling event as written as: ים (YM) / *Glyph meaning: Efforts to bring forth the Life.*

Note: The functioning of the *life* cycle is observed as a splitting (or branching).

As the seed grows, it branches into roots and stalk; when the sprout grows, it forms branches.

As other *life* evolves, it functions by *branching off* into related variations, but each stem from a common predecessor (ancestor). [Aka: the Family Tree].

The concept of the *branching* is expressed as the Glyph/Letter:

Chet, ח (Ch) / *Glyph meaning: Branching(Diversity) of ...*

The "Path" of **Creation**

The idea of something **reflecting** as a *"Greater"* thing to a *["Lesser"]* thing is also expressed in the relationship of the *"Path of Creation"* as the *"Greater"* and the *"Path of Life"* *["Lesser"]*, which it's reflecting.

> Concept of *How things are expressed in the Heavenly/Divine/Meta-Physical realm*
> *[Afterlife | non-Living things]*

The linguistic expression of this is linked to the Glyph/Letter: *Shin,* שׁ (Sh) – / *Glyph meaning: Aspects of Creation (and Destruction)* and adding the cycling event as written as: שׁי (YSh) / *Glyph meaning: Efforts to bring forth the* **Creation***.*

> **Note:** The connection to the other worldly relationship to the **patterns** of all things and the human observation of them. In other words, the observation of everything around us. One of the early examples is *the stars in the sky* and the *patterns they form,* and how they map out the story of the *divine path,* extending to *life* unfolding *reflectively.* Another example is *Prophecy* and the connection it has to events in *Life* that repeat themselves in similar ways.
>
> In other words, how we perceive the *repeating patterns* and *what these reveals to us,* or what this becomes in our connection or relationship to the divine realm.
>
> This concept is linguistically expressed as the Glyph/Letter: *Hey,* ה (H) / *Glyph meaning: Revealing/Revelation of ...*

> The interplay of these letters is interesting: (M)/(Sh)/(H)/(Ch) and the words/Names they generate: Shem, HaShem, Moses, Messiah, Mashiach, Ham, etc... [**Note:** discussed in a later section].

The Formatting Structure
within these two concepts of *"Paths."*

The *Path of "Life"* and its relationship to the **Seed***.*

The relationship to the idea of how this is *reflected* in a *Life structure* is expressed in the *seed format* or the concept of the *"Seed's Journey,"* which will grow into **crops,** which eventually lead to the **"Harvest."**

Life format

The Seed's Journey
as a *"Path to the Harvest"*

1 - Dry Seed — Concept of *Potential*
(as: *inert*, and an action is needed)

This represents both symbolically and actually the *Concept of Potential* (as stored up or storing up potential.

Other related concepts of this would be: 1) the concept of *dehydration* [the absence of water or the water removed]. 2) the concept of *hibernation* [going into a *deep sleep-like* state to get through the winter "harder times."

The concept of *Potential* is connected to survival [weathering of "hard times"] — also, the idea of *basic needs*.

> **Note:** There seems to be a hint at the idea of *living in a desert (survival of the dryness and lack of water) –or–* the idea of the *suffering servant(s),* and the positive that comes after such negative events/periods/states.

2 - Watered Seed — Concept of *Inspiration*
(as, exterior event [action] influencing the spark of life to begin)
[from the Darkness — or under the soil].

The triggering of *germination or re-hydration* | aka: the *"watering."* As the relationship to the idea of bringing life back into something.

> **Note:** The "rare" *Fire* germination plants – born/re-born "of *fire*" [and *smoke*] to aid in... fire-stimulated re-sprouting, flowering, seed release and germination).
>
> An interesting relationship to types of germination and concept of *water* in Noah's Flood and the *fire* in Revelation's "Armageddon."

3 - Sprouting Seed — Concept of *Action(s) taken*
(roots = downward directions) and choices (branching = upward directions).

> The generalized life cycle of a seed *(as a foundational state)* is separated into a basic growth process of these three steps.

The process continues as a symbolic *path* to get to the **Harvest**.

As a more complex version of the three stages.

4 - Plant/Tree — Concept of *Structure* (or *System*)

(as: the identification of what comes from the seed)

— *as grass yielding herb plant/tree and bearing fruit* [as described in Gen. 1:11].

5 - Grass-Herb/ Tree-Fruit — Concept of *Outcome*

(as: the Potential of Duality of Crops)

Grass to Flour *(becomes Bread, etc...)* | Flowers to Fruit

All of which is Food (Concept of *Nourishment*).

6 - "New" Seed(s)

The cycle repeats...

<As a beginning -to- end process, which is launches a (*or* many *"potential"*) *"New"* beginning(s)>.

The idea of a single seed *branches* into *branching* roots and *branching* stalk & limbs [aka: *"branches"*].

-versus-

The Tree/Plant produces many seeds as a way to *branch* [itself] out into the world to become many more.

Note: The symbolic connection to ABRAM-*Exalted Father* becoming ABRAHAM-*Father of the Multitude.*

-or- Constructed of/on a "Fractal Framework" = <Fractal Repeating>.

The concept of layering over time and of repeating the 3-stage process.

Symbolically, the Process of *God bringing forth Creation*, but as the *"potential"* or as *God's Seed* = aka: אָן (AN), and "watered seed" as *"God brings forth Life"*= אָם (AM) <translated as: *"Mother"*>, then growing into *God's Sprouting Seed,* as the *"actions taken"* = אָח (ACh) <translated as: *"Brother"*>.

85

Creation format

(as the 6 Days of Creation)

This process becomes part of a larger format of a repeating the **reflection** concept, while also aligning with the *Life/Seed* format.

Dry Seed	**Day 1** *[yom] echad,* אחד (AChD)
Watered Seed	**Day 2** *[yom] sheni,* שני (ShNY)
Sprouting Seed	**Day 3** *[yom] shelishi,* שלישי (ShLYShY)
Plant/Tree	**Day 4** *[yom] rebii,* רביעי (RBYaY)
Grass-Herb/ Tree-Fruit	**Day 5** *[yom] chamishi,* חמישי (ChMYShY)
"New" Seed(s)	**Day 6** *[yom] hashishshi,* הששי (HShShY)
Watered Seed 2	**Day 7** *[yom] hashebii,* השביעי (HShBYaY)

Day 1, or the *"first day"*

* Yom, יום (YVM) *<H3117>* translated as: *"Day"*

Is the *"flowing river"* (YM) = The concept of *Time* – specifically, the interactions within the flowing river (YVM) = the *interactions* within *Time*— the visualization of this is the interacting within the flowing river [Time], and the *what comes out* of it or is *brought forth* from it, is the (A) *Mind of God* + (Ch) *Branching/Sprouting(Diversity)* from it, is the (D) *Path/Way.*

+ * Echad, אחד (AChD) *<H259>* translated as: *"First/One"*

– used in Genesis 1:5 *And God called the light Day, and the darkness he called Night. And the evening and the morning were the **first day**.*

Note: את (ACh) *<H251>* translated as: *"Brother"* + ד (D) *Path/Way,* as:

The Brother's Path(s)/Way(s).

The idea of the *"Story of Two Brothers"* is a common trope or motif in many ancient cultures. Ex.: the Roman origin story involving *Romulus* and *Remus;* the ancient Egyptian myth called the *Tale of the Two Brothers: Anubis/Bata;* and, of course, the multiple versions in the Bible: *Cain/Abel, Ishmael/Issac, Esau/ Jacob.* Other variations of this theme (concept of separation/ splitting/duality) are expressed as *Light/Darkness, Day/Night, Evening/Morning, Good/Evil, Greater/Lesser,* and *the Sun/Moon.*

Day 2, or the *"second day"*

* *Sheni,* שֵׁנִי (ShNY) *<H8145>* translated as: *"Second/Two"*

– used in Genesis 1:8 *And God called the firmament Heaven. And the evening and the morning were the **second day.***

> **Glyph meaning formula**
>
> *Seed(s)/"Potential" <born within> Aspects of Creation's + Efforts*
> -or- *Aspect(s) of Creation for Generations (Seeds) to come and the Efforts they [the "Generations"] will <bring forth>.*

Note: The perspective of Glyphs/Letters [*Alphabet*] as the *Seeds* — aka: The **collective potential** from within all/whole of creation.

> The basic Concept of the *"**Push**"* or the *"**Nudge**"*

The idea of *the **impulse** that nudges the directions one goes* or *the choices a person or people make in life.*

> **Note:** שִׁי (ShY) *<H7862>* as: *Gift* → נ (N) *Seed,* as:
>
> ### The Creation's Fruit
>
> The idea of the *"Creation's Effort"* and the *"Seed"* within.
> Symbolically similar to Genesis 1:11... *the fruit tree yielding fruit after his kind, whose seed is in itself...*

Day 3, or the *"third day"*

* *Shelishi,* שְׁלִישִׁי (ShLYShY) *<H7992>* translated as: *"Third/Three"*

– used in Genesis 1:13 *And the evening and the morning were the **third day.***

> **Glyph meaning formula**
>
> *Aspects of Creation + Learn/Teaching [Lessons] + Effort + Aspects of Creation + Effort*

The idea of *the directions one goes* or *the choices a person or people make in life.*

> **Note:** The ל (L) *learning/lessons <born within>* שׁי (ShY)
> = Language(s) + *<bring forth>* שׁי (ShY) *Creation's Efforts.*
>
> ### The Fruits of our Labors
>
> The idea of *"taken in" of the Fruit* or *the eating of the Fruit.*

> Concept of *what we learn from walking a path*
> — as the *lessons gained* from our way of life.

The idea that *we will develop based on one's own
language* (as well as *the actions and choices we make).*

> **Note:** Besides the intertwining of how people live their
> lives and language. There is the ***intertwining* and *evolving***
> of the function of *language as: oral* to *written; glyphs* to
> *letters; 2-letter root words* to *3-letter root words [as: seeds* to
> *fruits, whose seed is in itself].*

Day 4, or the *"fourth day"*

* *Rebii,* רביעי (RBYaY) *<H7243>* translated as: *"Fourth/Four"*

– used in Genesis 1:19 *And the evening and the morning were the **fourth day**.*

> Glyph meaning formula
>
> *Mind of Man + Blueprint[Plan] + Effort + Observational + Effort*

The idea of *analyzing how people live their life(s),*
either as a group [tribe/nations] or as a *personal
reflection [self-reflecting].*

> **Note:** The title of a *Rabbi* is a term of a spiritual leader or
> religious teacher in Judaism. The Mishnaic Hebrew word
> רבי (RBY), meaning: *Master.* The connection to the רב
> (RB) *<H7727>* meaning and translated as: *"abundance,
> many, great, chief, captain, etc..."* + עי (aY) *<H5856>*
> translated as: *"a ruin" [broken down into pieces].*
>
> ### The Great Breakdown through Observation

Note: Similar concepts to the use of *making observations* is the term from the Book of Enoch: *The Watchers* [the Book of the Watchers] – explaining the fall of the watchers and taking of wives and the birth of the Nephilim.

Day 5, or the *"fifth day"*

* *Chamishi,* חמישי (ChMYShY) <*H2549*> translated as: *"Fifth/Five"*

– used in Genesis 1:23 *And the evening and the morning were the **fifth day**.*

> **Glyph meaning formula**
> *Branching (Diversity) + Truth/Life + Effort + Aspects of Creation + Effort*

The idea of *the many diverse efforts or actions coming from Life and Creation.*

> **Note:** The concept of much *branching* = ח (Ch) and the leading to <*bring forth*> מי (MY) → שי (ShY)
>
> **The Orchard** [as the outcome of it]
>
> The idea of *"going into"* then *"coming out"* of an Orchard.

> Concept of *what we take away [from the lessons from walking a path].*

Note: Similar concepts to the *Trees of [Life* and *Knowledge]*, and the *Kabbalah "Pardes"* [translated as: *"the orchard"*].

Another concept connection to the *diversity idea* of (MY) and the (M) as the Glyph of *Water* – is the *Fish [as what is making action in the water]* versus the (ShY) connection to the *Sky* and the *Birds [as what is making action in the sky].*

The direct relationship to the biblical account of the fifth day:

Genesis 1:22 *Then God blessed them and said, "Be fruitful and multiply and fill the waters of the seas, and let birds multiply on the earth."*

Symbolically, the branching of two paths: both the vastness of diversity of life, and the separation of *Written* vs. *Spoken words.*

Day 6, or the *"sixth day"*

* *Hashishshi,* הששי (HShShY) *<H8345>* translated as: *"Sixth/Six"*

– used in Genesis 1:31... *And the evening and the morning were the **sixth day**.*

> ### Glyph meaning formula
> *Revealing + Aspects of Creation + Aspects of Creation + Effort*

The idea of *actions reveals intent.*

> **Note:** The הש (HSh) is the first two letters of *Hashem* and *Heaven*. Symbolic of the stage just before the מ (M) *"Life"*
> — *The Revelation + Creation +* שי (ShY) *"Creations Effort"*
> <which is used in word of [Day] 3 and 5>.
>
> ### *The Revealing Creation through Creation's Efforts*

> Concept of the *"How"* we act, take action, or *interact.*
> The *"What"* we are willing to do & actually doing.
> Is it for *oneself, oneself only,* or *for others?*

Ideas like: *Do we behave like Animals or Humans?*
(Are we behaving as *"Elevated/Exalted"* [above Animals]?)

> Concept of the *Garden [of Eden]* versus the *Orchard*
> [the *Kabbalah "Pardes"* story], which is a perception of what grew from the Garden, and what can be harvested from it.
>
> *<The younger version versus the older/later version of itself>*

The idea of finding the way back into the *"Garden [of Eden]"* and discovering the saplings (or crops) are now all fully grown, aka: *full of fruit* <potentially an overwhelming state>.
The essential understanding is that *it's just a matter of harvesting [properly]* and *then replanting it* for the next cycle.

> Concept of (HSh) and what it reflects is the שה (ShH) *<H7716>* as: *"**a member of the flock**, sheep, goat, young sheep or goat, and of course the "**lamb**."*

The idea of *"what can be sacrificed"* [aka: the *Lamb*] → *"to bring forth something new"* (ShY) = as Creating/Creation of something new by the Destruction of something else.

In the generalized way, the (HSh) is the *"What is being Revealed by Creation"* is being brought forth by (ShY) *"the Actions of Creation,"* as the *"Patterns"* [we can and have observed].

Note: the first word in Genesis 1 is *Bereshit* בראשית (BRAShYT) = *"In the Beginning"* and the last word is *Hashishshi,* הששי (HShShY) = *"Sixth/Six."* — Both have the (ShY) and also represent the concept of the *First and the Last, Beginning and the End* = As the 6 stages of the *Effort(s) of Creation* (ShY) and as the *cycle (or cycling)* of it.

Day 7, or the *"seventh day"*

* *Hashebii,* השביעי (HShBYaY) <H7637> translated as: *"Seventh/Seven"*

– used in Genesis 2:2 *And on the* seventh day *God ended his work which he had made; and he rested on the **seventh day** from all his work which he had made.*

> **Glyph meaning formula**
> *Revealing + Aspects of Creation + Blueprint(Plan) + Effort → Observed + Effort*

The idea of *"Greater Reflection"* [the Group as a Whole] or <from the "Bird's Eye View"> versus *"Lesser"* [as *"Self-Reflection"*].

> **Note:** The relationship of the Day 4 = רביעי (R+BYaY) versus the swapping of the (R) *Mind of Man* and the הש (HSh) <The first two letters of (HShM) *"HaShem"* – the meaning and concept of *"The Name"* as an informal reference to *"God"*>. Thus, generating the word השביעי (HSh+BYaY).
>
> (BY + aY) *"Efforts Planned and then Observed"*
>
> **The Revealing Creation through Origins and Observation**

The basic Concept of the *Final Judgment.*

The idea of a *How actions affect "Everything/Everyone"* and as *"Accountability."*

Overview of the Grammar Concept(s)

The repeated complexity, intertwining, and layering of the same patterns can be mind-blogging and overwhelming. This complexity begins to generate a perspective of **chaos**. As a method of bringing a perspective of **order**, a streamlined method of analysis can be applied by condensing down the general concepts of the vastness of the previous matrix of language *patterns*.

There is a connection to these *patterns (or formats)* and the Biblical Hebrew language, as a **Process** and **Construct** of *Reflection*.

Process vs. Construct

Process = as Divine/God's Path(s) | Connection to the (Y)
[as God's acts/perspective of the Divine/Heavenly Realm]

Construct = as Man's Path(s) | Connection to the (V)
[as Man's acts/perspective of being *tethered* to the Earthly Realm]

There is also the idea of the layering effect of the *Seed to Man* formats of the three stages, which is the perspective of *Mankind,* or the *Way/(Path)* of Mankind, and the *tethering* to Earth.

As the way to get to a concept of *understanding* or the deeper meaning of a word(s), there are basic concepts: God → Man (as, *Reflection* and *Effort*), and Masculine → Feminine (as, *Branching* and *Tethering*).

Summarized in four constructs *(A simplified method of word analysis)*:

1 - Linear Construct

(Masculine force) <Creating, as bringing forth> Man (Adam) | "masculine reading"

2 - Dimensional Construct

(Feminine force) <Creating, as giving birth> | Woman (Eve) | "feminine reading"

3 - Reflective Construct

The reverse order of letters of words – [to compare the function of meaning]

4 - Meaning Construct

(*Spirit of God*) <God's interaction with Mankind> as the *"Union of Minds"*

Section Four

My focus is not just on the *current, traditional,* or *accepted* interpretations and the translations they have produced, but also on delving into the ancient Hebrew language.

Expanding the analysis through the lens of what I consider the origin of the Hebrew letters themselves: the *Glyphs*, and what I refer to as the influence of the layers of time and culture: *Sacred Etymology.*

The obvious place to begin is: *"In the beginning..."*

Genesis 1:1

English translation (King James Version)
In the beginning God created the Heaven and the Earth.

בראשית ברא אלהים את השמים ואת הארץ
(BRAShYT) (BRA) (ALHYM) (AT) (HShMYM) (VAT) (HARTs)
In + Beginning | Created | [God] | + (the) Heaven | and + (the) Earth

In the beginning

In English, both the one-word title "Genesis" and the first three words, "In the beginning." It is understood to convey the concept of a starting point — *"As a moment of Origin."*

> **Note:** In general, it's answering the "When" [as something that had a beginning action] and as "the How God began," as the how "God created" and the steps along the way (as to an ordered process) [formatted in the "6" days].

Bereshit | בראשית

The original word written in Hebrew is one word: *Bereshit*, בראשית (BRAShYT) <*H7225*>. The traditional view of understanding this word is with a grammar construct focused on a [root word] and with prefix and suffix letters. In this case, it's the ראש (RASh) <*H7218*>, defined and translated as *"Head, chief, top, beginning, leader."* The relationship to these words can be understood as *"At the head of...",* as a place where something begins, or as the top (as the most elevated) position, like the *"Chief."*

> **Note:** There is a similarity to the Hebrew letter ר (R) is pronounced as Rosh/Resh ריש (RYSh) and is the Glyph of the "Head" of man.

תי ש←ראו←ב   B → R A Sh → YT

The root word, ראש (RASh) <*H7218*>, describes objects (as a concept of *"that which [something] comes from"*) in other textual writings and is translated as:

- *"the head of rivers"* [used in Genesis 2:10],
- *"your head/thy head"* [used in Genesis 3:15],
- *"the top of mountains"* [used in Genesis 8:5],
- *"the top of towers"* [used in Genesis 11:4].

> **Note:** Its seems from the modern perspective of this word as referencing a moment of **time** — the focus on the relationship is to the water as, the place the "**river [begins]** (also, called the "headwaters") and flows from the mountain top," then making the **top** (or **head**) as, the **place of origin** [this is a relationship to the when, or where as well as *in the physical world* or as *in "Creation"*].

The ב (B) used as a prefix and translated as: *"In"*, and the י (YT), the feminine plural suffix — this is conceptually like translating to an "ing" ending [as related to the English root word *"begin"* to *"beginn**ing**."*]

The grammar function of suffixes: **Feminine** plural word endings.

The use of feminine plural, יִת (YT) versus the masculine plural, יִם (YM) has an interesting change function to the root word, רֹאשׁ (RASh) <H7218>.

The feminine plural version: רֵאשִׁית (RASh+YT) <H7225> is (a feminine noun) translated as, *"choicest, finest, first, first fruits, foremost."*

* **Note:** The addition of the feminine suffix transitions the definitions to denote "fruit-bearing," symbolically similar to the concept of childbearing.

** **Note:** The connection to Eve (life-bearing) and the Fruit of the Trees in the Garden within Eden is described in Genesis 3.

The grammar function of suffixes: **Masculine** plural word endings.

Whereas the masculine plural version of the root is רָאשִׁים (RASh+YM) <H7218> is (a masculine noun) [used in Genesis 2:10] as *"headwaters, rivers"* described in the text as "becoming four rivers which parted from a single river."

* Note: The use of the masculine suffix focuses on "water."

The difference between masculine and feminine seems to denote the distinction between "life-giving" vs. "life-bearing," — as concepts of "bringing forth" vs. "giving birth."

Another interesting detail about the 3-letter root word, רֹאשׁ (RASh) <H7218> is the breakdown of the word into a prefix of the ר (R), and the two-letter root word, אֵשׁ (ASh) <H784>, defined as *"a fire,"* but also translated as: *"blazing, burning, fiery, flaming, flashing."*

The use of letter ר (R) [traditionally described as meaning "first/top/beginning,"] as a prefix to the אֵשׁ (ASh) as generating a concept of *"First Fire,"* or *"the Spark."* Furthermore, expanding the

Glyph imagery of the ר (R) as representing the *Mind of Man* — The concept of man's thoughts or ideas are like a ***spark*** compared to God's thoughts or ideas | the א (A) as the *Mind of God,* which brings forth *"Aspects of Creation"* [ש (Sh)] -or- אש (ASh) as, ***fire.***

This symbolically relates ***thoughts*** to ***fire***, which leads to a relationship with ***Fire*** to ***Wisdom.***

Additionally, it could represent a **watershed moment** of ***man making fire***, and thus a correlation to the concept of the *Fire-maker,* as the *"Wise-man"* or *Mankind's Wisdom.*

When applying the **Glyph meanings** associated with the letters אש (ASh), the (A) as the Strength/Power *[Mind of God]* + (Sh) as an *Aspect of the Creation* (the relationship between *Creation* and *Destruction*) conveys the idea of the *"Power of the Sun (or Fire in the Sky<Heavens>)."*

From the traditional perspective of the (BRAShYT) — it conceptually represents, the "Human level" | the (BR) as *[The Plan of the Mind of Man]* to gives birth to *Wisdom* = (ASh) *"Fire"* as, Influenced [Inspired] by (A) *God's Mind* -or- the *Mind of Man* level is as a *Spark [of Fire]* = or a smaller piece of *Wisdom* compared of the full flame of *God's Wisdom* + (YT) as the how it weaves or is interwoven together.

> The generalized Concept of *How the human mind comprehends God's thoughts on how the Creation process is structured.*

Another way to view the בראשית (BRAShYT) *<H7225>* is as a union of two (2) three-letter root words.

שית ← ברא   BRA → ShY T

— The first is the ברא (BRA) *<H1254>*, defined as *"to create; to shape,"* and is used as the next word after the *"Bereshit,"* in Genesis 1:1, and translated as: *"created."*

— The second root word is the שית (ShYT) *<H7896>*, defined as *"to place; put; set."*

SHAPED + PLACED

Note: The combination of the two root words conveys the idea that "Creation -or- the beginning of it" is/was both *shaped* (created) and *set* in place."

The Hebrew word order of Genesis 1:1 ***In the beginning** [God] **created**...* is the (BRAShYT) (BRA), which is understood as the *shaped + placed,* then *shaped* again. This perspective is a pattern of a *first shaped* [as a state of existence] + *placed* [as an interaction of movement to somewhere different] + *another shaping* [state of existence].

Symbolically, this is a visual representation of the *process of making pottery:*

— **Step 1:** wedging/kneading the clay [to prep it]
A pre-shaping [pushing out/removing the air bubbles and improving the workability of the clay].

— **Step 2:** place/set a ball of prepped clay on a potter's wheel.

— **Step 3:** start to mold/shape into [something]
The shaping of it [into something], as it spins on the wheel.

Note: This clay analogy is also the Sumerian myth [process] of the creation or formation of man. *As well as a basic and modern understanding of the Earth as it continues to spin, evolve, and change over time.*

> The Symbolic Concept of *Creation,*
> as Processing of making *"Clay into Pottery"*

This union of two words represents the process of creating as the physical aspects of *Creation* itself — as the continuing process which is like the working of pliable clay into the many and diverse things of creation [not as a singular moment] — which can describe the pliability of the Human mind, as well.

> Another concept of these is the *"Was, Is, and Will Be"*
> [as referring to a placement in time]

BR+A → Sh+YT

A further breakdown of the view can be the בר (BR) *<H1247-53>*, defined as *"son,"* but also as *"grain"* + א (A) *Mind of God* + the ש (Sh) *Aspect of Creation* + ית (YT), as the feminine suffix.

> **Note:** The grammar concept is the making/changing of the word from *"son"* to the feminine by adding the ית (YT) to create the word *"daughter."*

בנ (BN) = *"Son"* to the בנית (BNYT) = *"Daughter"*

> **Symbolic representation:** The personified or physical representation of a concept of the *body/flesh* as the *potential/plan* of the *seed* -or- the *potential/plan of the family* = בנ (BN) [in an adolescent state].

[Repeating *"variant"* tropes]
Union of Son(s) + Daughter(s) | [Male + Female]

* The idea or act of a father giving his daughter to another family's son for marriage. The *union* of **not just** between the children[offspring], but of the families as well.

> Concept of making *separate families* become *united* is to have a union [marriage] between two family members from each family.

> *(Symbolically and sometimes actually, as an offering up one from each **side**).*

* In the case of God's Creation of *"Humanity"* — the *created* offspring being represented by the (ADM) and the bonded/offered partner will be from *within* or *part of itself*, as translated: *the woman.*

> Concept of making *humanity* whole is to reunite them or "the union of the two."

*Symbolically and literally, as an offering up one **rib** from Adam's **side**.*

Note: the Hebrew word translated as: *Rib,* also translated as: *"Side"*

-versus-

בר (BR) = *"Son,"* but ברית (BRYT) = as a concept of a *"Daughter"*

Symbolic representation: The personified or physical representation of a concept of *rational mind* to *emotional mind* as the *potential/plan* of the *Mind of Man* -or- the *potential/plan of the family of mind* [the idea of a collective consciousness] = בר (BR) [in an adolescent state].

The actual translation of the ברית (BRYT) <H1285-1286> is *"Covenant"* – not as: *"Daughter."*

Symbolic representation: The concept of the *marriage* of a *daughter to another family's son* (as making a union between both families and the children).

Is the concept of making a **Covenant** *with God,* as a state within oneself [and of your personal binding to *"God."*]

Also, the idea of *God* (as the *Father*) giving his offspring to another to bind the families in a union (of marriage).

Note: A concept that relates to the *"Bride of God* or *Christ"* [that is used in later books] — symbolically as the making of a *"Covenant."*

* The *"Covenants"* from **God to Man** *

The first use of the word: ברית (BRYT) <H1285> *"Covenant"* is in Genesis 6:18 with *Noah* – when instructed to build the Ark to save a selected grouping of life from the flood.

The next was in Genesis 9:9 *And I, behold, I establish my covenant with you, and with your seed after you...* [aka: *The Covenant of the Rainbow*] after exiting the Ark.

Additional *"Covenants"* | *Abram* becomes *Abraham*, with *Issac* (not with the firstborn, half-brother: *Ishmael*), with *Jacob* (not with firstborn, twin-brother: *Esau*), with *Moses* (again not the firstborn, which was his older brother: *Aaron* [and separated at birth]).

Note: If specific Biblical figures [aka: *Patriarchs*] whom God made/gave a *Covenant* (BRYT) = representing the *[betrothed] "Daughter."* They symbolically represent a concept of *"Sons of God"* [aka: *"Sons-in-Law"*]

If comparing the (BRAShYT) as representing the (ASh) *"Fire"* (or *"Wisdom"*) born within the (BRYT) *"Covenant,"* then the concept of the *Patriarchs* represents the *Wisdom* brought forth by their *Covenant with God.*

B + RA → ShY + T

Yet, another way to break down the בראשית (BRAShYT) is as:
(B) *Plan/Blueprint* + (RA) *Mind of Man + <bringing forth>* → *Mind of God*

Note: Although (RA) isn't actually used as a Hebrew word, it can be found within other words:

* ראה (RAH) <H7200> as: *to see, look at, inspect, perceive, consider*
* ראה (RAH) <H7201> as: *"bird of prey" | "glede/red kite".*
* ראה (RAH) <H7203> as: *seer, a vision*
* ראי (RAY) <H7209> as: *a mirror*
* ראי (RAY) <H7210> defined as: *seeing, vision, sight*

Concepts like: *Seers/Prophets* or *Prophetess/Oracle*
<as the earlier state or connection to God>

Also, the Concept of *Birds of Prey*
The idea of selecting its prey is like a personal bias as:
[picking what we like or want to take-in].

Even the Concept of *Reflection*

> The generalized Concept of comparing the *Mind of Man's* attempt to bring forth the *Mind of God.*

Note: The Egyptian god: **Ra** is the sun god of ancient Egypt, and the image drawn of his representation is that of a *falcon-headed* man with a circle/sphere on top of his head [said to be the "Sun"], but also with a snake [a Cobra lying on top of it.

+ (ShY) *Aspects of Creation + Efforts* = as: Patterns of/in Creation + (T) *Weaving together* = How they are connected.

Symbolically, as (RA) + (ShY) as *"Seeing the Patterns"* [as observational expressions in the physical world] and how they *weave together* – as: the ideas of *Fractal repeating, the Fibonacci sequence (also, connected to the "Golden Ratio" and represented as the Greek Letter "Phi" Φ); as well as, the idea of Sacred Geometry, etc...*

> Concept of *How Human's see the patterns in things*
> Including, *"Seeing what they(we) what to See"*

[From one's own experiences and bias] – [As the direction that influences the way a person interacts in life].

The Overview

The relationship to Biblical Hebrew words and their development is evolved from making connection and observations, thus creating a link between Creation/Life and Language itself [aka: the Grammar reflects it, which in return is creation reflects life, which reflecting the creator [one, or the first cause] = aka: the concept of God as the Most High – as the furthermost back in the reflected process also, represented/*"reflected"* by the Letter/Glyph of the *"Head of the Ox"*/ א/(A).

> **Glyph meaning formula:**
> *Blueprint(Plan) + <brings forth> → Human Mind + <brings forth> → Mind of God + <brings forth> → Aspects of Creation + <brings forth> → Effort + <brings forth> → Weaving together*

> Concept of *the Plan of Human mind*
> *is to bring forth our connection to Mind of God*
> *and Creation and how Everything is Weaved together.*

Note: But there is a notion that because it's coming from the Mind of Man [it will/has/will have flaws or be flawed].

There is a lot packed into this word: *Bereshit,* בראשית (BRAShYT), which is what brings me back the method of the four constructs as a simplified or a streamlined version of word analysis.

The general idea is to have a useful tool to get a good grasp of the concept of meaning of a Biblical Hebrew word. As well as attempting to list the various usage and translations of words and in which *books* they're located.

Note: I will be more encompassing of words in the beginning *(pun intended),* but I will streamline the listings of word usages down for the sake of keeping the pages manageable.

1 - Linear Construct (B+R+A+Sh+Y+T)

* בֻ (BR) <H1247> translated as: *the son [of]* used in Ezra 5:1-2, 6:4 and <H1248> used in Psalms 2:12 and Proverbs 31:2

* בֻ (BR) <H1249> as: *beloved, pure, empty* | translated as, *innocent | and I am clean* used in Job 11:4

* בֻ (BR) <H1250> as: *grain, the open country* | translated as: *[store] up the grain* used in Genesis 41:35, 49 | *[buy] grain* used in Gen. 42:3 | *with grain* used in Gen. 42:25, 45:23

> **Note:** Concepts of the *Son* or *Grain* [as the yield of the Herb Seed] = Concept of the *"Potential of a future Nourishment"* -or- the idea of *"Feeding the Future,"* but also from the idea of the *natural/open/ vastness of land* [to *"Live off the Land"*] → is the (BR) which leads to *bring forth* the *[Mind of] God* (BRA).

* בְרָא (BRA) <H1254> translated as: *created* — used in Genesis 1:1 and repeatedly in Genesis

* רָא (RA)   **Note:** *Is not a biblical Hebrew word!?*

Other variants or words built from (RA):

** רָאָה (RAH) <H7200> defined as: *to see, look at, inspect, perceive, consider* — used in Genesis *"[God] saw..."* — but written as (VYRA) / translated as the (V) as "And [God] saw...

** רָאָה (RAH) <H7201> as: *"bird of prey"* | used in Deuteronomy only once as: *"And the glede/red kite.. [a bird of prey]..."* — but written as (VHRAH).

** רָאָה (RAH) <H7203> as: *seer, a vision* | used in 1 Samuel as: *"a seer"* (HRAH) — as an older term used to describe the later term: *Prophet* — used in Isaiah as, *"having visions"* (BRAH)

** רָאָה (RAH) <H7204> as: a Name — used in 1 Chronicles (HRAH)

** רְאִי (RAY) <H7209> as: *a mirror*

** רְאִי (RAY) <H7210> defined as: *seeing, vision, sight* | used in Genesis 16:13 *"[God] who sees [me]..."* — used in 1 Samuel *"appearance/[good- looking]"* — used in Job *"of him who sees [me]"*

* רֹאשׁ (RASh) <H7218> defined and translated as: *Head, chief, top, beginning, leader.*

** רֹאשׁ (RASh) <H7219> translated as: *bitterness, gall [bold and impudent behavior]* | meaning: *a poisonous [plant], (bitter, poisonous herb), "Venom" [of Snakes]* // also: *"the poppy plant"* [of which — The ripe seed is only non-harmful part of the plant]

* אֵשׁ (ASh) <H784> defined as: *"a fire"*

Other variants or words built from (ChV):

* שַׁי (ShY) <H7862> translated as: *gift, present, gift offered, as a homage present* — used in Psalm 68:29, 76:11 and Isaiah 18:7

* שִׁית (ShYT) <H7896> as: *to place* | translated as, *to put, set, has appointed* — used in Genesis 3:15, 4:25, 30:40, and repeatedly in Genesis

* שִׁית (ShYT) <H7897> translated as: *a dress | garment, attire* — used in Psalm 73:6, Proverbs 7:10

* שַׁיִת (ShYT) <H7898> as: *briers/brairs, wild growth of weeds, trash* | translated as: *thorns* — used in Isaiah 5:6, and repeatedly in Isaiah.

> **Note:** Interesting that in Isaiah — the use of what is translated as *"briers/briars"* from (ShMYR) and the *"thorns"* from (ShYT). [* *which also makes a connection to Shem (ShM) and Seth (ShT)*].

> Concept of *what* is <brought forth> as,
> *"briers/weeds [thorns]"* or as *"clothing"*

* [The Concept of Thorns] is often used metaphorically to describe *desolation, judgment,* or *the consequences of sin.* It conveys the idea of something that is *troublesome, obstructive,* or *indicative of a curse.*

> **Note:** the relationship to *"Thorns"* and the Consequences of Sin: the covering with fig leaves (as *"Clothing"*) of Adam and Eve's nakedness after eating the fruit in Genesis 3.

> Also,
> Concept of *"Living off the Land,"*
> which *will provide for the people*
> [but it will be as *"thorns"* as the idea of *"blood, sweat, and tears"* | hard work leads to survival | the idea of the suffering servant.]

2 - Dimensional Construct (BR + YT →ASh)

The *"what"* is [Born within] is אֵשׁ (ASh) <H784>, defined as *"a fire,"* but also translated as: *"blazing, burning, fiery, flaming, flashing."*

> **Glyph meaning formula:**
> *Mind of God + <brings forth> → Aspects of Creation*

> Concept of *Wisdom,* as *finding the balance*
> in the duality nature: *Destruction/Creation*

The idea of *"Fire"* as the method of what is used to destroy in order to create and bringing a balance to nature [as: to clear old growth and bring in new seedling growth].

The female aspect [aka: the feminine plural suffix] is the יׄת (YT).

> *Glyph Meaning: Effort of the Weaving together*

> Concept of *putting together,* as to *do work for a purpose*

Note: When the (BR) and the (YT) are made as a union, it becomes (BRYT) <H1285> translated as: *"covenant"* → gives birth to → (ASh) <H784>, defined as: *"a fire,"* but also translated as: *"blazing, burning, fiery, flaming, flashing."*

> Concept of the *Wisdom* born within the *Covenant*

* (BRYT) <H1287> translated as: *"soap"* – used in Jeremiah 2:22 and Malachi 3:2 | **Note:** Ancient Soap was made using ashes [the by-product of fire].

Concept of representing a *purity of cleanliness.*

> Concept of the *Human mind exists to fasten together*
> *the purpose that will bring forward "Wisdom"*

The idea that the Human mind has the function to bring about purpose, as (BRYT) versus the (BNYT), as swapping the (R) *"the Human Mind"* with (N) *"the Seed"* <Dry Seed>, as the *Potential* to bring it.

Another *Dimensional Construct*   (BT →RASh)

* בת (BT) <H1323> as: *"Daughter"* + giving birth to the * ראשׁ (RASh) <H7218> defined and translated as: *"Head, chief, top, beginning, leader."*

Concept of *"a Daughter giving birth to a "Leader/Chief"*

Similar to the idea of the *sons of God* took wives from the *daughters of men* and giving birth to *Nephilim,* נפילים (NPYLYM) *<H5303>* (translated as: *"Giants")* – used in Genesis 6 & 13.

3 - *Reflective Construct* (T+Y+Sh+A+R+B)

> **Glyph meaning formula:**
> *Weaving together + <brings forth> → Effort + <brings forth> →*
> *Aspects of Creation + <brings forth> → Mind of God + <brings forth> →*
> *Mind of Man + <brings forth> → Blueprint/Plan*

Note: The idea of Weaving together of a basket or a net [*the Matrix*] — in other words, the patterned effect is its outcome and purpose, or the *Concept of Complexity* of/from/come out as → the *Effort(s)*
　　* This could also be understood as the intention of *Form* or the mold of a *Shape* (which reflects of the actual outcome)
　　— the idea of an action that is complex, but with an impressive outcome.

　　Note: From the Glyph meaning perspective, it's the concept of "how the weaving together is done.": (TY+_) Weaving together of the Effort as the action of [a thing/event] as the key factor vs. the outcome from the action (_+YT).

　　* תי (TY) Although there is not a two-letter word used in this format, there are words that begin with these two letters — denoting location or direction [described as meaning: North, South, Central/Middle, Desert]. Also implies the idea of: *with or as an intentional effort.*

　　* תיש (TYSh) *<H8495>* translated as: *"male goat"*
　　— the idea of *"actions with impressive outcome"* as, *the balancing and sheer footed-ness of a goat on a cliff side.*

> Concept of *the Balance of Nature,*
> *as sheer-footed – like the Goat but also the bold,*
> *craziness of accomplishment and actions.*

　　* שא (ShA) * used in the prefix position of words that denotes the idea of the *coming of a destructive force*; also infers the concept of the duality of outcome [Creation/Destructive].

107

> Concept of... *"If we observe → Nature [Creation]*
> *we can see aspects of God's Mind"*
>
> [Words ending with the (A) usually have the
> outcome: as the negative aspects of the positioning]

* שׁאב (ShAB) <H7579> translated as: *to draw [water]* — used when *drawing water from a well for the camels.*

* שׁאג (ShAG) <H7580> translated as: *roaring [of a lion -or- as-like one]* | additionally, translated as: *a rumbling, groan/moan*
— also used to relate to *water = the sound of water rapids, as the fast/ wild waters.*

* רב (RB) <H7227> translated as: *abundant* | רבה (RBH) <H7227> translated as: *much, many, great*

> ## Concept of *Great*
> [as, *abundance of* -or- *the too much of* → can lead to a negative]

Also, ideas like: *too much Ego can bring Arrogance*
- as a *Fine-line* of balancing -or- like: *Walking a Tight rope.*

* רב (RB) <H7228> translated as: *arrows* | used in Job 16:13 actually as (RB)=*his arrows/archers* and used in Jeremiah 50:29 (RBYM)=*archers*

* רבב (RBB) <H7231-7233> translated as: *to cast together, increase, in number, to multiply by the myriad* | *to shoot an arrow*

> **Note:** the visual concept of "having a steadiness" [as to hold the bow steady (TY) + the "pulling back of the string of the bow" [aka: to draw back the string] (ShA) + the release or shooting of the "arrow" (RB)

* There is the implied accuracy [visual of the steer footed-ness of a goat on a cliff] of someone who is a Skilled Archer - not the random person shooting arrows for the first time.
— The positive spectrum of this concept is the "Hitting the Bull's Eye" -or- even the Splitting of the Arrow, which is already in the Bull's eye {The Robin Hood story}.
— The negative direction of this concept is the idea of Sin as "missing the mark"!

> ### Concept of *pinpoint accuracy*

Note: The idea of location as *"Hitting the Bull's Eye* [of the target]" - versus - The idea of direction as aiming or heading towards it.

[As this is the reflective nature of the concept of the *Bereshit,* it would imply that Human perceptions are *not pinpoint accurate* or *have difficulty of achieving it.*]

Note: רב (RB) is also connected to the title of Jewish spiritual leaders: ***Rabbi(s)*** | the Mishnaic Hebrew construct רבי (RBY) meaning *"Master"* / also translated as: *"Teacher"*

The observable message here is … In a general way, *not all people [people's ideas/plans] are as good* as a goat walking the steer cliff. In other words, we have a great potential to slip and fall.

4 - Meaning Construct

> Concept of *what Mankind has knowledge about* or *is capable of knowing <as an ongoing process>*

Also, the idea of staring into the ***chaos*** looking for the patterns (or ***order***) within it -or- looking deeper to find the *"Fire* or *Wisdom* within"].

Note: The overall concept of the word: *"Bereshit,"* בראשית (BRAShYT) is not just: *In The Beginning,* but infers the ongoing process of *Creation* itself, and as *"a patterned/fractal repeating one."*

In addition, there's an interesting relationship to the idea of equating a 6-letter word to the concept of *"Fruit,"* in which *Bereshit,* בראשית (BRAShYT) is made up of 6 letters = [aka: symbolically inferring the concept of the *"Fruit from the Tree of Knowledge of Good and Evil."*

The Hebrew word, ברא (BRA) *<H1254>* defined as: *"to create; to shape,"* and translated as: *"created."* When paired with בראשית (BRAShYT), it generates a type of encapsulation, implying the idea of the whole of *creation (was/is/will be) placed* within all of its existence, and not just as a beginning point that was created.

> Glyph meaning formula:
> *Blueprint(Plan) + <brings forth> →*
> *Human Mind + <brings forth> → Mind of God*

1 - *Linear Construct* (BRA)

Note: Breakdowns are already listed previously with the (BRAShYT)

An additional concept is the בר (BR) *<H1247>* translated as: *Son,* and the א (A) *Mind of God* = ברא (BRA).

> Concept of the *Son of God*

Note: The ברא (BRA) = *(Son of God)* is begotten from within the (BRAShYT) (BRA) (ALHYM) = *[In the beginning God created...]* but also is *(Son of God) <brings forth>* the *Elohim.*

> Concept of the *Union with Bereshit* and *Elohim* as the origins of the
> אב (AB) *<H1>* and אם (AM) *<H517>* *[Divine Father and Mother].* As
> well as the ברא (BRA) = *Son of God*, as both born from and part of
> the *Bereshit* as an aspect of the ongoing *Creation* process.

2 - *Dimensional Construct* (BA →R)

* בא (BA) **Note:** *Although this is not a biblical Hebrew word,
it can be found within other words.*

** באה (BAH) *<H872>* defined as: *an entrance to [a building/temple]* — used only once in Ezekiel 8:5 and actually written (BBAH) and translated as: *"in the entrance."*

Note: The reflection of בא (BA) is אב (AB) = *Father*

<The idea of *what the "Father" reflects is an entrance* [aka: *door/path/way]*>

As the full word, it functions as:

* באר (BAR) <H874> as: *to dig, engrave, to explain*
* באר (BAR) <H875> as: *well, pit, spring*
* באר (BAR) <H876> as: *well <an oasis rest in desert during the Exodus>*
* באר (BAR) <H877> as: *cistern, well, pit*

> Concepts of *securing / structured importance / life-saving*

> **Note:** The function of the (A) used as a suffix ending in combinations of letters usually has a negative or the potential of a negative outcome. It's an aspect of the relationship of *creation & destruction*. The idea of *In order to create something is destroyed* — but also that which is destroyed is being sacrificed for the *"new"* created thing.

God

The most common word translated as *"God"* [in the Bible] and appears in Genesis 1:1 *"In the beginning God created..."* — is the Hebrew word: *"Elohim,"* אלהים (ALHYM) <H430>.

The "masculine" plural name of God as the *"Elohim,"* אלהים (ALHYM) <H430>. The singular versions are the two-letter root word, *"El,"* אל (AL) <H410> and 3-letter root word, *"Eloh,"* אלה (ALH) <H433>.

The fact that it has a plural ending has caused much debate.

> **Note:** A simple way to look at this is: If the word: *Yahveh* (YHVH) represents: *"I am that I am,"* then the *Elohim* (ALHYM) could represent a statement like: *"All that I am"* – which is both plural and singular.

> The [All *(or Everything)*] is many (or the plural) and I is singular, so *Elohim* represents more of an explanation rather than a name. Using that word Elohim would be like saying: All of God's creation or Everything that is God/of God.

> It also appears to be a generalization of a reference to that which is an individual's personal choice of his or her God they chose to worship within a time when there were considered to be many gods, for example: My *Elohim* is *El* name... rather

than saying *Elohim* is my *Elohim*. (All that is, was and will be; the oneness of all/everything; the Divine Mind/Council).

Note: By removing the plural ending from Elohim (ALHYM) to Eloh (ALH), which in the Islamic faith, the name of God is pronounced as "Allah".

1 - *Linear Construct* (ALH+YM) | (A+L+H+Y+M)

* אלה (ALH) *<H428-9>* as: *This, These*

* אלה (ALH) *<H424 & 427>* as: *"there under the oak [tree] — most likely the Terebinth tree* [a more common tree and used for many purposes in the biblical regions] and the relevant European version was the oak tree.

* אלה (ALH) *<H426>* as: *"God, of God, of the God, of their God"*

* אלה (ALH) *<H422-3>* as: *"an oath | adjuration, curse, of swearing [an oath]"* – but actually mixed with (ALYT, VYAL, LHALTV, ALVT)
— used in Hosea 4:2 / translated as: [By] *swearing* | but really it's because of the perspective of the speaker and whom it's spoken to...<as spoken from YHVH/Lord referring to (ALH) as the God's Wisdom but in an inappropriate way> {as in the similar way of the "taking the lord's name in vain = swearing or cursing}

* אלה (ALH), but actually (ALY) *<H421>* *"Wail, Lament"* – used in Joel 1:8

> **Glyph meaning formula:**
> *From the Mind of God + Lessons + Reveal*

> Concept of *God's Wisdom*

* ימ (YM) *<H3220>* as: *"Sea"* | *a sea, large body of water, the Mediterranean Sea, large river, an artificial basin, the west, the south.*

> **Glyph meaning formula:**
> *Effort + [Water] = Life/Truth*

*The visual imagery of the **"flowing river"** -or-*
"the ebb and flow [of the waves] of the ocean/seas."

> Concept of *God's Will* and as *the passage of Time*

A = **Knowledge** *"All-Knowing"*

+ **L** = Learning/Lessons

= **AL** = *"God's Lessons"* = **Understanding**

+ **H** = Revealing/Revelation

= **ALH** = *"God's Wisdom"* = **Wisdom**

+ **YM** = *"God's Will"* *<Time>*

= **ALHYM** = *"The Path to Enlightenment"* = **Enlightenment**

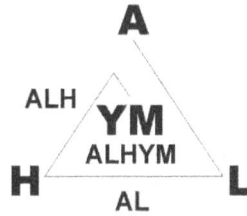

A

ALH

YM

ALHYM

H _____ **L**

AL

Concept of *Enlightenment*

but over time, and with a concept of changing or evolving
As growing/increasing-decreasing, also like or as
the fluid movement of the waters <river or ocean>

---

2 - *Dimensional Construct* (AL+YM →H)

Glyph meaning formula:

*The what is [Born within] is * (H) "Revealing" or "Revelation"*
— from (AL) as, "God's Lessons"
+ (YM) Time, as an aspect of "God's Will"

---

* אל (AL) *<H408>* as: *"not, no, do not"* | — used in Genesis 13:8 *Please let there be **no** strife...* [in many cases it's expressed as a *pleading for a condition*, rather than a command — for example: The lines commonly begin with the (AMR) *<H559>* as: *[someone] said...* – as well as, used with the word נא (NA) *<H4994>* translating as: *"please, I (we) pray, now | beseech"*].

* אל (AL) *<H409>* as: *"not, once, nothing"* – used in Daniel as: *[let] not.*

* אל (AL) *<H410>* as: *"El"*, singular for *"God,"* *mighty one*

* אל (AL) *<H411>* as: *"these, those"*

Glyph meaning formula:

Mind of God + Teach/Learning = [God's Lessons]

Concept of *"Strong Understanding"*
or the strong position of understanding.

The idea of *leadership through knowledge/education* -or- God as the top *teacher* or chooses a person as a *representative* and *exalted.*

+ *יָם (YM) *<H3220>* as: *"Sea"* | *a sea, large body of water, the Mediterranean Sea, large river, an artificial basin, the west, the south.*

> Concept of *God's Will* and as *the passage of Time*

→ *ה (H) as *"Revealing" or "Revelation"* – used to change a Name by adding the "H" as when a covenant is made with that person in regard to Human life [Example: *Abram,* אברם (ABRM) *<H87>* to *Abraham,* אברהם (ABRHM) *<H85>* and his wife, *Sarai,* שרי (ShRY) *<H8283>* to *Sarah,* שרה (ShRH) *<H8283>*].

> Concept of a *Process/Cycle* of from *Understanding*
> comes over *Time* will *[gives birth]* to *Revelation*
>
> *The idea of the Human attempt/trying to do so -or-*
> *symbolically, the "what" we are to give birth to.*

Another *Dimensional Construct*   (A+M →LY+H)

*אמ (AM) *<H512>* as: *"Mother"* *<birthing>* → (LYH)

Note: *Although (LYH) is not an actual word, variants similar to it are:*

*ליל (LYL) *<H3915>* as: *"Night"* | Also, described as a *"twist [away of light]"* — actually written as (LYLH).
  – used in Gen. 1:5 *[when naming the darkness as: the Night]*

*לילית (LYLYT) *<H3917>* as: *the night monster, screech owl*

Note: A connection to the name and character of: *"Lilith"* [the name of a female goddess known as a *night demon* who haunts the desolate places of Edom. [In the Akkadian language of Assyria and Babylonia, the terms *lili* and *līlītu* refer to a meaning of *spirits*]. Additionally, in other Jewish lore/myths she was Adam's first wife and the mother of night monsters/demons.]

> Concept of the *Mother of the Night* or *Mother birthing the Night*

*ליה (LYH) *<H3914>* translated as: *wreath* – used three times in 1 Kings (7:29, 30,36) but actually as ליות (LYVT).
  – [A connection to the *twist [away of light]* of *"Night"*]

3 - Reflective Construct (MY+H+LA)

* מִי (MY) *<H4310>* translated as: *Who?*

Note: If יִמ (YM) represents *"All-Time,"* then the reflective nature would be the *"focused" Effort of Time* — as in the *"Moment to/by moment"* interaction of *Effort(s)* [a person makes within Life].

Symbolically, the (YM) as *"the Flowing River"* and the. movement of all of what is in or on it, then the (MY) can be that which is pulled or drawn out of it *<like a fish by a fisherman [to take for oneself, family, or others>*.

> Concept of *What is done by Man* <as the action taken>, and by "*Who.*"

Note: An interesting connection the English use of *"My,"* as what is *mine*, as *"to own it"* or *"to claim/take ownership."*

+ * ה (H) as *Revealing/Revelation*

+ * לא (LA) *<H3808>* translated as: *"No, Not"*

> **Glyph meaning formula:**
> *Teaching/Learning (Lessons)* + *<bringing forth>* → *Mind of God*

The idea of being the *reflective* of *God's Lessons* is *God's Wrath.*

The generalized concept of *What is done* and *Who is doing it,* but also the *Why* [as the *being done* or *coming from "Mankind"*].

Simply put, this is the idea of *paying attention to a person's outcome from their actions* or *efforts* – which implies that Human perceptions should be analyzed by the outcome of the actions and effects.

4 - Meaning Construct

> ## Concept of *Enlightenment*
> -or- the Process of *Seeking a [the path to] Enlightenment.*

"The idea of the *Wisdom of "Life is a Journey, not a Destination.*"
Symbolically, as *"Riding down a flowing river."*

(untranslated)

One of the most commonly overlooked Hebrew words is the את (AT) *<H853>* — used in Genesis 1 over 20 times. As a word, the את (AT), *pronounced: 'ēṯ,* is not typically translated – *used as a direct object marker | an untranslatable mark of the accusative case.*

1 - Linear Construct (AT)

* את (AT) <H852> as: *a potent | sign, miraculous signs, wonders |* translated as: *"signs"* – used 3 times in Daniel (ATYA), (ATVHY), (ATYN)

* את (AT) <H853> as: *self* [usually not translated]

> **Note:** The את (AT) is used over 11000 according to Strong's Concordance but also divides this into two other uses of the word.

* The את (AT) <H853> is disregarded, but when there is a prefix, ו (V) [written as ואת (VAT)], it's translated as: *"and."*

* את (AT) <H854> as: *nearness, near, with, together with | among, against, before //* translated as: *"with"* (denoting proximity) in Genesis 4-9.

* את (AT) <H855> as: *mattock/coulter/plowshare | a hoe, or other digging implements.*

> **Note:** In English, if this word את (AT) gets translated, it's used as pronouns: *"me, him, her, us,"* and in the plural form אתמ (ATM) <H855> as: *"them."* This is understandable from the grammatical perspective because in the English language, the only words that occur in the accusative case are pronouns: *"me, him, her, us, whom,* and *them."*

2 - Dimensional Construct (A_T) <2-letter words can't have this function>
Reviewing words that represent the concept of a letter <born within>:

* אמת (AMT) <H571> as: *stability, certainty,* **truth**, *truth-worthiness | firmness, faithfulness, right way.*

> Concept of the **Life/Truth** *born within all the potential [that God will weave into existence]*

* אות (AVT) <H225> translated as: *consent, agreed* – used in Genesis 34:15 ...on this *[condition] we will consent* to you.

> **Note:** As the idea of an interaction (V) within the (AT) or as the monument of the full or *Greater* potential is conceded to a *Lesser* one.

3 - Reflective Construct (TA)

* תא (TA) <H8372> translated as: *room/chamber* [of the guardroom]

<the residence of the king's protectors> — inferring the idea of a *lesser* space within a *greater* space [as within a building like: a *Castle*].

> — used in 1 Kings 14:28 and 2 Chronicles 12:11, as well as several variants used in Ezekiel 40 | <describing the *House of the LORD* (BYT YHVH)>

4 - Meaning Construct

> ### Concept of *All that was/is/will be*
> [of what God will weave into existence]
> *– that contains all the potential (greater) of all the
> seeds of creation (the alphabet)*

> **Glyph meaning formula:**
> *The Mind of God + <brings forth> → Weaving together*

In other words, the Concept of "From the *First Cause* comes that which is *Woven Together*" — the idea of *how a thing is woven together* or *the complexity of the creation of a particular thing.*

> **Note:** The idea of the (TA) as *"Lesser"* is a chamber of a room -versus- the (AT) as *"Greater"* is the whole/all [or more specifically, the how God will weave into existence. — as the [was/is/will be] *woven together* — the idea of the specific cause [as: output or results of...] from the first cause [or the *First Causer* = (A), and outputting as: (AT) = *God's Matrix.*

Conceptually, the phrase: *"It shall come to pass"* — The denoting of the process of "The things [something] that will *come to pass* or *become.*

> **Note:** The other aspect is that the two letters are the "First and Last Letters of the Hebrew alphabet," and like the NT (which was or when written in Greek) are the Greek letters: Alpha and Omega. Of course, I must note the phrase in Revelation 22:13 *I am the Alpha and Omega, the First and the Last, the beginning and the end!*

The basis of the idea of the whole of the alphabet or all of the seeds of creation, as each expresses an aspect of the *"potential"* and as *the building blocks of all of Creation.*

Symbolically, this concept is also represented as: a *Conifer cone,*

a.k.a. *"Pine cone."* [Many cultures refer to this as a symbol of the spring rebirth
- because it is actually the function of the rebirth of *"Trees"*].

> **Note:** *Conifer cone,* defined as: the conical or rounded woody
> fruit of a pine tree, with scales that open to release the seeds.
> It's where seeds are stored—by definition it's a seed-bearing
> organ on gymnosperm: a plant that has seeds unprotected by an
> ovary (from Latin *ōvārium* 'egg') or *fruit.* [non-flowering] plants/tree].

> Concept of the *Tree of Life* and the "fruit" from it.

> **Note:** This is a similar function to a *"Corn Cob"* and connects to
> the *"Harvest."* | As well as, references in Sumerian[Assyrian/
> Babylonian] imagery of Annunaki *"holding the pine cone."* | Also, the
> references to looking like the *"Pineal Gland."*

The generalized concept inferring "[who/he/they] who holds
the power of all of the potential (or what will come from) of the
God's/gods Plan, as the (AB) = as a *"Beginning"* or what comes *First.*

And the as the whole of the *God's Matrix* <the (AT)> = as a
Greater what comes *First* and the*"End/Last."*

> **Note:** Ancient authors used it as a *"strong sign"* [as a sign
> of respect or "reverence," as to honor the authority of the
> divine creator/creation - "the awe of the Divine"], literally from
> the meaning of the Aleph א (A) meaning *"Strong"* and the Tav
> ת (T) meaning *"Sign."*

> The deeper connection is the visual imagery of the Glyphs
> as Head of the Ox, *or as the Mind of God* = the primordial First
> Cause, and the ending with Crossed sticks, as *weaving together*
> as the primordial *Basket of Creation.*

the Heaven

The Hebrew word השמים (HShMYM), which has the prefix
letter ה "Hey" (H) usually translated as: *"the"* is added to the root
word שמים (ShMYM) <H8064>, which is defined as: *"heaven, sky (air)."*

> **Note:** More often than not [in Genesis 1] it has the (H)+(ShMYM)
> *השמים (HShMYM) used in Genesis 1:1, 1:9, 1:14, 1:15, 1:17, 1:20,
> 1:26, 1:28, 1:30 — and — שמים (ShMYM) in Genesis 1:8

> **Glyph meaning formula:**
> *Aspects of Creation + <brings forth> → Life/Truth + <brings forth> →*
> *Effort + <brings forth> → Life/Truth*
> *-vs.-*
> *Revealing [Revelations] + <brings forth> → Aspects of Creation +*
> *<brings forth> → Life/Truth + <brings forth> →*
> *Effort + <brings forth> → Life/Truth*

Note: A revealing (H) that brings forth [anything] would infer the idea of a new understanding about it. The use of the (AT) (HShMYM) is making the statement *"all that it is/will be"* and *"all that is revealed"* [as how it will be understood] of the (ShM) and the (YM) is referring to how this *"plays out over time"*.

1 - Linear Construct (H+ShM+YM)

* שׁמים (ShMYM) *<H8064>* as, *Heaven, "sky"* | <Noted to have a word origin from an unused root meaning *lofty.*>

* שׁם (ShM) *<H8033>* as: *there, then, thither* | First used in Genesis 2:8 "And the LORD God planted a garden eastward in Eden; and *there he put* the man whom he had formed. | The actual order in Hebrew is first the (VYShM) *<H7760>* as: *"He put"* + (ShM) *<H8033>* as: *"there."*

* שׁם (ShM) *<H8034>* translated as: *"name"* [associated with a name] — inferring the idea of: *"to be **put** [by God]."* | Also, described as *an appellation,* [as a mark, memorial of individuality] and by implication: *honor, authority, character.*

* שׁם (ShM) *<H8035>* as the Name: *Shem* (one of Noah's sons)

> Concept of *"the assignment"*

The idea of the purpose of what something is/does <both as *"label* and *duty."*>

* *Hashem,* השׁם (HShM) *<H2044>* used once in 1 Chronicles 11:34 (BNY) The sons (HShM) of Hashem (HGZVNY) the Gizonite.

> **Note:** Doesn't list (the sons) by name(s), just references them as part of David's Thirty Mighty Men.

* ים (YM) *<H3220>* as: *"Sea"* | *a sea, large body of water, the Mediterranean Sea, large river, an artificial basin, the west, the south*

> **Note:** The idea of the (YM) as a masculine plural ending to (ShM) is the symbolic nature of *Time [All-time/God's Will]* as the *multiple ["Name(s)"]* or the Concept of *"the assignment(s)."* As the purpose of what something is/does <both as *"label and duty"*> and assigned to

the many individuals = aka: *the idea of the "Chosen" people.*

The addition of the prefix of the (H) as the *Revealing/Revelation* of... -or- as *"what was/is/will be"* <*brought forward*> in the (ShM+YM) or *Names.*

> Concept of *all aspects of how things will be done* -or- *the influence [the spirit realm will play out]*

The idea of *How people will express [or play out] their internal nature [as what is truly in their minds or spirit].*

Symbolically, as the souls of all people playing out.

Note: There is also the idea that this is an *elevated condition of the Mind or Spirit of "Man(kind),"* which in later beliefs becomes a separated place, as *God's realm/place [palace]* as: the *"elevated"* [as up in the sky] or divine[Godly] natures get to exist -or- has the place go (as to achieve to be placed — the rewarded place) — in the Afterlife!

2 - *Dimensional Construct* (HM →ShMY)

* הם (HM) <*H1992*> translated as: *"they"* | *themselves* — used in Genesis 3:7 *as "they, themselves"* <describing (Adam and Eve as their eyes were opened after eating the fruit>

<*Bringing forth*> → is the שמי (ShMY) = ש (Sh) *Aspect of Creation*

<*Bringing forth*> → מי (MY) *Life/Truth + Efforts = The Path of Life*

> Concept of *How "They"* – as *"the "Names" are* <*bringing forth the "Efforts"*

Another *Dimensional Construct* (HSh+YM →M)

* הש (HSh) <as a connection to the *HaShem, the Day 6 and Day 7*>

+ ים (YM) <as *God's Will/Time*> + <*bringing forth*> → מ (M) *Life/Truth*

> The Concept of *How the Revelations from God's Creation Efforts over time will bring forth "Life."*

The idea of *a special place or circumstance of an ideal condition* [and that it *will take time*].

Example: *"The Goldilocks Zone"* [aka: "The Habitable Zone"]

3 - Reflective Construct (MYMShH)

* מִי (MY) <H4310> translated as: *Who?*

Note: If יֹם (YM) represents *"All-Time,"* then the reflective nature would be the focused *Effort of Time* — as in the *"Moment to/by moment"* interaction of *Effort(s)* [a person makes within Life].

Symbolically, the (YM) as *"the Flowing River"* and the movement of all of what is in or on it, then the (MY) can be that which is pulled or drawn out of it *<like a fish by a fisherman [to take for oneself, family, or others>.*

> Concept of *What is done by Man* <as the action taken>, and by *"Who."*

Note: An interesting connection to the English use of *"My,"* as what is *mine*, is *"to own it"* or *"to claim/take ownership."*

+ מ (M) *Life/Truth* + * שֹה (ShH) <H7716> translated as: *member of the flock [lamb, sheep, goat, young sheep, young goat].*

-or- * מֹשֶה (MShH) <H4873> translated as: *"Moses"*

> Concept of *"Who is like* or *brings forward* the *"Lamb,"* or *"Moses"*

The idea of the *Messiah* [which is also the base letters (MShH)].

4 - Meaning Construct

> Concept of the *Aspects of the Name(s)*
> [And of *Understanding the Name(s)*]

The idea of *Returning to* or *Being with God* is the relationship to the concept of a *Name* and *Meaning*.

and + (untranslated)

The next use of the word *'ēt,* אֵת (AT) <H853> has the prefix letter ו (V) pronounced as *wə'ēt,* וְאֵת (VAT). The letter ו (V) is most often translated as: *"and."* Although the translation functions properly, it lacks its original meaning. It's not just an aspect of adding, but something "tethered" to (or from) another.

* (VAT) = The "All-Revealing Patterns," or rather "the tethering/connection [God level] as the Matrix (as All "Potential <pine cone>" Patterns)!"

> Glyph meaning formula:
> *The denoting of the process of...*
> *The Mind of God + <brings forth> → Weaving together*

the Earth

The translated words, *"the Earth"* or הארץ (HARTs), which has the prefix letter ה (H), usually translated as: *"the"* is added to the root word, ארץ (ARTs) *<H776>*, which is defined as: *"earth, land."*

1 - Linear Construct (A+RTs)

* א (A) *Mind of God*

+ * רץ (RTs) *<H7518>* as: *fragment | piece, bar*
— used once in Psalm 68:30 (BRTsY)

> Concept of *God's Fragment* or *a fragment/piece of God*

The idea of the *relationship between the Mind of God and the Mind of Man is that the human mind is a piece or fragment of God's Mind.*

— as *the place for the pieces to exist when separated from the oneness of God's mind.*

Another Linear Construct (AR+Ts)

* אר (AR)

Note: *Is not a biblical Hebrew word, but it can be found within other words.*

> Glyph meaning formula:
> *The denoting of the process of...*
> *The Mind of God + <brings forth> → Mind of Man*

** ארא (ARA) *<H690>* a Name meaning: *Lion*
— used once in 1 Chronicles 7:38 [describing the *"The Sons of Asher"* (one of Jacob's 12 sons/tribes) <as a generational offspring>.

** ארב (ARB) *<H693>* meaning as: *to lurk* | *to mix, to pledge, to exchange, to become surety* // translated as: *lies in wait, an ambush* — used in Deut., Joshua, Judges, Samuel, Chronicles

** ארבה (ARBH) *<H697>* as: *locusts* — used in Exodus, Leviticus, Deut., Judges, Kings, Chronicles, Job, Psalms, Proverbs, Jeremiah, Joel, etc.. [but with variants: (BARBH) (HARBH)(KARBH) (LARBH) (MARBH)]

** ארי (ARY) *<H738>* as *"a lion"*

Note: Symbolically, as the proper direction of understanding (or a true understanding), the how God thinks (AR) as the *"Greater"* versus the reflective (RA) as a *"Lesser"* or mankind's version of understanding — [as in the BRAShYT]

+ * צ (Ts) *the Glyph of the Snare/Trap/Fallen Enemy*

> ## Concept of *"The Fall [of man/mankind]"*

The connection and relationship of concepts of *being trapped/snared/ netted [like an animal]* as well as the *"fallen enemy"* and *"taking a knee."* The idea of *submitting/submissive (as either forced or by choice).*

2 - Dimensional Construct (A+Ts →R)

* אצ (ATs) *Mind of God + Snare/Trap/Fallen Enemy*
Note: *Is not a biblical Hebrew word, but it can be found within other words.*

The idea of *being held in a limited space/place — restricted movement*, is **how** humans move through time.

** אצבע (ATsBa) *<H676>* as: *something to seize with* | *a finger, a toe* — used in Exodus 8:19 in describing the *finger of God.*
[+ ** בע (Ba) is connected to בעא (BaA) *<H1156>* as: *to seek, ask, or as a desire]*

** אציל (ATsYL) *<H678>* as: *extremity* | *a noble*
[+ ** יל (YL) is connected to ילד (YLD) *<H3205-6>* as: *to bear young, to beget, to show lineage, something born, a lad, offspring]*

Concept of *something both connected* but *yet independent* [in both function and movement]

The idea of *a person in leadership over others* but *disconnected from them.*

→ * ר (R) *Mind of Man*

Concept of *"Mind of God limits or restricts movement of the Mind of Man [Mankind]"*

The idea of the *possibility of the leading to <seizes or rules over>.*

3 - Reflective Construct (Ts+RA)

* צ (Ts) *the Glyph of the Snare/Trap/Fallen Enemy*

{* צר (TsR) <H7200> as: *narrow, a tight place, a pebble, flint, adversary, foe, oppressor*}

+ * רא (RA) **Note:** *Is not a biblical Hebrew word!?*

Other variants or words built from (RA):

** ראה (RAH) <H7200> defined as: *to see, look at, inspect, perceive, consider* — used in Genesis *"[God] saw..."* — but written as (VYRA) / translated as the (V) as: *"And [God] saw...*

** ראה (RAH) <H7201> as: *"bird of prey"*
— used in Deuteronomy only once as: *"And the glede/red kite.. [a bird of prey]..."* — but written as (VHRAH)

Note: Egyptian god, Ra *(Sun god)* was *the falcon-headed* [a bird of prey]

** ראה (RAH) <H7203> as: *"seer, a vision"*
— used in 1 Samuel as: *"a seer"* — written as (HRAH) [described as an older term used to describe the later term, Prophet] — used in Isaiah as: *"having visions"* — written as (BRAH).

** ראה (RAH) <H7204> as: a Name — used in 1 Chronicles | written as (HRAH).

** ראי (RAY) <H7209> as: *"a mirror"*

** ראי (RAY) <H7210> defined as: *seeing, vision, sight*
— used in Genesis 16:13 *"[God] who sees [me]..."* — used in 1 Samuel as: *"appearance/[good-looking]"* — used in Job as: *"of him who sees [me]"*

Concept of the *"being trapped"* will bring a mental wrath [within oneself or others]

The idea *extends to others having* or *taking power over another,* as well as [*to capture/take what one sees*].

4 - Meaning Construct

> ## Concept of *"Earth"*
> *– as the place in which the mind(s) are ensnared.*

Note: The relationship of *Heaven* and *Earth* is the *Metaphysical* tethered to the *Physical* aspects of Creation/ Existence, similar to the *Human Mind* tethered to the *Body.*

Genesis 1:26 *And God said, Let us make man in our image, after our likeness...*

<see next page → Fig. 3 Generations from the *"Beginnings"*>

Trinities of Creation

TETHERING TO EARTHLY REALM

ShT
Seth
(Generations from the son of Adam to Noah)

ShM
Shem
(Generations from the son of Noah)

ShYT
"to place, put, set"

The process of an "Incubation" to "Birth"

AR
Reflective / Aspects of Creating w/o (B) Grouping

HARTs
(Earth)
Revealing the Physical
Incubation process from the elements

AVR
(Light)
Creation of the elements

(V)

BRA
"to create; to shape"

BRASHYT
(Bereshit)

H ShM YM
(Heaven)
Revealing the Non-Physical

YM
Effort of Life/Truth

YVM
Yom (Day)

(V)

Ⓑ

RASh
Head Ends

Trinity of Bereshit

Primordial Feminine

Trinity of Elohim

Primordial Masculine

ShM
(Heaven)
Revealing the non-Physical

Ⓐ

AL

ALHYM
(Elohim)

The Efforts (Y) of El

(Unseen Effort (Y) of Revelation (H) is "Yah")

The path of "Revelation" to "Truth/Life"

AB Divine "Father"
The Union of Primordial Parentage

TETHERING TO EARTHLY REALM

YHVH

(V)

H

126

The Overview

The complexity begins to generate a perspective of **order to chaos,** by separating into categories: (the idea of what is reflected versus what it's reflecting). Specifically, the concept of the *Divine/Heaven realm* versus the *Earthly realm,* and what is *brought forth* versus *born out of...* [the idea of the *masculine creation process* versus the *feminine creation process*].

The common themes repeating and building a layered complexity [the Concept of the *"Matrix"*] = aka: the idea of the word *et,* אֵת (AT) *Glyph Formula: Mind of God + Woven together* = *God's Matrix* — used as a way to denote the complexity of things built into the word that is placed after it.

> **Note:** The complexity of the *woven together* <ת(T)> in the (BRAShYT) and the (ALHYM) to the layered connections building into <אֵת(AT)> the Heaven, Earth, then branching out to other words and key **Names.**

> Concept of the *"layered/layering"* Matrix
> *as the inner workings of God's Matrix*

The *complexity* of the *"Path of Creation"* (YSh) is formatted in a pattern of the six (6) days [in Genesis 1], which presents the idea of *place (as: location)* versus the *what was* or *is set in place*: as the **Concept of Names (characters),** and how this relates to the *"Path of Life"* (YM).

> **Note:** This transition is also the idea of (ShT) *Seth to* (ShM) *Shem,* which is impeded in Genesis 1 (as: the ShT) Creation's Weaving versus the Life Weaving (as: the MT) *in Genesis 2, which is the first use of the word* (ShM) *as Naming concept* (translated as and there in Genesis 2:8 and put (VYShM) and named (ShM) and placed.

Additionally, the continuing *"Concept of Reflection"* as expressing the idea of how things *branch out* and the *Efforts* they produce [as *attributes*] = which are expressed as Names.

Section Five

The Concept of a "Name"

In ancient times, when someone asked your name, they were asking the question, *"Who are you and what do you do?"* Some cultures even waited to give a child a name until they witnessed some action or event to make this connection to who the child would be, to link a name to them (as a form of earning one's name). In some cases, an additional name or a new name was given to describe events, changes in a person, or surroundings.

The function of *naming [a thing]* is to capture its essence, which correlates to what it does and who it is. In other words, describe its *attributes* and its *character*.

> **Note:** This idea of *"capturing the essence"* seems to be the case for all ancient [biblical] words, including the letters/glyphs themselves.

The concept of a *Name* or *Naming* is also connected to the ideas of *personification, incarnation,* and *manifestation*.

> **Personification**: representing or assigning attributes of a personal nature to a non-human entity as a human-like figure.

> **Incarnation**: actually has a meaning of *vested [clothe* or *embody] in flesh*. Also, used to describe the union of the second person of the Godhead with manhood in Christ.

> **Manifestation**: using the term *embodies [to have a body]* to define the concept of its meaning. Making a connection to a broader range of physical theories or abstract ideas, often associated with divine or spiritual aspects.

There also seems to be a similar attribute or function of the concept of *flesh* or *body* to *clothes* or *garments,* as *something* that is *containing* [or *tethering*] to an Earthly realm from the Heavenly realm. The idea of the unseen *Divine* or *Spirit* realm having entities or an entity is then expressed in *Names,* which are connected to attributes.

Name(s) of God

[Names associated with God]

HaShem

HaShem, הַשֵּׁם (HShM) *<H2044>* translated as: *"the Name."* This is a title in Jewish tradition used to refer to God without using any particular name, terminology, or aspect of God — serving as a sign of respect and to honor. In Judaism, *HaShem* is used in regular conversation when referring to God, but when in prayer, the term *Adonai ("my master")* is used. The *"Name"* terminology is referencing *YHVH [Yahveh/Yahweh → Jehovah]*, translated as *"Lord."*

שמ ← ה   H → ShM

Note: As I mentioned in the {Process vs. Construct section} about the function of prefix letters: the ה (H) translated as: *"the"* and the שמ (ShM) *<H8034/H8036>* translated as: *"name."*

* שמ (ShM) *<H8033>* translated as: *there, thither | where, here, in it*
— used over 800 times in Genesis 2:8, 10, 11, 12 *[in reference to the Garden of Eden]*, many other times in Genesis, Exodus, Leviticus, Numbers, Deuteronomy, Joshua, Judges

* שמ (ShM) *<H8034>* defined and translated as: *"[the/a] name"*
— used over 800 times in Genesis 2:11, 13, 14, 19, 20 *[in reference to the "Names" of things connected to the Garden of Eden]*, many other times in Genesis, Exodus, Leviticus, Numbers | also: [translated as: *[men of] "renown" and "fame"]* in Deuteronomy, Joshua, Judges, Ruth, 1 Samuel

* שמ (ShM) *<H8035>* defined as the Name: ***"Shem"*** (*one of three sons [the oldest] of Noah*
— connected to the root word שׂוּם (ShVM) *<H7760, 7761>* translated as: *"to set, place, put, appoint, make"*

* שמ (ShM) *<H8036>* defined and translated as: *"[the/a] name"*
— used in Ezra, Daniel

Note: There is a relationship to the word as the intertwining of function when something is *"set in place"* – as: (ShT) *Seth* and its purpose as: (ShM) *Shem,* and the reflective nature of this function, as it's "Name."

The concept of the *Name* is also describing its purpose, which was the way in which ancient people viewed names [as being connected to who someone was].

In other words, to be a [thing] is to be placed and is to name it [this is also the "Concept of becoming or being personified"] — the establishment of who a person is [which is why names were often given later in life, or changed, or given added names.

Note: Over time, this concept of Names has transitioned into the use of surnames, like "John, the carpenter" became "John Carpenter" or "William, the son of John" became William Johnson." As well as evolving [branched/split-divided] into [as expanded terminology in the use and separation] of titles and job descriptions.

1 - *Linear Construct* (H+Sh+M)

* השׁמ (HShM) *<H2044> Hashem*

— used once in 1 Chronicles 11:34 *"The sons* בני (BNY) השׁמ (HShM) *of Hashem* הגזוני (HGZVNY) *the Gizonite"*

Note: Listing as part of David's Thirty Mighty Men

Other variants or words built from (HShM):

** להשמעות (**LHShMaVT**) *<H2045>* translated as: *to you with information | unto thee, to cause {thee} to hear | to let [you] hear [it] with.* — used once in Ezekiel 24:26

> Concept of *"One of the Senses or as "Getting a Sense [of something/anything/everything]."* Also, the idea of *"Making sense of [something/anything/everything]"*

Note: This implies the idea that a *Name* is also *information* received *[from God].* A perceptive view [by a Jewish/Rabbinic? Tradition] as: *"A person's mission in life"* {as in the *mission of a person is built in* or *within* the Name a person was/is given}. The idea of a *Name* is a representation, or the concept of *"getting a sense of who a person is/will be/or was."*

2 - *Dimensional Construct* (H+M →Sh)

* הם (HM) <*H1990-1992*> translated as: *"themselves"*
(relates *the idea of unto oneself* or *making part of one's own*)
[Born within] → is the שׁ (Sh) *Aspect of Creation*

— used in Genesis 3:7 as: *"they, themselves"* <*describing them along with the function of* <*what they did as they made [a thing] for themselves*>

> Symbolically, as *How we are part of Creation itself* and *How we are creating within in it, as well.*

3 - *Reflective Construct* (M+Sh+H)

* משׁה (MShH) <*H4872*> as the Name: *"Moses"*
*** The details of the Name: *Moses* describes at the end of this section ***

> Concept of *[what is reflected from...]* or *[what is personified]* of *"HaShem"* (HShM) is the *"Moses"* (MShH)
> – which also relates to the assemblage of the word *"Messiah"*

4 - *Meaning Construct*

> Concept of *"Getting a Sense [of something/someone]"*
> < the idea of receiving a *"hint"* or having a *"gist"*>
> (like: *smelling* or *hearing* [something] without *seeing)*

Note: The concept of *"reflection"* in regard to *perspective*: God's versus Mankind's. The idea that mankind can't know the *"All"* [of a thing], only a part of it, so if mankind **names** a thing – it's only identifying a limited aspect of it (via *human senses*).

> Concept of *Mankind's understanding* of a Name (or *Naming)* of *"God"* is actually **unknowable.**

Examples: [Commandment of ... *"Do not take the Lord's name in Vain"*], and as an explanation of Moses asking what is your name [to God] and getting the reply meaning: *"I am that I am"* [(YHVH)].

Adonai

Adonai, אדני (ADNY) *<H136, H113>* | Not a name, but rather as a *Title*. Traditionally in Judaism, the name יהוה (YHVH) is not pronounced, but read as *Adonai* (defined as *"Master"* and translated as *"O Lord"*).

> **Note:** The term is used during prayer and referred to as *HaShem* (*"the Name"*) at other times.

> **Glyph meaning formula:**
> *Mind of God* (A) + *Path/Way* (D) + *Seed(Potential)* (N) + *Efforts* (Y)
> *"The God's Path brings forth Potential Efforts from it"*

1 - Linear Construct (AD+NY)

* אד (AD) *<H108>* as: *mist, vapor, fog* + *<bringing forth>* + נ‬י (NY) *<H5204>* as, *wailing (a crying out)*

> **Glyph formula:** *Mind of God + Path* (*bringing forward of a Path from the Mind of God*) – as the direction one takes or goes.

> **Note:** The idea of following *God's Path* – as something difficult to see *<fog:* blocks visibility > | *mist/vapor* (is like the spirit form of water) and is the gas state or attribute of the liquid water *(life/truth).*

> Concept of *"Not so clear <or as a type of lacking>"*
> *but with an Authority or Power*

+ * נ‬י (NY) *<H5204>* translated as: *wailing | lamentation.* Also, connected to denote *"a river or a flowing body of water."* — although not actually used as a two-letter word, and is linked to (**BNYHM**) and translated as: *[their] wailing* — used only once in Ezekiel 27:32.

> **Glyph formula:** *The Seed (Generations) <Potential> + Effort* as the potential of the efforts that come from it.

> **Note:** The idea of the *collection of things to come* and what *efforts* are brought forward:
> – The relationship of the need or necessity of the *"watering"* to assist in or to make a *Seed* begin to *Sprout.*

– The connection to *crying out/wailing* could symbolically represent: the idea of *"Having a cry is a perceived need to move on from a hard event or situation."* As well as the concept of a newborn baby as its *"needs"* and *crying out* to be nursed [*for its mother's milk*].

> Concept of a type of communication of *"lacking clarity of words, but with an authority or power* [of the need of an infantile wanting]

The idea of *"lacking deep thought."*

– In a positive way, *it's to take care of the baby's needs.*
– In the negative, as *an ignorant/infantile position of authority.*

Word Example: [of building off the base concept]

* נִיד (NYD) <H5205> translated as: *solace, moving,* and identified as the *"quivering [motion] of lips."* | Meaning as: *"motion."* — also defined as: *wandering, exile, fugitive, lamentation.*

2 - Dimensional Construct (A+Y →DN)

* אִי (AY) <H335> translated as: *"Where? How | Alas! | "a howler [a howling beast], any solitary creature (a jackal)"*

→ <born within> + נ (DN) <H1835> a Name: *Dan* | meaning: *"to judge"*

The idea to *make others feel the sorrow [of oneself]*
+ The idea of *judge* [from] or the *judging* of others.

> Concept of *Announcing One's Sorrow*
> Ideas like: *"Misery likes/loves Company,"* and terms like: *"being a Karen"*]

Symbolically, *"A Jackal (the howling beast)* is comparing an Individual = who has a judgmental viewpoint.

> Concept of *Passing judgment on others from a position of solitary authority."*

3 - *Reflective Construct* (YNDA)

Note: the (YNDA) *is not a biblical Hebrew word!?*

* **יַ** (YN) *Note: Although not a word, it is used as a plural suffix to words!?*

> Glyph Formula: *Effort + <bringing forth> the Seed*

Note: The *Seed* is released from the fruit or plants as they die, in order to re-populate [as a resurrection or rebirth process].

Other variants or words built from (YN):

* **יָנָה** (YNH) *<H3238>* as: *to rage, be violent, to suppress, to maltreat* | as the *Revealing* from the (YN)

* **יָנַח** (YNCh) *<H3240>* as: *to deposit, to allow to stay, to rest, settle down & remain* | as the *Branching/Diversity* from the (YN)

— used in Genesis 2:15 *And the LORD God took the man* (HADM), *and put him* (V**YNCh**HV) *into the garden of Eden to dress it and to keep it.*

Note: The actual word (YNCh) has the (HV) added to the end, which implies a *<holding back> Revealing/Revelation* -or- the idea of "prior to eating from the *Tree of Knowledge*."

> Concept of *Heading towards a "Potential"*

The Idea of *Something having potential to lead somewhere.*

+ * **דָּא** (DA) *<H1668>* translated as: *"this"*

> Glyph Formula: *Path + <bringing forth> Mind of God*

Note: The attempt to bring forth an understanding of God.

> Concept of *Attempting to do* or *live the Right Way/Path*
> or having the desire for *"God's Will"* to be done.

The idea of *an Authority from God as a speculation [or a desired state] of what should, would, or could be a thing [or something].*

Note: The (DA) as a desire to do *God's Will* or to *serve God* versus the reflective nature (AD) *God's Path* or *Way,* [aka: (ADM) *Adam*] = The actual *Right[ous] way of doing things.*

4 - Meaning Construct

> ### Concept of *a Master (Lord)*
>
> *[as the Lesser]* — *the crying baby in need of its mother's milk*
> versus
> *the reflective nature is of being "needy"*
> *[as the Greater]* — *the "The return of the right[ous] way of doing things"*

The idea of *what someone "serves"* [as a fine line between a right or wrong way]. In other words, the difference between our selfish needs and the needs of others.

Note: Symbolic of the relationship of the Moon, as *Lesser [light]*, because it only reflects the light of the Sun, as *Greater [light]*.

YHVH

Yahweh/Yahveh(Jehovah), יהוה (YHVH) *<H3068>* translated as: *"Lord"* and described as: *"I am that I am"*. Also, known as the proper name of the God of Israel.

> **Note:** Also called, *"The Tetragrammaton"* or *"Tetragram"* [from Greek -> *tetra-* (four) + *-grammos* (letters)].

1 - Linear Construct (YH+VH)

> **Glyph meaning formula:**
> *The* (Y) *Effort* + (H) *Revelation/Revealing* +
> (V) *[held back]* + (H) *Revelation/Revealing*

* יה (YH) *<H3050>* also translated as: *"Lord"* and described as a contracted form of יהוה (YHVH) *<H3068>*.

> The (Y+) *Effort* or *Actions of...* <inferring a value [of time passing]
> + (H) *Revealing* <as reaching a moment [of wisdom]>
> = (YH) | the idea of *what will be revealed in time = outcome(s)*

Note: The correlation to the Canaanite *"Moon"* god [known as: **Yah**]. He was celebrated for his ability to change and control the seasons – an important aspect of Canaanite agricultural life, specifically getting to the *"Harvest."*

> Concept of the *bringing* of the *seasons* or *harvest*
>
> – as the *"Bringer of the Harvest"*

The relationship of *Duality* and the *Cycle of Creation/ Destruction*, in context to the *Harvest*, is the *act of creation to grow crops*, then to the *destruction of crops [to take the life of the plant]* for the *"Fruits of the Labors".*

Connection to this concept of *Harvest* and *Fruits of Labor* is used in Exodus 23:16. *The Feast of the Harvest of the Firstfruits* of their labors... and used in Leviticus 23:9-14 titled: *The Feast of Firstfruits* or *The feast of the Harvest.*

The perspective of the *"Positive"*

At the basic level, there's the idea of *"The harvest of success"* or *"The successful harvest."* There are numerous of references to the concept of the *successful harvest* in both OT [Old Testament] and NT [New Testament] – in terms of *harvest* being *plentiful.*

As it relates to *God*, it's a concept of a "Name" or "Title" – making the statement: *"He who brings forth the successful harvest,"* as: the *"Successful Harvester* or *"Harvester of Success."*

> Concept of the *Success of the Crops*

A connection to using a *Tool* – as in *"The Glyph of a Mattock"* [aka: *"Plowshare"*].

The perspective of the *"Negative"*

As a related Concept of *Success [of Harvest/Crops]*, by comparing to the concept of *Conquest*, which is a connection to using a *Tool* – as a *"Sword."*
The idea that success itself is brought by *"God"* – by means of a battle.

Note: The relationship to this *duality* idea is used in Isaiah 2:4 as *the pounding swords to plowshares...* [as the Messianic future of "returning to Godly ways" or the idea of a *"redeeming."*

* יהו (YHV) symbolizing the (V) *<hold backing>* as *restraining* the *"Negative"* conquest and war-like version of (YH) [aka: worship or serving the *"War god"*].

Also, the idea of *<holding back> growth* or *expansion* – as an *over-reaching* or *excessively growing crops* = the concept of *guiltily*.

+ *<bringing forth>* (H) *Revealing/Revelation* = (YHVH) [as the *"Good"* or *"Good thing(s)"*] = the *"Positive"* way, as a concept of *having patience* and *reflecting on a decision [prior to taking action]*.

* + (VH) – not used as a word

The (V) tethering to + (H) revelation/revealing
The connection to mankind is the "Earthly tethering"

Another *Linear Construct* (Y+HVH)

* (Y) *"Effort" [leading/brings forth to]* →

+ * הוה (HVH) *<H1942-3>* as: *"ruin, desire [in a bad sense], Iniquity, naughtiness, mischief, perverse thing, very wickedness, calamity, etc..."*

Note: Ideas like: *"The actions taken based on selfish desires"* – *to stand rigid/firm* [but in a *stubborn way*].

versus

The concept of *lacking solid ground* (*not taking a stand* or *being a pushover.*)

2 - *Dimensional Construct* (YH →HV)

* (YH) + *[Born within]* is the → (HV) *<H1930>* as: *Alas!*

Concept of *Making something good from something else [the attempting to]*, but in order to create there will be destruction.

Symbolically, but this can be like *the farmer [plowman]* must *till the soil* [destroy the top of the ground[soil] in order to plant and grow crops from the seeds — the idea *to feed the people of the community.*

Note: This is a connection to *Adam* as *a tiller of the soil!* (as well as: *Cain*, as a *tiller of soil*) — This is the *"How/What"* is to be *destroyed* or *to what degree* or *the negative impact of the destruction,* in order to get the *creation* (Crops for the feeding of humanity).

> Concepts of the (HV) as the *capacity* of "Re-building"

The idea of *making something "good" from something else* [or *attempting* to].

3 - *Reflective Construct* (HV+HY)

> **Glyph meaning formula:**
> *The (H) Revelation/Revealing + (V) [held back]* →
> *(H) Revelation/Revealing + <bring forth>* → *(Y) Effort*

* הו (HV) <H1930> translated as: *Alas!* *Revealing/Revelation + [Held back]*

+ * הי (HY) <H1959> as: *woe, wailing, lamentation*
– [an expression of *sorrow, mourning,* or *regret.*]

"Revelation" [held back] is to *bring forth* **"Woe,"** *as the "Revealing Effort"*

> Concept of the *"Negative"* [as *thought* or *actions*]

The idea of *making something "good" from something else* [or *attempting* to] + ["Woe"].

> Concept of *"thinking negatively of others* or *thinking you can do better,"* but *leads to sorrow for others.*

This idea extends to *allowing others to make decisions on one's behalf,* which can lead *to sorrow or negative outcomes for oneself.*

4 - Meaning Construct

> Concept of *"How the <internal> dialog works within us."*

The idea of *"How things are Revealed (Wisdom).*

versus

The idea of *(Understanding)* expressed with (AR) | (RA) *as:*

How the Mind of God (A) and the Mind of Man (R) *relationships work.*

In addition to the relationship to *Elohim* (ALHYM).

Note: The relationship to the Canaanite gods:
El <Sky "god" | Father "god" | "Sky Father"> + *Yah* <Moon "god" [which is linked to the cycles of the moon]. Also, to Storm/Thunder "god" + *Yam* <Water/Sea god> = (AL+H+YM).

A similar format and function of the Sumerian gods:
"Anunnaki", as *An* (Sky god) + *Nanna* (Moon god) + *Ki* (Earth god).

<Note: *Nanna* | god of the moon and wisdom>.

The *"El"* variants
[Names associated with "Aspects or Attributes of" God]

The names of God also have a variety of meanings, not necessarily meant as a different God, but rather different aspects of Him, as well as a culturally, regional, or personal expression of a group or individual's relationship to Him.

Specifically, referring to as the *"El"* variants or the *"El + ____,"* as defined as the singular version of *Elohim*, אלהים (ALHYM).

Here are four examples (of the many formats):
El Avicha (God of your Father),
El Elyon (Most High God),
El Ro'i (God Who Sees [me]),
El Shaddai (Almighty God).

The **Understanding(s) of**... as *"El"*+ ___

El Avicha

El Avicha, אל אביכ **(AL ABYK) as:** *"God of thy Father"*
— used in Genesis 49:25 as (MAL) *By the God* (ABYK) *of your father*
<also in 1 Kings 12:4> (ABYK) *your father & of your father.*

> **Glyph meaning formula:**
> (AB+Y+K) *God's Plan* as the *Efforts*
> from it → leading to *Mankind's flesh/body*

Note: *Father* (AB) + (YK) as an element of primal *"desires"*
[*"God of My Desires"* — also the concept of *"Sins of the Flesh"*].

As well as *Elohei Avicha* (ALHY ABYK) as: *"God of thy Father"*
— used in Exodus 3:6 as: (ALHY) the God (ABYK) of your father...

1 - *Linear Construct* (AB+Y+K)

* אב (AB) <*H1-2*> translated as: *"Father"*

   + <*Bringing forth*> (Y) *Efforts*/[actions] + (K) *Flesh/Body*

* (B+AB+V) <*H3*> translated as: *Green(ness), Blossoms*

* (ANBH) <*H4*> as: *Fruit [it's Fruit]* = (AB) with (N) =
symbolically, *"Seed within itself."*

* (ABH) <*H15*> as: *My desire* | actually (ABY) used in Job 34:36
   — (ABY) as *"Desire"* → <*Bringing forth*> + (K) *Flesh/Body*
      = *"The desire of the flesh"*

> Concept of *"the unfolding of how things are [to be]"*
> — *God's Plan (& desire to..)*

+ * (YK) <*H3197*> as: *wayside*
   — is noted as a "scribal error" = *Yad* (YD) <*H3027*> *hand*

   * (YKCh) <*H3198*> as: *to decide, adjudge, prove*

   * (YKYN) <*H3199*> translated as: *to establish*

> Concept of *"the unfolding of how things
> are [to be]"* in relation to Mankind

2 - *Dimensional Construct* (AK →BY)

* אכ (AK) <H389> translated as: *surely, howbeit*

> *Mind of God + Flesh/Body ["God made Flesh"]*

→ *<Bringing forth>* + * בי (BY) <H994> as: *pray, excuse me* | and as: *"Oh" [my lord]* or *"Please" [Lord]*

> Concept of *[the realization of a thing that "is"]*

The idea of the *"Acceptance of the outcome of an Event/Action [in Nature or Life] in relation to Mankind*

3 - *Reflective Construct* (KY+BA)

* כי (KY) <H3588> translated as: *"that"* | defined as *"because, that, for, when"* → *<Bringing forth>* + (BA) as a *Concept of "Drunk-ness"* or *over-indulgence* [*destructive* = as a *Reflective of Creation* and the *Concept of Destruction*]

> Concept of *"that a thing is -or- because a thing is"* an *over-indulgence (destructive to one's life [or to others])*

4 - *Meaning Construct*

> Concept of *"What a person [mankind] is drawn to"*

The idea of *"one's passions"* (Also, the idea of *"Bias"*) [Emotionally, as *desire*]

El Elyon

El Elyon, אל עליון (AL aLYVN) <H5945> as: *"the Most High God"*

> **Note:** in Gen. 14:19, refer to *El Elyon* as the creator [possessor] of the heaven and the land/earth, which is the same as Gen 1:1 description of *Elohim* created the heavens and the land/earth.

1 - *Linear Construct* (aLY+V+N)

* עלי (aLY) <H5943> as: *"Most High"* | *supreme [upper]*
  [As a *position/location* to be *elevated*, but maybe not *exalted*]

  ** בעלי (BaLY) <H5940> as: *a pestle* [a Mortar & Pestle] –
  < aka: a *bowl* and *grinding club*]

  > Concept of a *"Tool,"* that is used to *grind down.*

  The idea of something that comes from the upper position
  [of a forceful/power position]

  → *[Held back]* + (V) = holding back *the power to crush,*

  → *<Bringing forth>* + (N) as the *Potential [or Generations]* to come.

  > Concept of *Position of Power/Destruction*
  > [but holding back], which will cause *ideas* to come from it.

2 - *Dimensional Construct* (aL+YV →N)

* על (aL) <H5922> as: *upon, over* [the surface/face] – used in Genesis
* על (aL) <H5922> as: *against, upon, over, above* – used in Ezra
* על (aL) <H5923> as: *a yoke* [round the neck] – used in Genesis

  + * (YV) = The reflection of (VY) *"Conception-Birthing"* as *"Trying to Force/Manipulate/Influence the Natural Order/Process*

  → (N) = *Seeds [the generations to come]*

  > Concept of the *Position* of being *"Yoked"* [or *tied up*]
  > [as a *Manipulated Influence*], and the *Generations* or
  > *Ideas* to come from it *will be* affected by this state.

  The idea of *the influence of one's bias' can led astray*
  or *manipulate what one's sees* or *wants to see.*

3 - *Reflective Construct* (NV+YLa)

* (NV) **Note:** *not a biblical Hebrew word!?*

> (N) *Seeds [Potential] "Generations"* + (V) *[held back]*
> (as the generations yet to come)

> Concepts like: *having "No fountain" | "no ground"*
> or *"grounds for" |* [as: *no soil* to *plant the seed*]

The symbolic idea of a *pre-stage moment [before the purpose is revealed]* — an *earlier stage,* but *coming from a cycled event/process.*

Examples of Hebrew words using the (NV) within them:

* נוא (NVA) *<H5106>* as: *to hinder, restrain, frustrate*

* נוב (NVB) *<H5107>* as: *"to bear fruit"*

As [something] holding back the Seed → but <bringing forth> a Plan/Blueprint

> **Note:** An interesting connection to the *interaction* of the (V)
> within (NB), and the word = נבא (NBA) *<H5013>* as: *"prophesy."*

* נוד (NVD) נוד *<H5110>* as: *"to wander, wanderer"*

As [something] being held back → but <bringing forth> a Path/Way.

→ *<Bringing forth>* ילע (YLa) *<H3216>* as: *devour, devoureth*

> The idea of *"a fast action or not taking time."* Additionally, it's a
> *"missed opportunity of learning"* or *"reflecting on it when it's too late."*

> **Note:** * ע (Ya) as: *"a shovel"* | symbolically, making the (YLa)
> *"digging oneself (or others) into a hole."*

> Concept of *"If you go too far [dig too deep],*
> *it can be impossible to get out"*

Examples of Hebrew words using the (NV) within them:

* לעד (YLD) *<H3205>* as: *"begat, became"*
* לעד (YLD) *<H3206>* as: *"child, son, boy, youth"*
* לעדה (YLDH) *<H3207>* as: *"girl(s), youth girl"*

> Concept of *"expanding into something"* - *"gathering*
> *knowledge/data/experiences/understanding/etc..*

The idea of *evolving* or *something new [a hybrid* or *new ways],*
but *coming from* [as *part of*] *something else [old ways].*

4 - *Meaning Construct*

> Concept of *being "Patience,"* as *"restraint"*

The idea of *not taking action,* especially when you
are in the dominant position.

Additionally, like the phrase [idiom]: *"Taking the high ground"* =
ultimately, the Concept of *being "Moral"* - as the *"Most High."*

El Roi

El Roi, אל ראי (AL RAY) / אל (AL) <H410> as: *"the God"* and
ראי (RAY) <H7210> as: *"who sees me."*

Note: The story of Abram's wife, Sarai, and her Egyptian maid,
Hagar [and Hagar's conception of Ishmael] in Genesis 16:13 *"And she
called the name of the LORD* (YHVH) *that spake unto her, Thou God
(AL) <H410> seest me* (RAY) <H7210>: *for she said, Have I also here looked
(RAYTY) <H7200> after him that seeth me* (RAY) <H7200>.

> Glyph word formula:
> *Mind of Man → <bringing forth> + Mind of God → <bringing forth> + Efforts*

1 - *Linear Construct* (RAY)

* ראי (RAY) <H7209> translated as: *"mirror, looking glass."*

— used [only once] in Job 37:18 as כראי (KRAY), but then
in Nahum 3:6 כראי (KRAY) is used, but translated as: *"[you up
as] a spectacle"* | *"thee as a gazingstock,"* but linked to <H7210>.

* ראי (RAY) <H7210> as: *"seeing, sight, looking | appearance"*

> Concept of *thoughts comes first before actions are taken*

The idea of *"thinking before we act"* or *"the
thinking that is the cause of our actions."*

2 - *Dimensional Construct* (RY →A)

* רי (RY) <H7377> as: *irrigation, a shower* → (A)

> *Mind of Man + Efforts* → *<giving birth>* (A) *Mind of God*
>
> **Note:** The connection of water in relation to the aspect of the *watered seed* (aka: *Manna*) as representing – *Inspiration*. The idea of *seeing* [as *making an observation*] can generate an aspect of *inspiration*. Specifically, the concept of being *observationally aware*.
>
> *Mankind's Efforts* to *give birth* to [aspects of *inspiration*],
> but in the *"Lesser"*/Earthly state.

Note: In addition, there's a relationship to *moisture* [as *sweat*] from doing *hard work* and the benefit received as: *Fruits of one's Labors*. As well as the relationship to *moisture* [as *crying*] – like: a baby does to get what it wants <as: *putting in minimal effort* or even, *taking the "sweat" effort of others>*.

> Concept of *"Being Observationally Aware"*

3 - *Reflective Construct* (YAR)

* יאר (YAR) *<H3372-3>* as: *fear, afraid, awesome acts* | to *show reverence* or to *stand in awe* — used to describe: *"the fear of God."*

> <as the *"proper"* way to reflect the *observation* of God – as the relationship to the *"Greater"* to the reflective *"Lesser">*.

* יארא (YARA) *<H3372b>* as: *to shoot, pour* — used to describe: *the archers shot, shooting* | as well as: *watering*

> **Note:** The (RA) part of words meaning *"seeing, experiencing,"* *"bird of prey [bird's eye view]"* and *"vision/seer."*

> Concept of *"Reverence"* → *the proper way*

The idea of terms, like *"Fear [of God]."*

> as the *Effort* to *<bring forth>* the *"Mind of God"* (YA+)
> but then as the *proper way* for man to think = *"Mind of Man"* (R)

Note: The connected relationship of letter orders and concepts between *Fear* (YAR), *Lion* (ARYAL), and even (YRD) *<H3381>* as: *descending down* <or *the idea of being pounced on by a Lion>*.

4 - Meaning Construct

> Concept of *"Firsts"* <as what comes *First*>

The idea of *from* the *Minds of [Man (of God) vs. God]*

<*Thoughts* come first before *Actions* are taken>

We *think* before we *act,* [but how much do we think
and where are the thoughts coming from?]

Note: This appears to make a connection to the
relationship of *Mind of Man* (R) and *Mind of God* (A).

<(RA) *"Lesser"* versus the *"Greater"* as (AR)>

> In addition, this extends to words like: *Bereshit* (BRAShYT)
> and *bare* (BRA) <the Hebrew words translated to *"In the
> beginning"* and *"creates"*> | As well as words like: *"Light"* (**AVR**)
> and *"Earth"* (**AR**Ts).

El Shaddai

El Shaddai, שדי אל (AL ShDY), translated as: *"God Almighty,"*
this title is not only used several times, its also used along with other
names or titles of God.

— used in Genesis 49:25 *"Even by the God of thy father* (El Avicha), *who
shall help thee; and by the Almighty* (Shaddai), *who shall bless thee..."*

— used in Genesis 35:11 *"And God* (Elohim) *said unto him, I am God
Almighty* (El Shaddai)."

> (AL) = *Mind of God + Teaching/Learning = (God's Lessons)*
> (D) *within* (ShY) = *Path within Creations Efforts*

* **שדי** (ShDY) <*H7706*> translated as: *Almighty* | as: *field, land*

> The (AL) *Understanding* of (ShD+Y) *Creation's Path
> + Efforts = * as a *Path of How to Live in Creation*]

1 - Linear Construct (ShDY)

* שֹׁד (ShD) <H7699> as: [female] "breasts"
— used in Genesis 49:25 and Jon 3:12, actually as the plural version, שׁדים (ShDYM).

→ <Bringing forth> + (Y) "Effort"

— used in Psalm 22:9 and Songs 1:13 as שׁדי (ShDY) referring to the action of nursing/feeding on a Mother's breast.

> Concept of the *Safety/Comfort "Feeling" [as a Nursing Baby]*

* שֹׁד (ShD) <H7700> as: "demon"
— used in Deut. 32:17 | actually לשׁדים (LShDYM) as: "demons"

Symbolically, this could represent a *"suckling" from the demon's (or the Devil's) teat* [aka: *"the selling of the soul"*].

> Concepts of *"Learning to be comforted by being dependent"*

The idea of *"Taking the easy way out"* [finding wealth/success/etc...] .

> Concept of *Understanding the Destruction*

The idea of *Duality* to the *aspects of creating [Creation]* <the Positive> and <the Negative> as the sacrifice needed to do so.

2 - Dimensional Construct (ShY →D)

> *Creations + Effort <giving birth to> → the Path/Way*

* שׁי (ShY) <H7862> as: *a gift (offered as homage)*

> **Note:** Used as Day 2 <*the seed within the* (ShY) = (ShNY)>, Day 3 <*the learning from/within the* (ShLY) *bringing forth* (ShY)>, Day 5 <*the branching/diversity of* (MY) *Life's efforts bringing forth* (ShY)>, Day 6 <*Revealing/Revelation of Creation* (HSh) *bringing forth* (ShY)>
>
> These words/numbers infer (or symbolize) concepts as being the *"Gifts"* from *"God's creation process."*

> Concept of *"making sacrifices"* is a *"gift"*

The idea of *If you make a sacrifice for another* = it's *"the greatest gift."*

3 - Reflective Construct (YDSh)

Note: the (YDSh) is not a biblical Hebrew word!?

> Glyph formula: *Effort+ Path/way + (aspect of) Creation*

As the reflection of *making sacrifices* [in an honorable/noble way] versus symbolically, as the *plowing* over others to *forcefully sacrifice.*

> Concept of the *greater good* as the *justification* of [negative] actions.

* יד (YD) <*H3027*> as: *hands, attempts* | even as: *power*
* ידה (YDH) <*H3034*> as: *to cast, throw*

---

* יש (YSh) = used in names (**Note:** connected to a meaning of *Salvation* as a *"Lesser"* version) and reflecting the *"Greater"* Gift [from God].

** *Isaiah*, ישעיה (YShaYH) | Symbolically, the Concept of the *Creation (Universe laws)*, which is *observed* or how it's *observed.* → *leading to an Effort* (Y) *of Revealing/Revelation*(H).

** *Jesus* ישוע (YShVa) | Symbolically, the Concept of the <*holding back*> [as: *having the "capacity"*] of *aspects of Creation.*

The idea of *Universe* [or *Universal*] *Laws"* which are *observed.* [The connection to the *Scientific Method*].

> Concept of *wielding the "Power of Creation" in [ones] hands.*
>
> Symbolic, like: the *wielding* of the *flaming sword* by *[angels/cherubim].*

4 - Meaning Construct

> Concept of *Creation's way of doing "everything"*
> = the ways of the Universe or *"Universal laws"*

The idea of observing the Creation [broadly the Universe] is the way to see the connections to *"Everything."*

Name(s) of People
[Names associated with Biblical Characters]

Adam, אדם (ADM) <H120, 121>

> Glyph meaning formula:
> *Mind of God + <brings forth> → Path/Way + <brings forth> → Life/Truth*

1 - Linear Construct (A+DM)

* אדם (ADM) *<H120, 121>* used as a Name: **Adam** *[of the first man/ "Human" created by God>]* and as representing the all/whole of Mankind.

> * אדם (ADM) *<H119, 122-123>* used as a root word and translated as: *being dyed red.*

> * אדם (ADM) *<H124>* translated as: <as describing the gemstone> *Sardine Stone* [a gem of a blood-red color, obtained from Sardis in Lydia]. Modern translations use: *Ruby* <probably because it's currently more recognizably known gemstone>.

* דם (DM) *<H1818>* translated as: *blood*

> [**Note:** the obvious relationship to *blood* and the *color red*].

> Concept of *God's Blood, the Blood that flows within God, God's Bloodline, or God's Lifeblood*

The idea that *"God's intended Path/Way to Live [Life]."*
Conceptually, like the *"blood flowing within our veins,"*
which is linked to the *"beating of the heart."*

Note: The symbolic nature of the *Adam* represents the whole of mankind [as all of human existence – throughout time] would correlate to symbolically represent the *flowing Blood of God*. This could represent the responsibility our existence was given to function as the blood within Life and Creation itself, as part of the whole or "oneness" of it.

As a perceptive, from ancient times, this probably connects to the *"blood sacrifices/offerings"* that were done — some connection to the *"what gives life to God."* Interesting, that from a modern understanding this now could represent each human existence as the blood cells within the Blood [of God] — each person has a function/purpose/task to perform in the service of the body [of God] - as to denote a personal responsibility in [All of] Creation "World as God knows it vs. World as we know it."

Note: This clay analogy is also the Sumerian myth process of the creation or formation of man: *Through a divine process, Enki mixed the blood and body of a slain god with clay, resulting in the formation of Adapa, the first human, often referred to collectively as "Adamu,"* which is translated as: *"man"* or *"human"* in Sumerian.

Another *Linear Construct* (AD+M)

* אד (AD) <H108> translated as: *"mist"*

> The glyph concept of meaning of (AD) as *"God's Path"* or *"God's Way"* will or "is to" <bring forth> → (M) *"life/truth"* = the [body of] water

Symbolically, this is the (AD) *"Mist"* to *"Water"* (M) = (ADM) = *"God's Path (or Way) is <bringing forth> Life and Truth."*

The relationship to the translated word as *"mist"* [*the droplets of water floating in air* (or *the seeing one's breath when the air is cold*) — a pre-stage or condition to the building up of a *body of* "water."

Note: The interesting relationship between the construct functions of blood and water in this word (name) is evident, and the transition from blood offerings to baptisms is seen as *"the making a connection to God."*

Other attributes of water and *mist* – like the visual image of the early morning *mist* floating over a body of water.

Note: The connection to the first introduction to the waters in Genesis 1:2 *And the Spirit of God moved upon* (also translated as: *"was hovering over"*) *the face of the waters.*

> Spirit = [the *Ruach*] (RVCh) of God = [the *Elohim*] (ALHYM)
> *Inferring a potential connection to a*
> The (R) in the (RVCh) *as the Mind of Man* and
> the (A) in the (ALHYM) *as the Mind(or Spirit) of God.*

Other variant or word built from (AD):

* אדיר (ADYR) <H117> translated as: *"mighty, nobles, magnificent, lordly"* | described as: *majestic*

> **Glyph meaning formula:**
> *Mind of God + <brings forth> → Path* (AD) = **"God's Way"**
> *<brings forth> → the Effort* (Y) *of Mankind Mind* (R)

— Inferring a meaning of *"majestic,"* as connecting to the idea of *"God's Way"* = (AD) + *<bringing forth> → the Efforts* (Y) *of Man* (R).

2 - Dimensional Construct (A+M →D)

Note: *the* (AMD) *is not a biblical Hebrew word!?*

* אם (AM) <H517> translated as: *"Mother"* — used in Genesis

* אם (AM) <H518> translated as: *"If, lo!"* (*oh that, or, though, not...*)

— used over 1000 times in many books: Genesis, Exodus, Leviticus, Numbers, Deuteronomy = (the *Torah* /the 5 books of Moses / *Pentateuch*)

– The first use in Genesis 4:7 ***If you do well... and if you do not do well...*** [which is the אמ היטיב (AM) (TYThYB)... אמ לא היטיב (AM) (LA) (TYThYB)...

Note: Symbolically, as *"Mother of [being] Good(Fine/Pleases)"* versus *"Mother of Not [being] Good(Fine/Pleases)."* Essentially, a figure of speech term that is translated as the intended function of the expression.

> **Glyph meaning formula:**
> (A) *Mind of God + <brings forth> →* (M) *Life (and Truth)*

> ### Concept of *giving birth* [aka: Mother(s)]
> The idea of *what Life does = "Reproduction."*

In other words, the dimensional construct represents the *"Feminine reading,"* as: *"the Path* (D) *born within [Divine] Mother* (AM).*"*

> ### Concept of *God's Way(Path)* of Life/Truth
> The *"Godly"* (or Divine) path/way to life = as the proper way to live

The idea of *living life* to be *productive* or *"reproductive"* [to bring about the continuation of *Life – "thinking and bringing about the future [generations]"*].

Note: An interesting relationship to the concepts of *blood* and *water* as part of the *<bringing forth>* process of the word: *Adam,* and the representation of all mankind (male and female).

– The idea of the phrase: *"Through blood, sweat, and tears"* – as the types of *"waters"* that come from [exit] the body through *hard work* [a concept of a *"suffering servant"*].

– The relationship to human reproduction (via the female body) as the menstrual cycles [*blood* exiting the body], then the *water breaking* [exiting the body] at the moment of giving birth = both are part of the *birthing process.* Also, as part of the concept of the *"suffering servant."*

Also: The connection of the *separation of waters* in Genesis 1:6 ... *and let it divide the waters from the waters.* [as the difference between *salt water* and *fresh water*]. — The water needed to *take in* [to the body] is the *fresh water* versus the *waters* that *come off* the body, which are *salty* [*blood, sweat, tears,* and *urine*].

3 - Reflective Construct (MDA)

Note: the (MDA) *is not a biblical Hebrew word!?*

* מַד (MD) *<H4055>* as: *extent, height, a measure, a vesture [a garment] | clothing, a carpet*

> Concept of the *way a person dresses* will *reflect* the *measure* of *one's worth/value.*

– used in Judges 5:10 (MDYN) translated as: *[rich] carpets | judgment | judge's attire* <the connection to *height/extent* as the *elevated* statue>.

– used in Leviticus 6:10 (MDV) translated as: *robe, garment,* and associated with the word בַּד (BD) as: *linen* <symbolizes *purity, righteousness, holiness,* and often associated with the *garments* of priests and the heavenly realms>.

Note: The suffix of the (V) as the *<holding back>* of the (MD) – maybe inferring a *difference in approach* in *how* to present one's *"elevated-ness"* [as the *measure* of one's *worth*] — as to be *humble before God* when doing so.

– used in Genesis and Exodus (MDBR) *<H4057>* translated as: *wilderness, desert.*

> Concept of a *person* or *group of people* "elevate" their ideas *(or agendas)* — is like *wandering in the wilderness/desert*

The idea of (MD) *"Elevate (in vain)"* + (BR) *Plan of the Mind of Man.*

> Concept of *"Life"* *bringing conflict, having difficulties or challenges.*

The idea that we can learn more from our mistakes
[or hard lessons] aka: learning the hard way.

Also, the idea of *taking a risk*
[as a making a *sacrifice,* which is a kind of *suffering* as well].
— *positive:* if it fails, but still a lesson to be learned].
— *negative:* if one group uses another to make a sacrifice to selfishly
benefit themselves.

+ * רא (DA) <H1668> as: *this, together, one another*

> Concept of *making contact*

The idea *"to butt heads"* [the visualization of two rams head-
butting] <as to be in conflict or having difficulties>.

4 - Meaning Construct

> Concept of the *"Direction(s)" we take in our own lives.*

The idea of *How we live our lives.*
– Also, *"How we get along while living our lives.*

Essentially, it's about the connection to *"The way of living life,"*
and how we face the *"reflected" nature* of it. In other words, the
challenges/suffering that life may put in front of us, which includes
the *"challenges of getting along."*

> **Note:** There is a relationship to concepts connected to *"Blood"*
> and *"Blood flow or flowing."* **Examples:** 1) *If we don't get along, the*
> ***blood will flow,*** *which leads to injury or death.* 2) The idea of
> *Challenges* can make us stronger (if a person stays positive, it has
> potentially a better version of oneself) -versus- the idea of *Suffering*
> making a person weaker (or kept down). Concepts of the *Suffering*
> *Servant.* 3) Additionally, the idea of *Blood Brothers* and *blood bonding*
> traditions like "Making a *Blood Oath."*
>
> *Blood rituals* played a crucial role in ancient times, often
> symbolizing *purification* and the *establishment of sacred*
> *covenants.*

(Including in the Bible) One prominent example is found in Exodus 24:6, which describes a *covenant ceremony between God and the Israelites at Mount Sinai.*

> Concept of (ADM) as (A) *Mind of God* + (DM)
> *"Blood"* + the (Y) *Efforts* = (ADMY)

The idea of persons representing [an Adam] and their *Efforts or Actions taken.*

Note: Example of this can be found in Exodus 25:5 *And rams' skins dyed red* (M**ADMY**M)... describes the *"Offerings for the Tabernacle."*

Symbolic concepts of the Names of Key Figures:

1) The story of *Job,* יוב (**Y**VB) *<H3102>* is the telling of [*challenges and suffering*] — as the relationship of *Life <God's Way/Path of Life/Truth* = ADM> | [God and Satin *(the adversary)*] and the impact it makes on (us) as Humans (mankind).

2) The story of *Jacob,* יעקב (**Y**aQB) *<H3290>* is the telling of [*challenges and suffering*] — as the relationship of *Life <God's Way/Path of Life/Truth* = ADM> | [God and Man] and the impact it makes on (us) as Humans (mankind) = as "Wrestling with God"!

3) The story of *Joseph,* יוסף (**Y**VSP) *<H3130>* is the telling of [*challenges and suffering*] — as the relationship of *Life <God's Way/Path of Life/Truth* = ADM> | [Family] and the impact it make on (us) as Humans (mankind).

4) The story of *Joshua,* ישוע (**Y**ShVa) *<H3442> Yeshua* [meaning: *Yahweh is salvation*] is the telling of [*challenges*] — as the relationship of *Life <God's Way/Path of Life/Truth* = ADM> | [Establishing Community] and the impact it make on (us) as Humans (mankind) **Note:** Actual Name was *Hoshea,* הושע (HVSha) *<H1954>* but Moses called him, *Joshua.*

5) The story of *Jesus,* ישוע (**Y**ShVa) *<H3442> Yeshua* is the telling of this [*challenges and suffering*] — as the relationship of *Life <God's Way/Path of Life/Truth* = ADM> | [Community] and the impact it makes on (us) as Humans (mankind).

Eve, חוה (ChVH) <H2332> *Chavvah*

> **Glyph meaning formula:**
> *Branching(Diversity) + [held back] Interaction*
> *+ <brings forth> → Revealing/Revelation*

The Hebrew word used as a *Name,* not used until Gen. 3:20 and Gen. 4:1 and only twice as a *Name.* The traditional meaning is associated with the meaning *"life-giver"* or *"living one."*

Note: Described as having a connection to the Phoenician word: חוא (ChVA) translated as: *"live";* and the Hebrew word: חיה (ChYH) as: *"live."*

* חיה (ChYH) <H2421> as: *to live, to be alive, to revive, to restore to life | to breathe* — used times in Genesis as (VYChY).

* חיי (ChYY) <H2425> *to live, to revive*
— used in Genesis 3:22 ... *of the tree of* **life** (HChYYM) <H2416> ... *and* **live** (VChY) <H2425>

* חי (ChY) <H2416> as: *"living"* — used in Genesis 1:20 ... *let the waters bring forth swarms(abundance) of* **"living"** (ChYH) *creatures and birds let fly...*

1 - Linear Construct (ChVH)

* חוה (ChVH) <H2332> as the Name: *Chavvah | Eve* [from the Greek: Εὕα (Eva)] — Only used 2 times in Genesis 3:20 and 4:1.

* חוה (ChVH) <H2331> as: *to declare, show, make known* — used 5 times in Job: (AChVK), (MChVT), twice as (AChVH), (VAChVK); and once in Psalm 19:2 as (YChVH).

— Defined as the function of a verb to emphasize the act of communication and the importance of making something known by expressing or revealing information, intentions, or feelings.

* חוה (ChVH) <H2333> as: *an encampment (tent village), village |* translated as: *town, or small town*

— used 4 times: Numbers 32:41 as (ChVTYHM); Joshua 13:30; 1 Kings 4:13; and 1 Chronicles 2:23 as (ChVT).

Note: There is a link to this version with the association of the word: יאיר (YAYR) translated as: *Jair* <*"Town(s) of Jair"*>.

Jair, the son of Manasseh → the connection to *Towns* = something similar to *Eve*, as a *Mother* — and *Village* = as something similar to a *Daughter* — Symbolically, the similarity to the *Sons of God* taking *daughters of men* and they birth *Giants* (Nephlim) = mighty men of old.

Another *Linear Construct* (Ch+VH)

* ח(Ch) *Branching* <*brings forth*> or *"Diversity from"* [something]...

+ * וה (VH) *Tethering + Revealing/Revelation*

The (H) is the idea of The *"All-Revealing (Wisdom),"* and the (V), or rather the *"tethering/connection"* that <*brings forth*> *Revelation (or Wisdom)* is inferring the connection *humans* have to it.

Note: This idea could imply *"focusing in/on"* aspects of the [thing]. <as what it *"reveals"* or the *revelation* from it>.

Symbolically, the ח (Ch) *Branching* is like the *tree* or *plant's branches.* Also, all life branches off from a common stem, trunk, and roots <aka: *"Family Trees"*>.

> Concept of *How this is the "reflected notion" from Divine(Heavenly)* to *Physical(Earthly)* or <*God to Man*>.

Note: Coming from the (D) = *Path* [of *Elohim*, אלהים (ALHYM) *Process*] = (A) *Knowledge* → (AL) *Understanding* → (ALH) *Wisdom,* as a process = (YM) *Movement of Time [God's Will]* = (ALHYM) *Enlightenment.*

Also, connecting the (D) = *Path* [of *Yahveh*, יהוה (YHVH) *Process*], which is the (H) = (YH) *Effort of Revealing* [connection to the *Divine (Heavenly)* <aka: *Spiritual/Metaphysical*> *Realm*] and the (VH) *Tethering to Revealing(Revelation)* [connection to the *Earthly* <*Flesh/ Body/Physical*> *Realm.*

The (VH) concept used with *Eve* (ChVH), *Yahveh* (YHVH), and also used in Genesis 1:2 *"And the Earth..."* | actually (VHARTs) | translated: (V) as: *And* + (H) as: *the* + (ARTs) as: *Earth.*

In other words, the *Tethering/Connection* to *"All-Revealing,"* to Humans on *Earth* [aka: *Revelation/Wisdom(s) brought forth* from the Human perspective].

Concept of the *focusing on one of the various Revelations/Wisdom giving to mankind"*

The *cause <desire/need>* to *"focus on"* / *"care for"* a specific [thing]. *<As when a mother has a baby and the instinct to shift to care and protect>.*

The idea of the negative and positive (pros and cons) of *focusing in.*

The negative effect of hyper-focusing is like: *a thorn* [As to *stab in* and *to make bleed*].

* חוח (ChVCh) *<H2336>* as: *a thorn, thorn-bush* | *a ring for [the nose]* | translated as: *briars, thickets, thistle, bramble, hooks.*

A modern perspective on concepts like having a *bias* and the relationship to emotion.

2 - *Dimensional Construct* (Ch+H →V)

Note: *the* (ChHV) *is not a biblical Hebrew word!?*

* חה (ChH) **Note:** *not a biblical Hebrew word!?*

* נחה (NChH) translated as: *to guide, transport*

Seeds (Potential) that transport *many (diverse) revealings*

Note: * נח (NCh) as a Name: *Noah*

The idea of *guidance* to go a particular direction is (N) *Seed* [as the *potential*] versus actually *going* (or *gone*) *to...* and the (ChH) is the *destinations* [*many possible destinations*] and the (V) is the *holding back [of the many destinations* or even the *selection of one*].

Symbolically, (ChVH) is the concept of *[holding back] diversity* or *branching* the vastness of a discovery of wisdom, [and maybe as just selecting one], which also connects to *emotions,* and the idea of having a *bias.*

In other words, the *<holding back>* or the *"**Interaction** within"* the *Branching(Diversity) of <bringing forth> Revelation.*

Note: Like, the (YM) as the *flowing river* is the idea of *God's Will* and *the Movement of Time,* and (YVM) as: *"day"* as the (V) = *"**interaction** within" <the Tent peg as a stick stuck in the river and the wake the interaction is making>.*

Another way to understand the (ChH) is as a *state of the overall "Revelation,"* or as the *"Vastness of Wisdom(s)."*

Also, as a *Concept of Love* [for all] or *"All-encompassing Love."*

Symbolically, the (ChVH) as *interaction with* or *focusing within* is the *focused love* [of another].

[Positive Version] – *"Mother's love for her baby."*

[Negative Version] – *"Love of oneself"*
[aka: The eating of the fruit of the Tree of Knowledge of good and evil].

Concept of *"what a person will focus on or care about."*

The idea of *what are our passions* or *biases* within the vast diversity of available things (topics).

> **Note:** *We can't handle everything, but the diversity of people [and their interests or expertise] can fill in the gaps. If we work together, we can accomplish [great things], but in order to do this, we need to understand that it takes diversity.*

3 - Reflective Construct (HVCh)

Note: *the (HVCh) is not a biblical Hebrew word!?*

* (HV) *<H1930>* translated as: *Alas!* | *oh!* – used in Amos 5:16 *"...they shall say Alas! Alas! and they shall call..."* [a connection to *"wailing in the streets"*].
– used as the be asking *"what is the optimum way of doing* or *being,* because of needing help *knowing the way?"*

Revealing + [holding back] + → Branching/Diversity

The *Reflective to the "All-Revealing,"* or as *Revelation [held back],* but as having the *"capability"* of *"Revealing/Revelation."*

Concept of the *yet revealed* [from all that will be revealed].
(as knowledge/learning/understanding/wisdom)

* (HV+Ch) **Note:** *not a biblical Hebrew word!?*

Symbolically, *"what was prior to the known = unknown*
The idea of *Darkness,* then what comes from *Darkness* is the *Light.>*

Concept of being at the *moment of the precipice.*

159

The idea of *being at the edge of* [*being revealed*] or *all possible* or *potential* from what is capable of being *Revealed*.

<The *Everything* versus The *Reflective* [as: The *Focused*]>

Note: This represents all the ways of being *humble* or asking for help, then the reflection of this word is the not state of not being humble or asking for help.

4 - Meaning Construct

Concept of *focusing on one (or a few)* from the diverse (or many) "Revealing" concepts.

<as *Lesser*, but part of the whole (*Greater*)>

As well as the relation that *"Emotion"* has to "the *"Rational"* mind.

The relationship of *Mind of Man,* as:

Adam [*Rational mind*] and *Eve* [*Emotional mind*].

Simplified as the Concept of *One's Biases*
[as a "focused" way of thinking]

Generations of Adam/Eve

Genesis 4:1

English translation (King James Version)
And Adam knew Eve his wife; and she conceived, and bare Cain, and said, I have gotten a man from the LORD.

Cain, קַיִן (QYN) <H7014> Qayin

Glyph meaning - word formula:
Past/Ancient + Efforts + Seeds

The idea of *Influence* of/by the *Past + Efforts/Works,* as what was build upon for *Generations,* but also for the *Self.*

The name, **Cain,** is described as meaning *"acquisition or acquired"* – from the קָנִיתִי (QNYTY) *<H7069>* defined as: *acquired |* translated as: *"gotten."* In addition, he was the firstborn and the first human *born* [from a human].

1 - Linear Construct (QY+N)

* קִי (QY) **Note:** *not a biblical Hebrew word!?*   *Past [time] + Efforts*

+ *<Brings forth>* **(N)** *Seeds (Potentials) | "Generations"*

The idea of *"looking back"* / *"dwelling in the past"* + the *actions* one takes from these perspectives or the *potential* which they *<brought forth>*.

Note: Symbolic concepts leading to a spectrum like: From family and cultural influences (demands) — to more extreme cases, such as *P.T.S.D.* [Post-traumatic stress disorder].

At the core, the idea is: The *structures* or *things* that *hinder* *"free will"* [influencing our *way of thinking*] — this is an outside influence that affects how a person *"defines oneself."*

Other variants or words built from (QY):

* קיה (QYH) *<H7006>* as: *to vomit up, spew out*

* קִינוּ (QYNV) *<H7013>* as: *of whose spear [a spear]*

— used in 2 Sam. 21:16 / describes the *weight of the spear* [which is the [holding back] of the word, *Cain* — which could infer [someone] is not *swayed* or *influenced* by *emotions.*

The idea of having *"No fear"* | similar to the phrase *"a measure of a man"* and relates to ideas like: *they give back as much as they received* [the level of commitment of character one has] and symbolically, the relationship of those who used a *"spear in battle"* which also correlates to this idea of having *no fear.*

* קִים (QYM) *<H7010>* as: *Adversary* | *<H7010>* as: *Statute* | *<H7010>* as: *steadfast/enduring.*

Efforts of the Past <bring forth> Life/Truth

* קיטור (QYThVR) *<H7008>* as: *[Thick] smoke / clouds*

* קיר (QYR) *<H7023>* as: *a wall*

Concepts of *hindrance/interference*

The idea of *that which is holding something back* (blocking or making difficult to see beyond/past) — and *not* [or thinking it was not] *by one's own choice* or *doing.*

Another **Linear Construct** (Q+YN)

Note: the (YN) *is not a biblical Hebrew word!?*

* יָנָה (YNH) *<H3238>* as: *to rage, be violent, to suppress, to maltreat*

> A connection to the ideas of *Rage, Violence, Suppression, and Maltreatment* to the concept of *Hindrance* and *Interference.*

2 - **Dimensional Construct** (Q+N →Y)

Note: the (QNY) *is not a biblical Hebrew word!?*

* קַן (QN) *<H7064>* as: *nest [bird], room*

+ *<gives birth to>* (Y) *Efforts [from]*

Note: The concept of *building a bird's nest*; origins (or process) of building *"structure"* related to family, but as bit by bit (twig by twig) building up to make what will become the nest.

> The idea of *small (weak) construction* or *structuring* to *<brings forth> Mind of God* = קָנָא (QNA) *<H7065>* translated as: *to be jealous, envious; to purchase/buy/acquire; to erect, create, procure, to own; a reed, a rod, shaft [of lamp stand], branches [of lamp stand], shoulder-joint; Hunter; possession.*
>
> > <Maybe as a connection to the Tower of Babel and its *"Fall."*>
>
> Even one of the *three principal spices* [the LORD spoke to Moses] as to make the *"oil of holy ointment"* | The spice of *Cinnamon* translated from קִנָּמוֹן (QNMVN) *<H7076>* — used as *part of the holy anointing oil.* <Concept of *"Weak <interaction within> Manna"*>.

* קִנִּים (QNYM) *<H7064>* plural ending of (QN) translated as: *Rooms* — used in Genesis 6:14 *Make thee an ark of gopher wood; rooms* (QNYM) *shalt thou make in the ark, and shalt pitch it within and without with pitch.*

Concept of *action one takes* from a *condensed/contained [narrow] place,* but *within it has an elevated (wide) view.*

The idea of being *stuck in the nest,* but still *looking out over* into the world, and applying a limited perspective to what one hasn't experienced yet.

Also, as the idea of *[spectrum]* of *being narrow-minded,* then *extending the value to what is beyond.*

Spectrum of concepts includes: *Bigoted, Biased, Intolerant, Illiberal, Self-righteous, Dictatorial, Disdainful, Dogmatic.*

* קָנִיתִי (QNYTY) *<H7066>* as: *"I have acquired"*

— used in Gen.4:1 [describing the birth of Cain]

Symbolically, *the first "Mama's Boy"* — kept in the Nest by the *emotionally* or feminine influence over the rational mind, which also leads to jealous, zealous, envious traits.

Concept of *the potential humans have within ourselves to be affected by "negative" emotional influences.*

The idea that *"Another"* will direct *[influence] your direction* or *development* — as an attempt to control or protect.

Note: The relationship to *"Another"* or *"Other"* is assigned to both the *body* [as other people] and the *spirit* (as thoughts within one's own mind).

<This is also connected to the concept of *bad/evil spirits/demons*>

3 - *Reflective Construct* (NYQ)

Note: *the* (NYQ) *is not a biblical Hebrew word!?*

The *"Potential"* *<brings forth>* *"Past"* and *Effort [born within it]* — the idea of perspective of time [as a *fractal repeat*].

Concept of *Something that was set up in a past [moment of time],* but *cycles in the future,* which itself causes the *action to be taken* [or *born within it*]

* ‫נִי‬ (NY) <H5204> translated as: *wailing* + (Q) as the *"Past"*

The idea of a *perspective of time* [as a *fractal repeat*] is similar to the concept of *"reincarnation"* or *"re-birth."*

> **Example:** If a tax is *created/decreed/generated*, then the *efforts* to *pay it* will be *"as the pains [efforts] of giving birth."*

Other variants or words built from (NQ):

* ‫נְקֵא‬ (NQA) <H5343> translated as: *clean, pure*

The idea of *"Paying Tribute"* to <bring forth> the Mind of God is *"pure."*

* ‫נְקָב‬ (NQB) <H5344> as: *to appoint, to name* [to *dictate terms*].

— used in Genesis 30:28 *And he* [Jacob asks of Laban (the Father of Rachel) when Joseph was born] *said* [asks] *appoint/name* (NQBH) *me your wages and I will give* [pay] *it.*

> Concept of *"What is it you are demanding/or expecting"*

The idea of a *payment/compensation* of me to give to you [as a tribute for one to another] — like: a *Tax [burden].*

versus * ‫נְקָב‬ (NQB) <H5344> translated as: *blasphemed*

— used in Leviticus 24:16 *And [whoever] blasphemes* (V+NQB) *the Name of the Lord* (YHVH)...

The idea of *"What is it you are demanding/or expecting"* as a *payment/compensation* from what a person expects from God, as *"What God should give to you."* [as a *Tribute* from God to a Human] or like: a *Tax applied in behalf of* or *to* God by a Human.

* ‫נְקִי‬ (NQY) <H5355> translated as: *free from [guilt], clean, exempt,* | also translated as: *released*

> Concept of the *Efforts* <brought forth> by the *demanding(expectation) of payment/compensation"*
> — like: a Tax [burden] that has been paid.

Idea of [a person] is making an *Effort,* [they] shall be... *innocent/clear/free/unpunished/blameless/guiltless/free of obligation/etc...*

* נָקַם (NQM) <H5358> translated as: *Vengeance/Avenge*
— In Genesis 4:15 // as: *[a sevenfold] <u>vengeance shall be taken on him]</u>* in regard to anyone who kills Cain

The idea that *Paying Tribute(Tax)* to *<bring forth> Life(Truth)* is *"a violent act"* [maybe because in Nature (the concept of *paying a tribute*) is a [Primal act] *predator/prey existence*].

> Concept of *a "Fine-line."* and a *Balance*
> between dealing with *Pain* in order to have a *Gain.*

The ideas of *"no Pain, no Gain,"* | *"Making a Sacrifice,"* and *"Suffering Servant(s)."*

<But the difference is when it's not being imposed by oneself [or by choice], but imposed by others.>

4 - Meaning Construct

> Concept of *"Holding on to the past"*

— can be both a limitation to growth and the result of growth,
— but when restraint is taken too far, it's to strangle to death.
— as one's own (within oneself), and to others around us (as the "how we affect others").

The idea of a connection between *holding on to the past* and *it having an [emotional] effect on us.*

It's principal [or baseline] of our *actions/efforts* (Y) that we *become introduced to* or *born into* and *grow up with* or *around*, *like:* by the *Family* or *Community* [aka: *Culture*] as that which *influences* us → *<bringing forth> Seeds* (N) = as that which will *grow from* or *out of* [as a "small" or indirect influence].

The idea of the *"Human mental collective"* is like the *"Nest."* — We are all born into [something], but it takes leaving the nest to expand it for the future.

Abel, הבל (HBL) <H1893> Hebel/Habel

> *Glyph meaning - word formula:*
> *Revealing + Plan/"Blueprint"/Family + Learning*

The idea from the meaning: *Revealing + Family + Learning* in relation to the *Adam-Eve bloodline family* as *"All that will come..."* as a reference to all the names [and what they will reveal], then what one can learn from it.

The idea from the meaning: *Revealing + Blueprint + Learning* in relation to *"God's Plan,"* revealed as *"All that will come to pass"* [and what we learn from it].

... And the idea of the coming of *"Heaven on Earth"* -or- representing the *How the Names* will play out [revealed] and what we learn from it. <The movement from (H) to (L)>

1 - Linear Construct (HBL)

* הבל (HBL) <H1893> as the Name: *Abel* | but in Hebrew pronounced as: *Hebel* or *Habel* — used 8 times in Genesis 4

* הבל (HBL) <H1891> as: *to act emptily, become vain*

— used in 2 Kings 17:15 translation of back-to-back variants of the root:

* ההבל (HHBL) as: *become* + ויהבלו (VYHBLV) as: *vain* | but in Hebrew ההבל (HHBL) as: *idols* + ויהבלו (VYHBLV) as: *and became idolaters*

— used in Job 27:12 (THBLV) as: *vain [do you act foolishly]*, but in Hebrew as: *you behave with complete nonsense.*

* הבל (HBL) <H1892> as: *vapor, breath*

— used in Deuteronomy 32:21 בהבליהם (BHBLYHM) translated as: *"with their idols"* | *"with their vanities"* — used in Job 7:16 (HBL) translated as: *breath*

Other variants or words built from (HB):

* הבהב (HBHB) <H1890> as: *Gift*

* הבנים (HBNYM) <H1894> as: *Ebony*

Revealing + Blueprint(Plan) + Seed(Potential) + Efforts + Life/Truth

<(H)+(BN)+(YM)the plural ending = The Sons or the "Revealing" Sons>

-versus-

* הובנים (HVBNYM) <H1827> as: *Ivory*   {Revealing [held back]}

— both words used in Ezekiel 27:15 *The men of Dedan* (DDN) *were thy merchants; many isles were the merchandise of thine hand: they brought thee for a present horns of ivory* (HV<u>BNY</u>M) *and ebony* (H<u>BNY</u>M). Symbolically interesting that these words describe objects of white (ivory) and black (ebony), as referencing *color* <and the connection to *light* and *dark* as well.

<born within> → * נִי (NY) <H5204> translated as: *wailing*

Note: Relates to Day Two | sheni שני (ShNY) = as *Creation's Wailing* vs. (HB+YN+M) *The Gift of Wailing* <brings forth> *Life*

<born within> → * בני (BNY) <H1129> as: *built | fashioned | "made"*
— used in Genesis 2:22 [when describing the *fashioning/ building/"made"* of the woman [from the side/rib of Adam].

<brought forth> → * בנים (BNYM) <H1143> translated as: *Champion |* and meaning: *"a double interval"* and *"the space between two armies"* — used in 1 Samuel 17:4, 23 [*when describing "Goliath"*].

* הברי (HBRY) <H1895> as: *Astrologers* — used in Isaiah 47:13

Revealing + Blueprint(Plan) + Mind of Man + Efforts

* (HB) *Revealing + Plan* +

Concept of *having a perspective* of the *"Intention"*

The idea of *Why* [something is the way it is]"

<bringing forth> → * רי (RY) <H7377> translated as: *moisture*

Note: The symbolic view – that (RY) *"moisture"* is connected to the function of looking to the stars [in the black of night]. As the relationship to the *"Watered Seed* [aka: *manna]* = "Concept of *Inspiration,"* and the expanding connection to *"Rain"* symbolizing *inspiration* from God [also: The trigger to making plants grow as the <bringing forth> *Life* (M)].

Concept of *"Theory"* or *"having a theory"*

-or- *making a theory* [but, *based on observing patterns*] and *launching into them*, as *"New Ways"* of doing things.

The idea of *unknowns* (guessing what is in the dark) from the *sparks of light* (stars) - rather than the patterns from the *stars.*

2 - *Dimensional Construct* (H+L →B)

Note: the (HLB) *is not a biblical Hebrew word!?*

Revealing/Revelation + Learning/Teaching [giving birth] → Blueprint/Plan

Other variants or words built from (HL):

** הלא (HLA) *<H1972>* as: *to be removed [cast] far off, outcasts*
— used in Micah 4:7, actually the word is (VHNHLAH)

** הלאה (HLAH) *<H1973>* as: *[stand]aside, [stand]back | out there, onward, further*

Note: This is the reflection of (ALH) from Elohim — idea of the direction [or as a Road to...] to the Concept of (ALH) as, [knowledge, understanding, wisdom] -vs.- (HLA) as: [wisdom, understanding, knowledge].

** הליכ (HLYK) *<H1978>* as: *a step [taken steps]* |

** הליכה (HLYKH) *<H1979>* as: *a going [goings on], way, traveling company | "a procession" | the travelers / the company*

** הלכ (HLK) *<H1980>* as: *flowing*
— used in Genesis 2:14, actually word is (HHLK) and describes the Tigris river as "*it flows*" -and- used in Genesis 3:8, actually word is (MTHLK) and translated as: "*walking*" [in the garden].

> Concept of *"Going in a direction"*
> [*A way of thinking*] // aka: *"Setting a Heading"*

There is an idea of *reflection* [being reinforced] that is a key component to *"Everything/All things."*

<Everything is reflecting another [on and on]>

3 - *Reflective Construct* (LBH)

* לבה (LBH) *<H3826>* as: *the heart* <actually as (LBVT)/(LBT)>

* לבה (LBH) *<H3827>* as: *flame* <actually as (BLBT)>

— used once in Exodus 3:2 [describing the *burning bush* | the *flame* (BLBT) *of fire* (ASh) *from midst the bush,* but also be "*the heart*" *of fire...*]

Other variants or words built from (LB):

* לב (LB) <H3820> as: *inner man, will, heart*
  → <*bringing forth*> + (H) *Revealing/Revelation*

> Concept of *One's own thoughts* [providing a
> *Revealing/Revelation*] <aka: *Perception*>

* לבט (LBTh) <H3832> as: *to thrust down, out,* or
away; and translated as: *to be ruined, fall*

> Concept of *One's own thoughts* [being held in a *bowl/container*]

The idea is that *if one stays in their own head,* it will lead to *"ruin [or a fall]."*
— as to *"go mad/insane* or *a spectrum of it* [like: *becoming a narcissist]."*

4 - Meaning Construct

> Concept of *having* a *new [simple/basic]* *"Belief/Theory"*

> *From the idea of the Glyph formula*
> (HB) *Revealing + Plan* + (L) *Learning/Lessons*

<*Having a perspective* of the *"Intention"* + the *"Lessons" that come from it*>

A generalized idea of *"Lesser"* moment/idea becoming or
reflecting the *"Greater"* moment/idea.

Examples: The *"Spark"* that becomes the *"Fire;"* The *"Moisture"*
[*dew* or *drops*] that builds up into a *"Pool of Water;"* or comparison of
a *"Star"* [in the night sky] versus the *"Sun"* [in daytime], but then
reading in or generating *"meaning"* or *"purpose"* to it.

Additionally, the concept of *seeking a relationship with God* → as a
way to *get to know* or *have a relationship with God.* Ideas like: *New
Ways [New gods]* from *the Old Ways [Old gods]* or *the transitioning
from* and *to* [religious beliefs].

Note: Conservative and Progressive/Liberal relationship →
new ideas being presented are "Progressive/Liberal," but if
established, will in time become "Conservative" ideas, and the
cycle will continue.

Generations of Cain

The idea of Cain [as: *not leaving the "Nest"*] and the influence of Eve [as: representing the *Emotional Mind of Mankind]* expands to *"How the human **"Senses"** and how they have an effect on our input/output relationship to our surroundings.*

Specifically, the *"Generations of* and *from Cain,"* as representing the idea of one of the *five (5)* **senses** – presenting in each of the *"Names".*

Genesis 4:17

English translation (King James Version)
And Cain knew his wife; and she conceived, and bare Enoch: and he builded a city, and called the name of the city, after the name of his son, Enoch.

Enoch, חנוכ (ChNVK) *<H2585>*

> **Glyph meaning formula:**
> *Branching (Diversity) + [that which] Seed(s)/[Generations] + Tethered (Interactions) [held back] + Flesh(Body) "Physical Aspect"*

The **Sense** of **Touch**

[2 hands, 2 feet]

Note: Like the correlation to the (RASh) has a watershed moment of *"Man making Fire,"* this would denote the watershed moment of *"Man walking on two feet"* [transition from walking on all fours to two] / [Also: when or the moment an infant begins to walk]. Additionally, the watershed moment of *"Man making and using tools."*

1 - Linear Construct (ChNV +K)

(ChN) + *[held back]* (V)

* חנ (ChN) *<H2580>* translated as: *"graciousness | favor, grace, charm"*
— used in Genesis 6:8 "Noah found *favor/grace* (ChN) in the eyes of the LORD" [many occurrences from Genesis, Exodus, and Numbers — almost always phrased as: *"found favor in his/your/the sight"*].

Other variants or words built from (ChN):

** חנה (ChNH) <H2583> translated as: *"to encamp, to pitch tents* – as well as: *to dwell, to rest"*

Ideas like: *"Where one takes a stand"* | *"Plants one's feet"* | *"Stand your ground".*

> ### Concept of *"Sitting around the campfire"*

The idea of *"being in the comfort of the campfire* [in which God provided or in the presence of God at the campfire] is the *<bringing forth> Revelation* [Symbolically, representing the *Fire = Wisdom*

Symbolically, the *Campfire* located at the center of community/ cultural influence and development = serves as a separation that leads to a potential and revealing kinship = tribe → nations, etc...

[The idea of *having discussions* around a campfire].

> ### Concepts of *"What one chooses to believe in,"* but inferring both the idea of *having discussions* and *having comfort* [in doing so].

The idea of *resting* or *getting rest* as *comfort* or *rejuvenation* [*from rest*] = the idea of *taking a deep breath to calm oneself.*

All connects to the *"making a choice [decision] of what to believe"*

- versus - *<Holding back>* of this state.

The idea of *"not resting"* is to move about <the connection to two hands and two feet>. Symbolically, like: walking on a tight rope <slight shifting action or movements to stay *balanced.*

(ChN) *Branching Seeds ["Diversified Potentials"] <bringing forth>* (K) *Flesh/Body*

* חנך (ChNK) <H2596> as: *"dedicate, train [up]* | *to narrow, initiate*

Note: As the *many possibilities* or *capabilities* are being brought forth in the Physical world = representing the aspects or outcomes of the achievements of these actions [as: *the wonders of the world*]. The meaning of: *Dedicated, Trained, Disciplined*, because this relates to the idea of the *Hard Work* it takes to achieve such things.

The connection to the firstborn from Cain [and the emotions drive one to *"hard work"*] = is the *City Builder*, and relates to the name of this [first] city concept.

The חנ (ChN) *[holding back]* by the (K)

versus *<Interaction within>* * חנכ (ChNK) *<H2596>* translated as: *"to narrow, to initiate, discipline | to train, inaugurate"*

> **Note:** Symbolical of *"not being graceful in one's training."* Ideas like: *Just going for it* [an earlier approach = as a *child jumping into anything* [including: *touching* or *grabbing* everything and anything] = *"Fearless(Naive) Child"* | Symbolically, reflecting a *Sprouting,* but as *Rooting[Roots] Seed* [as a *Fountain* to the *Plant/Crop]"*

> The idea of being *driven by pure curiosity,* as tactile input.

+ * וכ (VK) *Tethering + Flesh/Body[Physical]*

Note: Symbolically, as the *"Rooted Seed"* or *"Anchoring to the Soil [Earth]."*

> Concept of *"transition from wild [to domestic]"*

The idea of *"Unstructured to Structured."*

Symbolically, as: the concept of *"Chaos"* to *"Order".*

2 - Dimensional Construct (ChK →NV)

> **Note:** the (ChKNV) *is not a biblical Hebrew word!?*

* הכ (ChK) *<H2441>* translated as: *"palate, [roof of] the mouth, taste"* *<born within>* is the (NV)

> — used in Job [describing the function of speaking, as it relates to the function of the inner mouth] <but not the sense of taste/eating>.

> Concept of *"From inside the mouth"*

The idea of a *stage before/pre-staging* [actions of the mouth].

Symbolically, like: *chewing* [of food] <leading to the swallowing of food> -or- as *speaking words* <an earlier approach to communication>.

→ is the *[held back]* * ונ (NV) *"the Seed" (Potential) + [held back]* as relating to the stage before the seeds are ready [for planting].

* נוב (NVB) as: *"to bear fruit"*

* נוד (NVD) as: *"to wander, wanderer"*

> Concept of *"earlier approach and earlier stage."*

The idea of an *Ancient of Ancient ways.*

3 - *Reflective Construct* (KVNCh)

> **Note:** the (KNVCh) *is not a biblical Hebrew word!?*

* כו (KV) *<H3551>* as: *"a window"*

— used in Daniel 6:10 as: (VKVYN) translated as: *and with windows | he had windows | and his windows.*

> **Note:** Seems to be a reference to the *"looking upon* [something] *out in the physical world"* as what is observable [maybe as a limited perspective]. Comparison and connection to the phrase *"Eyes are the window to the soul."*

* כון (KVN) *<H3559>* as: *"to be erect" | to be firm, be stable, be established, to be set up, be fixed* | translated as: *is determined, make ready, prepared*

> **Note:** * כן (KN) *<H3651>* as: *"to set upright"* | translated as: *and it is so…*
> — used in Genesis 1 *<repeatedly>* as [God making things come into existence]

* כון (KVN) *<H3560>* as city Name meaning: *"established"*

* כון (KVN) *<H3561>* as: *"cake, sacrificial cake [wafer]"*
— used in Jeremiah 7:18 & 44:19 [as offerings to the *"queen of heaven"*]

Other variants or words built from (KV):

* כוכב (KVKB) *<H3556>* as: *"a star"*

— used in Genesis 1:16 as (HKVKBYM) [translated as: *the stars*]

> **Note:** Symbolically, to compare to the *descendants* or *key people to stand out [in the future/present/past]* = as the *"stars of heaven"…*

> There is a symbolic relationship to (KV) as the way in which Humans connect/see the world [creation].
> The (K) = the *body (flesh)* as a relationship to the *head* [as *mind*] = (R)

If *body/flesh* **(K)** *[held back]* **(V)** *<interaction within>* and *<brought forth>* …

→ * נח (NCh) *<H5146>* as the Name: *"Noah"* <see page 229>

> *"Seed"/(potential) + "Branching"/(diversity) = **Many Potentials**

Other variants or words built from (NCh):

→ * נחה (NChH) *<H5148>* as: *"to guide, transport"*

> *as the what was revealed from the seed(s) = what will sprout = sprouting seed*

→ * נחש (NChSh) *<H5175>* translated as: *serpent, <snake>*

Concept of *"Establishing Guidance"*

The idea of *transitioning from "Chaos to Order."*

Symbolically, a process (cycle) going from
Seed(s) to *Sprouting Seed(s).*

4 - Meaning Construct

Concept of *the Sense: "Touch"*

There are a multitude of ideas that also connect to
parts of the body that function directly to *touch.*

Hands [*Actions, Efforts, Interactions,* and *Creation*],
Feet [*walking* – specifically as *"down a path"* and *Life*],
and the Tongue [as a pre-state before *Taste*].

Note: The connection to the *transitional* relationship regarding
Hands and Feet, and the *"Beginning"* stage/part of the *"Cycle of Life
and Creation."* Specifically, letter connection to the *Process/Cycle* (Y)
of *interacting* (V) and *learning* (L) from *Life* (M)/*Creation*(Sh) = (MSh).
Extending to the relationship of (MSh), which leads to what is
revealed (H), as the (MShH) or personified as *Moses,* and also the
concept of the *Messiah.*

The concept is directly related to the *transitioning* and
the *"attempt"* to **balance.** The idea of being on a tightrope
as the *shifting/swaying movements* in order to stay
balanced. Additionally, connecting to the *ebb and flow* of
the sea and the relationship between *Chaos and Order.*

Note: There is an interesting relationship to the Name:
Enoch, specifically to the four different characters with
the name in Genesis. [aka: *The Four Israelites* — as the
Sons of *Cain, Jered, Midian,* and *Reuben*].

Enoch #1 of 4

(*The newborn/infant version of Enoch*) = An earlier stage/
approach, but coming from a cycled event/process.

A connection to the relationship to the *"flesh/body"
development* (rather than a *mental one*).

Genesis 4:18
English translation (King James Version)
And unto Enoch was born Irad: and Irad begat Mehujael: and Mehujael begat
Methusael: and Methusael begat Lamech.

Irad, עירד (aYRD) <H5897>

The **Sense** of **Sight**
[2 Eyes]

Tradition associated the name with the
meaning of *"runner"* or *"fugitive."*

A connection to the idea of *first walking, then
running,* or *"walk before you run."*

1 - *Linear Construct* (aY+RD)

* עי (aY) <H5856> as: *"a ruin, heap of ruins"*

> *Glyph Formula: Observation + Effort*

> Concept of *"All things become a ruin at some future date"*

The idea of *"Watching where* [someone] *is heading to..."*

+ * רד (RD) **Note:** *not a biblical Hebrew word!?*
<but has a connection to meaning: *"treading, walking"*>

Other variants or words built from (RD):

** רדד (RDD) <H7286> as: *"to beat down, to conquer, to overlay"*
** רדה (RDH) <H7287> as: *"to tread down, subjugate, to crumble off"*
** רדי (RDY) <H7287> as: *"trampling"*

Symbolically, the *trampling down* to *ruin.*

The idea of *completely crushing a thing* or *laying waste.*

> Concept of *Perceptions from Observation*

The idea of *"Snap judgment"* or *"Judging a book by its cover."*

2 - *Dimensional Construct* (aD →YR)

* עד (aD) *<H5703>* as: *perpetuity | all, continually, and/for ever*
  — used in various books like Exodus 15:18, Numbers, and Job

* עד (aD) *<H5704>* as: *as far as, even to, up to, until, while, against*
  — used in various locations in Genesis

* עד (aD) *<H5705>* as: *unto, until | before, order*
  — used in various locations in Ezra and Daniel

* עד (aD) *<H5706>* as: *the prey, booty*
  — used in Genesis 49:27 *devours the prey* or [as *the object/thing*]

    Note: The "predator" *saw* [or *witnessed*] | the hawk/eagle *seeing* its prey [aka: *"a bird of prey"*] — as from the *bird's eye view* as it flies above, then drives in to snare.

  — used in Genesis 49:27, Isaiah 33:23, and Zephaniah 3:8

* עד (aD) *<H5707>* translated as: *a witness*
  — used in Genesis 31:44/48 (L+aD)(aD)
  — used in Genesis 31 as: *"witness"* | in Exodus 20:16 as in a *commandment* — ...*do not bear false "witness" | "evidence."*

* עד (aD) *<H5708>* (aD+YM) as: *[are] as filthy, filthy*
  — used in various locations in Isaiah 64:6 as: *"filthy" [rags]*, *"garments"*, but this seems a consequence of the context of the overall sentence message — it may actually be referring to a cycle [repeated] of a noticeable occurrence [which may be the connection to meaning: *the menstrual flux, soiling.*]

    Note: * עוד (aVD) *<H5750>* as: *to return, repeat,* or *do again*

    + * יר (YR) **Note:** *not a biblical Hebrew word!?*
    <but has a connection to meaning: *"fear/reverence"*>

  Other variants or words built from (YR):

** ירא (YRA) *<H3372>* as: *to fear, to revere*

> Concept of *how others perceive you* can lead
> to an *attack* or *being victimized.*

The idea of *being a "mark"* [Con Artist term]
or *"being prey* to a *predator."*

Note: *Scaring* someone into *"bearing false witness"* | *"If you act like a scared victim, you will become one"* | *"If you think your a victim, you will be fearful."*

> Concept of *how someone's perceptions* can *give birth* to *fear*, which is then *projected onto others.*

The idea of *lacking courage.*

3 - Reflective Construct (DRYa)

* דר (DR) *<H1858>* as: *a pearl, pearl-stone, mother-of-pearl, alabaster, [white]* | *<H1859>* as: *an age (generation)*

+ * יע (Ya) *<H3257>* as: *a shovel*
<Defined as: *to appoint, to designate, to meet, to assemble*>

The idea of *what comes out of [the event]* [as: *result of actions taken*]

Symbolically, the idea of *"the pearl white* [wealth of wisdom] *can bring useful tools* [but also *dig yourself a grave* or *get into trouble*]."

Note: Also as the *<born within>* format/construct:

* דע (Da) **Note:** *not a biblical Hebrew word!?*
<but has a connection to meaning: *"knowledge"*>

Other variants or words built from (Da):

** דעי (DaY) *<H1843>* as: *knowledge*

<as the (D) *Path* to עי (aY) *<H5856>* as: *"a ruin, heap of ruins"*>

→ * רי (RY) *<H7377>* as: *irrigation, a shower, moisture [watering]*

The idea of *"knowledge"* gives birth to *"water"* *<Life/Truth>*
as a *birthing process* or even a *method.*

Symbolically, the irrigation that brings forth life
<the crops> that will feed the people.

4 - Meaning Construct

> Concept of *the Sense: "Sight,"* [Perception]
> *as a wandering Sight (looking around)*

The idea of being aware of one's surroundings – as an external awareness, like the traits of *Hunter/Gatherers.*

Note: The duality of negative and positive outcomes of awareness is observing how the results of our actions play out [in comparison to nature's balance].

Mehujael, מחויאל (MChVYAL) <H4232>

> **Glyph meaning formula:**
> *Life/Truth + Branching(diversity) + Tethered(interactions) +*
> *Effort + Strength (God's Mind) + Teach/Learn (Understanding)*

Concept of *"Listening within the World/Life*
→ the Diversity(Increasing) of Awareness"

The **Sense** of **Hearing**
[2 Ears]

1 - Linear Construct (MChVYAL)

*מח (MCh) <H4220> as: *"fat, rich"* | <H4221> as: *"fat, marrow [from the kill of the Hunt]"* − <snapping/breaking the bone open>.

+ (V) *[held back]*

Other variants or words built from (MCh):

*מחא (MChA) <H4222> as: *"to rub, strike hands together"*

> Concept of *"Clapping"*

The idea of *making sound* (to push prey, later to "herd to flock")
- origins to "smite, kill, impale .

> Concept of *"Hunting"*

+ *יאל (YAL) <H2973> as: *"to be slack, to be foolish"*
— used in Numbers (NVALNV); Isaiah (NVALV); Jeremiah (NVALV)
Note: There's not a (Y) used, and it ends with the (V) *[held back]*.

+ *יאל (YAL) <H2974> as: *"to yield, assent, to undertake"*
— used in Genesis (HVALTY); Exodus (VYVAL); Deuteronomy (HVAYL); Joshua (HVALNV), (VYVAL); Judges (VYVAL), (HVAL), 1 Samuel (HVAYL), (VYAL); 2 Samuel (HVAL); 2 Kings (HVAL); 1 Chronicles (HVALT); Job (VYAL), (HVAYLV); Hosea (HVAYL)
Note: Rarely is (Y) used as a prefix, and most endings don't have (V).

The primary common function is the (AL) *Mind of God + Learning/Lessons [God's Lessons]* = *"Strong Understanding"*

> Concept of *"Effort" to <bring forth>* (AL) *El* [God]"

The idea of *action* as *"taking it upon myself."*

Symbolically, as *actions* or *understanding* of a triggering [impulse to..]
a *fight/flight response* — being alerted to the potential dangers | also,
distracted/worried/mentally paralyzed [as in having phobias].

2 - Dimensional Construct (MCh+AL →VY)

* מֹחַ (MCh) <H4220> as: *"fat, rich"* | translated as: *fat beasts, wealthy*

* מֹחַ (MCh) <H4221> as: *"marrow"* [as from the "Kill of the Hunt"]

> Concept of *full completion of the act and benefit*

The idea of *the final treat* [as having the dessert at the end of the
meal], but when at the *extreme*, it's an "over-indulgence"

+ * (AL) <H410> the singular *[El]* as: *"god, god-like one, mighty one"*

→ *<birthing within>* * (VY) *"Conception-Birthing"*

> Concept of the *"result of understanding"*
> but as an *over-indulgence.*

The idea of *completely devouring a resource* leads to the *strategic/
planning* of a *beneficial outcome* of repeating/long-term/generations.

3 - Reflective Construct (LA+YV+ChM)

* אַל (LA) <H2524> as: *"not, No"*

+ * יִ (YV)   *Effort + <brings forth> Tethering [held back]*

*Symbolically, the sexual act brings forth the conception,
but also the "birthing pains" bring forth.*

Note: On its own, it's not seen as a word, but used with words:
translated as *Desert, Ram's Horn* [the blast of it], *Stream* [a
flowing of water], the name *Job* [he who was *"persecuted"*].

> Concept of *"Pain"* can bring *"Pleasure/Joy"*

The idea is akin to the phrase: *"No pain, No gain."*
-or- *"The Joy [and Difficulty] of having children."*

+ * חָם (ChM) <H2524> as: "father-in-law" | (ChM)+(YK)/(YH)

+ * חָם (ChM) <H2525> as: "hot, warm"

+ * חָם (ChM) <H2526> as a Name: "Ham" [Noah's son] <pg 235>

+ * חָם (ChM) <H2526> as: "heat, hot"
   – used as the idea that [being hot/heat] → "will lead to anger."

> **Concept of *a result* from *something* [an external influence]**

The idea of "Not putting in an effort, which leads
to bitterness or anger towards those who do.

4 - Meaning Construct

> **Concept of *the Sense:* "Hearing"**

The idea of being aware of one's surroundings – as an
external awareness, like the traits of *Hunter/Gatherers.*

Note: As two aspects of *Hunting: Stalking prey* by listening
and [making sounds] = *to push the prey* [to an ambush].

Symbolically, connection to *mediation* [or *inspiration*]
<the *listening* to *oneself* [inner voice] or [inner man]>.

Methushael, מתושאל (MTVShAL) <H4967>

> **Glyph meaning formula:**
> *Life/Truth + Weaving + Tethered [held back] Interaction + Aspect of
> Creation + Strength (God's Mind) + Teach/Learn (Understanding)*

Concept of "Eating"
<as part of Survival within the World/Life>

[The Duality of the *Mouth* = *Eating* and *Speaking* <as a *Necessity*]

The **Sense** of **Taste**

1 - *Linear Construct* (MTV+ShAL)

*מת (MT) <H4962> as: *"an adult, a man"*

> Concept of *"un/under-developed maturity"*
> [versus *"developed maturity"*]

Symbolically, as *"eating like an animal"* versus *"the refined table manners"* <Also as a comparison of *"lesser* to *greater"*>.

+ (V) *[held back]*

+ * שאל (ShAL) <H7592> as: *"to inquire, to request, to demand"*

> ## Concept of *"Transitioning"*
> — from being *"like an animal* to *becoming human"* - both in how we eat and in speech [with the development of words]

The idea of *not being immature* and *not taking on responsibility.*

2 - *Dimensional Construct* (MT+AL →VSh)

*מת (MT) <H4962> as: *"an adult, a man"*

+ * אל (AL) <H410> the singular *[El]* as: *"god, god-like one, mighty one"*

→ <gives birth> * רוש (VSh) *[tethered to]* Aspects of Creation

Other variants or words built from (VSh):

** נורש (NVSh) <H5136> as: *"to be sick, distressed"*

> ## Concept of the *"Fine-line balance"*
> <as (N) *potential* to *over-stress oneself* by taking on too much responsibility.>

The idea *of the importance* and *delicate nature of finding balance.*

Specially, when *taking on responsibility* and *keeping the value of youth* [as one becomes *mature*].

Note: *"Staying curious"* – as a value of becoming an adult, but still maintaining *a child-like curiousness>.*

<The pre-stage of being *"Open-minded">*

3 - *Reflective Construct* (LA+ShV+TM)

* לֹא (LA) <H2524> as: *"not, No"*

> The idea of *having a lack of understanding.*

+ * שׁוֹ (ShV) **Note:** *not a biblical Hebrew word!?*

Other variants or words built from (ShV):

** שׁוּב (ShVB) <H7725> as: *"to turn back, to retreat, return"*

** שׁוּב (ShVA) <H7723> [LShVA] as: *evil, idolatry, uselessness*
— actually translated as: *in vain* and *false* [witness/report].

** שׁוֹא (ShVA) <H7722> [ShVAH] as: *devastation, tempest, ruin, waste*

** שׁוֹא (ShVA) <H7721> [BShVA] as: *a rising, arise*

> Symbolically, a *rising wave* [a tsunami] <a precursor to a *"flood"* [aka: a *"harbinger"* of the flood]

** שׁוֹא (ShVA) <H7724> as a Name: *Sheva*
— described as meaning: *to false* and *Jehovah contends*

+ * תֹם (TM) <H8535> as: *"complete, pious, gentle, dear"*

+ * תֹם (TM) <H8537> as: *"innocence"*

> The idea of *not understanding [pious/innocence]* leads to *being "closed/narrow-minded.*

4 - *Meaning Construct*

> Concept of the *Sense: "Taste"*

The idea that *once you taste something,* it leads to *eating, which can't be undone,* but only describes *what was experienced.*

<The "Attempt" to take in.>

Also, the *transition of what one accepts* [as truth] and *projects out* [as truth] as the perspective of a [or one's] personal truth.

Lamech, למכ (LMK) <H3929> meaning: *"powerful"*

> **Glyph meaning formula:**
> *Teach/Learn(Lessons) + Life/Truth + Flesh/Body(Primal)*

The **Sense** of **Smell**

Note: As an *"early warning"* | *"being down/up wind* [from something] | *testing before eating a rotten/spoiled thing* | *"verification"* of the *senses.*

[The Duality of the *Nose*]

Note: Another aspect of the *Nose* is to *Breathe,* which is described in Genesis 2:7 as the idea of the 1st Act of Life [...and breathed into his nostrils the breath of life.. <referring to Adam>], and by extension as: the *Final Breath*].

> Concept of *"At the precipice"*

The idea is *we find a way to save ourselves* or *make the necessary change.*

1 - *Linear Construct* (LM+K)

* למ (LM) **Note:** *not a biblical Hebrew word!?*

Teach/Learn(Lessons) + Life/Truth = Life's Lessons

+ * כ (K) *Flesh/Body*

> Concept of *"What is made Flesh"*

The idea of [something] *created in the Physical world,"* but what comes from *Life Lessons.*

Other variants or words built from (LM):

** למד (LMD) <H3925> translated as: *"to goad, to teach"*

The Path (D) that comes from *Life Lessons* (LM)

2 - *Dimensional Construct* (LK →M)

Note: *the* (LKM) *is not a biblical Hebrew word!?*

Other variants or words built from (LK):

** הלכ (HLK) <H1980> as: *"it flows"* | *to walk* | *"to go"*

— used in Genesis describing the *flowing* river and *walking* in Eden.

** למד (LKD) <H3920> as: *"capture, take, seize"*

** למד (LKD) <H3921> as: *"something to capture with, a noose"*

> Concept of *"Capture"* of *"Life and Truth"*

The idea of *"Seizing the Moment"* or *"Seize the Day"*

** למה (LKH) <H3922> as: *"journey"*

The idea of a *"journey"* to <bring forth> life/truth"

> Concept of *Life [experiences* and *lessons]*,
> but also *a Journey ("The Sacrifice of Time")*

3 - *Reflective Construct* (KML)

> ***Note:*** the (KML) *is not a biblical Hebrew word!?*

Other variants or words built from (KM):

** כמה (KMH) <H3642> as: *"to pine after"*

** כמס (KMS) <H3647> as: *"to store up, save"*

The generalized idea of *wanting to have or keep [something].*

Other variants or words built from (ML):

** מלא (MLA) <H4390> as: *"to fill, be full of"*

The idea of filling up after building up.

Symbolically, the filling up of grain silos.
(but this can lead to a *spoiling/poison if it sits for too long,* and also
like: *stagnant water* versus *flowing water [aids in keeping it fresh]*)

Note: The correlation to the modern concept of *cash flow -
keeping the economy in movement* [but, if too much is held
stagnant at the top and not flowing down, it's like a poison].

Another *Reflective Construct* (KL →M)

* כל (KL) <H3605> as: *"the whole, all, any, every"*

— used in Genesis 1:21 .. and *every* (KL) [living]... | and *every* (KL) [winged]...

→ <gives birth> to מ (M) *Life/Truth*

Note: When merging the two variations of ideas, it connects *Everything*
that is *life,* is somehow *restricted/contained,* but *full (or being filled).*

4 - Meaning Construct

> Concept of the *Sense: "Smell"*

The idea of *"Inquiry,"* and is connected to something *"Intuitive."*

Symbolically, as a duality of *scent:* The predator *sniffing* out prey ["tracking"], and the *warning* to prey [by *smelling* the predator].

> Concept of *being Educated/Taught,* but at a level of *intuitive* or *inquiry* rather than a complete knowledge of it.

A negative version would be the idea of *"Hubris."*

The Overview

The complexity of making sense of it all [the inputting data through our senses, in order to understand the world mankind lives in].

Formatted as the perspective of *"The Path of Adam* [Rational thought] *and Eve* [Emotional thought] *through Cain* [the Comfort condition] *to the offspring generations of Cain* [Five Senses].

<The Path of Cain>

Cain
Holding on to the past, as a way of interacting with the physical world [*"Earthly"* realm] and transitioning from the [unstructured] fearless, wild child towards being an adult.

1 *Enoch*
The transitioning attempt: to balance from Chaos to Order. [The Sense of *Touch*].

2 *Irad*
The attempt: to *be aware* or *find awareness.* [The Sense of *Sight*]

3 *Mehujael*
The attempt: to *meditate* or *find inspiration.* [The Sense of *Hearing*]

4 *Methushael*
The attempt: to *be in the moment* and *perceptions of* [one's] *personal truth.* [The Sense of *Taste*]

5 *Lamech*
The attempt: to *seek the opportunity* for one's *own truths* and *life experiences.* [The Sense of *Smell*]

The Wives / Offspring of Lamech

Genesis 4:19

English translation (King James Version)
And Lamech took unto him two wives: the name of the
one was Adah, and the name of the other Zillah.

Wife of Lamech [1st Wife]

Adah, עדה (aDH) ‹H5711›

> *Glyph meaning - word formula:*
> *Observation + Path + Revealing*

Concept of *Sight*, as: *What is "Revealed from the Seeing."*

The idea of *choosing a path* and the *outcome(s)* from that *choice.*

Note: Compared to the Name: *Irad*, עירד (aYRD) ‹H5897›
represents the sense of *Sight* as: *"The Effort of making
Observations + ‹bring forth› the Mental Path(direction).*

Perception versus *Perspective*

1 - *Linear Construct* (aD+H)

* עד (aD) ‹H5703› as: *"duration, perpetuity | for ever"*

* עד (aD) ‹H5704› as: *as far as, even to, up to, until, while, against*

* עד (aD) ‹H5705›as: *unto, until | before, order*

* עד (aD) ‹H5706› translated as: *the prey, booty*
    — used in Genesis 49:27 ...*devours the prey...* or [as the object/thing]
    that the predator *saw [or witnessed].*

* עד (aD) ‹H5707› translated as: *a witness | evidence*
    — used in Genesis 31:44 (LaD), 31:48 (aD)
    — used in Exodus 20:16 as a *commandment = "do not bear false witness"*

+ ‹brings forth› (H) *"Revealing/Revelation"*

Concept of a *"continual realization [of things]*

The idea of *as far as the eye can see."*

Another *Linear Construct* (a+DH)

Note: *the* (DH) *is not a biblical Hebrew word!?*

Other variants or words built from (DH):

** דהב (DHB) *<H1722>* as: *"gold"* <the assignment of value>

<The *path* of *revealing/revelation* is the plan from it.>

Note: The word (aDH) is adding the (a) *observation* aspect of
"gold" = *"Seeing the shimmer of [gold]."*

* דהוא (DHVA) *<H1723>* as: *"the sickly"*

(DH) *[held back]* + *<bring forth> Mind of God*

Note: The comparison of *the* <u>shimmer</u> *of gold* versus *the* <u>paleness</u> *of the sick.*

2 - *Dimensional Construct* (aH →D)

* עוה (aH) *<H5753>* as: *"to crook | to bend, twist, distort"*

→ ד (D) *Path <born within>*

Concept of a *"distorted view can lead astray"*

3 - *Reflective Construct* (HDa)

Note: *the* (HDa) *is not a biblical Hebrew word!?*

* הד (HD) *<H1906>* as: *"a [joyful] shout, cheer"*

Revealing/Revelation + <bringing forth> a Path

Note: This *Path* can lead to *Pride* and a *"Messiah complex."*

+ ע (a) *Observation <brought forth>* from (HD)

Other variants or words built from (HD):

** הדך (HDK) *<H1915>* as: *"to crush with foot"*

Note: The (HD) *"made flesh"* (K) = The *behavioral trait* or *outcome* of
a *"prideful"* (Messiah complex) *leader.* [aka: *False Messiah*]

— used in Job 40:12 *"to put others down"* | *"to think less of them"*

The idea of *a person who thinks themselves to be better* or *greater than
another* or *all others.* [The *negative* or *dangerous* level of *Pride.*]

** הדר (HDR) <H1921> as: *"to swell up, to favor, honor, be high, proud*

Note: The (HD) + *Mind of Man* (R) = The *behavioral trait* or *thoughts* of *"pride"* unchecked = *"Having a swollen head."*

Other variants or words built from (Da):

** דעי (DaY) <H1843> as: *"knowledge"*

> Concept of *prideful, overzealous knowledge* or *behavior*

The idea of *thinking [you're better than others]* and *what you know, is "right" way [just because you think you're better than others].*

4 - Meaning Construct

> Concept of the *Perspective*

The idea of *"If a person tries to look too far ahead, it can/will be a distorted view which can lead one astray."*

Positive: *Real value* -versus- Negative: *Perceived value*

When this is at the *personal* level, it's akin to *the desire to have or wear "bling"* [flashy jewelry worn especially as an indication of wealth, or status expensive and ostentatious possessions].

Shiny object syndrome: refers to the tendency to become easily distracted by new and exciting things, regardless of whether they align with long-term goals or not.

Note: The extreme version of this behavior leads to... *Hoarding disorder* versus <or as a *fine-line*> of just being *an avid "collector."*

The sons of Lamech via **Adah**

Symbolically, as a *marriage[union]* of two attributes.

Lamech: represents the *person who thinks they know so much [everything] that they know* and *can predict the future.*

The idea of *having everything all figured out.*

Concept of *"Hubris."*

Note: They have two sons [aka: *Two Brothers*].
Jabal, יבל (YBL) and *Jubal,* יובל (YVBL)

Genesis 4:20

English translation (King James Version)
And Adah bare *Jabal*: he was the father of such as
dwell in tents, and of such as have cattle.

Note: The *Father* of those who *dwell in tents* and *raise livestock.*

Concept of *"Shepherding"*

[Like: *Abel,* (H+BL)], but as (Y+BL) = (Y) *"Efforts"* move us [as *feelings*].

Son of Lamech [with Adah]   [1st Son]

Jabal, יבל (YBL) <H2989>

Glyph meaning - word formula:
Effort + Blueprint/Plan + Learning/Teach

* בל (BL) <H1077> as: *"a failure, nothing, not at all, lest"*

"Lesser" Understanding [Blueprint/Plan + Learning/Teaching]

Concept of *"the Way people will learn"*

The idea of *"How & What"* [born from *"Lamech"* | from the *"life lessons"*]

-versus-

* אל (AL) <H410> *"El"* | *"God"* = *"Greater" Understanding*

Mind of God + Learning/Teaching = God's lessons/teachings

Concept of *"the Way [How and What] people will learn"*
[from the "God's teaching/lessons"]

1 - *Linear Construct* (YBL)

* יבל (YBL) <H2986> as: *to conduct, bear along, to bring*

— used in Job 10:19 (AVBL) *carried* [from the womb]

— used in Job 21:30 (YVBLV) *brought forth* [at the day]

— used in Job 21:32 (YVBL) *brought forth* [to the grave]

> Symbolically, as **<First** and the **Last>** = *"Moving" through the womb* and then *"Carried" to the grave.* Functions as: *"Moments" of movement* by *another force* or *will* [not of one's own].

* יבל (YBL) <H2987> as: *to bring, carry*

— used in Ezra: [someone or something] being *brought* (VH<u>YBL</u>) to a [place]

* יבל (YBL) <H2988> as: *running/streams* [with water]

— used in Isaiah (YBLY)

> Concepts of *being "Inspired" — being "Moved"* by something

The idea of *putting into practice* | *set up an organized structure of teaching*

> **Note:** Seems to be linked to the *flight response* — as a degree or spectrum of *fear-worry-concern,* but as *pushing past one's fear(s).*

> Concept of *"to overcome"* the *impulse* (BL)
> to *run/hide/worry/procrastinate* (Y)

Other variants or words built from (YB):

** יבב (YBB) <H2980> as: *to bawl, to cry, cry out [shrilly]* | *lamented*

** יבמ (YBM) <H2993> as: *to perform the duty of a brother-in-law*

2 - *Dimensional Construct* (YL →B)

* יל (YL) <infers an *intent "to influence another"* [in some way]>

— This could go either in a *good/bad* direction.

→ *<giving birth>* to (B) *Plan*

> Concept of *attempting to teach* or *learn by its nature*

> The idea of *what gives birth to a plan or a blueprint one can/will use in one's future self [life].*

Other variants or words built from (YL):

** ילד (YLD) <H3205> as: *to bear young, to beget | to act as midwife | to show lineage* [begot]

3 - Reflective Construct (LBY)

Note: *the (LBY) is not a biblical Hebrew word!?*

* לב (LB) <H3820-1> as: *the heart, the feelings, the will, the intellect* | Also as: *"inner man"* [aka: *"Mind"*]

Note: The use of this word in Genesis is linked to both (LB) and (LBV).

— used in Genesis 6:5 (LBV) *man's heart [held back]* as: *wicked* and *evil*, in Genesis 6:6 implying God (YHVH) was *grieved* in the *heart* (LBV), and in Genesis 8:5 uses both (LBV) as God's *heart* and (LB) man's *heart*.

4 - Meaning Construct

Concept of *putting into "Practice," as what a person believes*

The idea of *working towards, service of,*
or *worshiping of what life teaches us."*

Note: As a *"lesser"* understanding = El (.AL) [aka: *lesser god*].

The Father *[of those who]*...

* ישב (YShB) <H3427> as: ***"dwell,"*** *settled, remain, sit down*

Effort + Aspect of Creation + Plan

Symbolically, it's the *place* where the **Mother** gives birth.

Note: As it relates to *"carrying in the womb"* [pre-birthing/birthing pains] <the moment just before giving birth>.

The idea of *giving birth* in **tents.**

Tents

* אהל (AHL) <H168> as: *tent, home, (dwelling)(place)* | *tabernacle, covering, side pillar*

Mind of God + Revealing + Learn/Teach

Construct A: (AH+L)

* אה (AH) **Note:** *is not a biblical Hebrew word!?*

> ### Concept of *"coming together"*
> [for the purpose of *love*, or *loving another* or *others*]

<brings forth> + (L) *Learn/Teach*

Other variants or words built from (AH):

** אהב (AHB) <H157-159> as: *"to have an affection, love for another or to God"*

Construct B: (A+HL)

(A) *Mind of God* + (HL) as *"departing from [to move/go away]"*

Other variants or words built from (HL):

* הלכ (HLK) <H1980> as: *"to walk, departing from, move, go away* | *to die, live, manner of life*
— used to describe the flow [of a river]"

Symbolically, this version of the word is the *Tent*, which carries a meaning and a duality relationship of the movement of *coming in* and *going out.*

> ### Concept like: *"walking the tight rope"*

The idea of *"If there is not a proper balance"* →
it can lead people away from *God* [or lead to *Death*].

The idea of *giving birth* to [*raising*] **livestock.**

Livestock

* מִקְנֶה (MQNH) <H4735> as: *[raise] livestock, cattle,
flock, herd, possession, purchase, acquisition [something bought]*

Life/Truth + Revealing + Past + Seed + Revealing

* מִקְנָה (MQNH) <H4736> as: *bought, purchase price*

Construct: (MQ+NH)

* מַק (MQ) <H4716> as: *"a melting, putridity
[corruption] | decay, rottenness [stink]"*

+ * נֹה (NH) <H5089> translated as: *Lamentation |
"wailing, eminence, distinction"* | a position of prominence
or superiority | distinction

> Concept of *"purchasing [something]*
> is both *valued* and has *"a rotten smell."*

The idea of *how one sees* what is *"good,"* but has a *negative side*
to it — as an *Earthly* [Human] Value.

> Concept of *Highly Valuing*
> [one's things/property/possessions]

Genesis 4:20

English translation (King James Version)
And his brother's name was **Jubal**: he was the father of
all such as handle[who played] the harp and organ.

Note: The *Father* of those who *play the harp* and *flute* .

The idea of *how "music" moves us* [as feelings].

(Y+V+BL) = (Y) *"Efforts" move us* [as *feelings*] + (V) *"interaction within."*

Son of Lamech [with Adah]   [2nd Son]

Jubal, יובל (YVBL) <H3106>

Glyph meaning - word formula:
Effort + [held back] Interaction + Blueprint/Plan + Learning/Teach

1 - Linear Construct (YVBL)

* יו (YV) = The reflection of (VY) *"Conception-Birthing"* as *"Trying to Force/Manipulate/Influence the Natural Order/Process*

+ * בל (BL) <H1077> as: *"a failure, nothing, not at all, lest"*

"Lesser" Understanding [Blueprint/Plan + Learning/Teaching]

Concept of *"the Way people will learn"*

The idea of *"How & What"* [born from *"Lamech"* | from the *"life lessons"*].

Note: The (V) as the interaction within the Concept of *his "Brother's Name."*

Concept of *putting into "Practice,"* as *what a person believes*

The idea of *forcing,* manipulating, or *influencing* the *Practices of Beliefs.*

Note: This can be either in a positive or a negative way.

The idea of *being overcome [emotional response]* is to embrace it through *musical instruments* or the *music* they are playing.

Concept of *being "Inspired"*

The idea of *being "Moved"* by something.

2 - Dimensional Construct (YL →VB)

* יל (YL) = *"working towards educating oneself"*

Other variants or words built from (YL):

** ילד (YLD) <H3205> as: *to bear, bring forth, begot* | *"begat"*

The idea of *needing to learn* [a process of *developing into an adult*]. Symbolically, it's *a path through life,* and is *precious* [to *grow the family*].

<give birth to> → * (VB)

> Other variants or words built from (VB):
>
> ** (NVB) <H5107> as: *to germinate, to flourish, to utter |
> to bear fruit | make cheerful.*

The combined ideas of *expanding* and *revealing knowledge.*

Symbolically, *to give birth/bring forward* and *to flourish.*

> Concept of *being "Inspired,"* but by means of learning things
> that will make *oneself* or *others* "*cheerful, flourish, fruitful*"

The idea of *"Making Music."*

3 - Reflective Construct (LBVY)

* בֹל (LB) <H3820-1> as: *the heart, the feelings, the will, the
intellect* [also as *"inner man"/ mind*]

> — used over 500 times in many books, formatted with both the (LB)
> and the (LBV) *[held back].*
>
> Symbolically, referring to as *the caring, emphatic state* and maybe
> even as the *increased beating heart* [increasing rate when *confronting
> stress*] = (LB) versus the (LBV) *<holding back>* = *staying calm,
> managing the stress* or *not caring.*

+ * וֹ (VY) = *"Conception-Birthing"*

> The idea of *choice* is a *duality* to a *deeper emotional response.*

> Concepts of *Courageous/Heroic/Compassionate/Selfless*
> -versus- *Selfish/Cowardly/Frightened/Un-Compassionate* traits.

4 - Meaning Construct

> The Concept of *Motivation
> behind what a person believes*

The idea that *outcomes* will be of a *"lesser" understanding.*

Harp

* **כנור** (KNVR) <H3658> as: *Harp, lyre*

Flesh/Body + Seed + [held back] Interaction + Mind of Man

* **כנ** (KN) <H3651> as: *"set upright, just"*

* **כנ** (KN) <H3652> as: [and it was] *"so"*

+ *[held back]* (V) + (R) *Mind of Man*

Other variants or words built from (KN):

** **כנה** (KNH) <H3657> as: *"a plant" [to be rooted]* | *"root"* | *support* (of tree), *shoot, stock*

> Concept of *"Grounded to Earth"* [and *growing* from it].

Symbolically, *"To take roots"* is to be *"Grounded to the Land/Earth,"* but to have this *[held back]* (V) infers the capabilities to be *"Grounded,"* but also *"Not Grounded."*

Note: inferring connection to music affecting people on a spiritual level [as *"soothing" the soul*]. In addition, *<bringing forth>* (R) *Mind of Man* = a mental capacity [as to be *"elevated" spiritually/creatively intelligent*].

Other variants or words built from (NR):

** **נר** (NR) <H5369> as Name: *Ner* | meaning: *"lamp"*

> **Note:** the (V) *<interaction> within* (NR) = (NVR)

Symbolically, the *light* from a *lamp* [*lesser light* or *understanding*] – as having an internally powered *"light"* [*good-hearted* or *understanding*].

As a generalized description,

> Concept of *having a [spiritual] Charisma*

The ideas of *being a "stand up" person [honorable]* and *inspirational [inspiring others].*

Flute

* עוּגָב (aVGB) <H5748> as: *Flute | Pipe, Organ*

Observation + [held back] Interaction + Gathering + Plan

* גַב (GB) <H1354-5> as: *(arch of) the back* [of man] | *"eyebrows"* [as *top (arch of)* of the eyes] | *top, rims*

The idea of *being on top* and *arched.*

* גַב (GB) <H1356> as: *beams* [of a house], *ditches/cisterns/pits* [maybe as being on *top* of the ground].

* גֹּב (GB) <H1357> as: *"locust"* — used once in Isaiah 33:4 ... as the running to and [fro] *of locusts* (GBYM) He shall run upon them.

The idea of *flying in from above,* then *landing* to *consume [crops].*

* גֹּב (GB) <H1358> as: *den* [of the lion] — described as a *pit* [for wild animals] | also: as *a cut out [of the land]*

* גֹּב (GB) <H1359> as a Place: *"Gob"*

Concept of *trying (attempting) to do [something] challenging*

The idea of being *difficult to see (unseen), but as a knowing it's there (awareness).*

As a generalized description,

Concept of *having Faith <as believing in [something]*

The idea of being a *"Believer."*

Note: Symbolically, the combined aspects of a person who plays the *Harp* and *Flute* are connected to the meaning of a person who is *Charismatic* and *Faithful.*

Wife of Lamech [2nd Wife]
Zillah, צלה (TsLH) <H6741>

> *Glyph meaning - word formula:*
> *Snaring"The Fall" + Learn/Teach + Revealing*

Concept of *Taste* | meaning: *"Shade"*

The idea of *loosely hidden* and the *outcome(s)* from a *blind taste test.*

1 - Linear Construct (TsLH)

** צל (TsL) as: *"shade, shadow"*

Concept of *Shade* = *"not complete darkness"*

The idea of *a place to hide from the Sun.*

+ (H) <bringing forth> Revealing/Revelation

Symbolically, *not fully known* but also *not unaware* of [something].

Concept of *unseen/unknown*

The idea of *"What is done in the shadows."*

Symbolically, a *realization* that will *trap/snare* a person.

> **Note:** as a pre-cursor, a hinting [or as a *"taste of"*] the
> idea of the Concept of the *"Fall of Mankind"* or *"Sins"}*

Other variants or words built from (TsL):

* צלא (TsLA) <H6739> as: *"pray"* [more likely as: a *"curse"*]
* צלה (TsLH) <H6740> as: *"roast"*

Concept of the *"Firing [cooking] of food"*

2 - Dimensional Construct (TsH →L)

* צהל (TsHL) <H6670> as: *"bellow, cry aloud (out), lift up, neigh, rejoice, shout, make to shine, glisten*

(TsH) *Capturing* then *Revealing* → *<born within>* (L) *Learning/Teaching*

> Concept of *"the harsh reality [truth] of things"*

The idea of *personal benefits* at the *expense of harming another.*

Also symbolically, what one can *learn* from being in *exile.*

Other variants or words built from (TsH):

** צהב (TsHB) *<H6669>* as: *"to glitter, be golden in color"*

As the (B) *Plan* [as the *tangle, the intention of looking tempting* = bait]

** צהר (TsHR) *<H6671>* as: *"to press out oil"*

3 - *Reflective Construct* (HLTs)

Note: the (HLTs) *is not a biblical Hebrew word!?*

Other variants or words built from (HL):

** הלא (HLA) *<H1972>* as: *"to remove, be remote"*

** הלכ (HLK) *<H1980>* as: *"it flows"* | *to walk* | *"to go"*

— used in Genesis describing the *flowing* river and *walking* in Eden.

<Also, connects to *Lamech* and *Abel* regarding *position* and *direction*>

Note: the (H) to (L) is the *directional order* used as prefixes and a *pattern* in Genesis. Inferring a *direction away* from *God* going to *Man* versus the idea of (ALHYM) as the direction to return [*Man to God*] = The *Path to Enlightenment.*

+ (Ts) *<brings forth>* *"Snaring/Trap"* or *"Fall"* – also as: the *"Fallen"*

> Concept of *getting trapped* in our [*sorrows* or *troubles*].

The idea of *having [emotional] baggage.*

<Extreme version would be "PTSD" [Post-traumatic stress disorder]>

4 - *Meaning Construct*

> ### Concept of the *Sense: "Taste"*

The idea is that *once you get a taste of something,*
it leads to *desiring/wanting more.*

Symbolically, a *pleasing favor* [tastes good, but came at a cost].

> ### Concept of "Sin"
> as the *personal benefit(s)* at the *harm of another.*

The idea of *"what is done in the shadows."*

Son of Lamech & Zillah

Tubal-cain, תּוּבַל קַיִן (TVBL QYN) <H8423>

> *Glyph meaning - word formula:*
> *Weaving [together] + [held back] Interaction + Plans + Learning/Teaching*
> *Past/Ancient + Efforts + Seeds*

Note: Combines *Noah's grandson* from *Japheth:* **Tubal,** and *Adam's son:* **Cain.**

Tubal

Concept of *Early Learning* (as *Bad Ideas*)
Also, *before making real connections* from the *past concepts.*

+ Cain

Concept of *holding on to the past*
It can be both a *limitation to growth* and the *result of growth.*

Note: ...but when *restraint* is *taken too far,* it's symbolically
a *strangle to death.* [as *one's own* or within *oneself,* and *to
others around* us (how we affect others)].

> * Described as the *instructor* [*forger*] of every
> *craftsman* in *bronze* and *iron.*
>
> Symbolically, as the *person who hammers down
> metal to make tools/weapons.*
>
> Additionally, there's the idea of *bad practices* or
> *stubbornly holding on to traditional practices.*

1 - *Linear Construct* (TBL)

* תבל (TBL) *<H8397>* translated as: *"perversion <in sexual sin>"* | *confusion <violation of nature or divine order>* | also described as: *"mixture"* or *unnatural bestiality (like an animal)*

* תבל (TBL) *<H8398>* translated as: *"the world"*

Other variants or words built from (BL):

** בלל (BLL) *<H1101>* as: *confuse, mingle, mix, confuse, confound*

Note: the god name = *Baal* (BaL) translated as: *owner, lord* |and used to translate as, allies/archer]

** הבל (HBL) *<H1893>* Abel [symbolic: *humility/hope*]

Note: Whom was killed by his brother - *Cain,* קין (QYN) (which represents the senses of mankind and how they interact with emotional states of mind.

Other variants or words built from (TB):

* תבה (TBH) *<H8392>* as: *box, ark, vessel*

The idea of *putting [something] in a box* or *being boxed in.*

2 - *Dimensional Construct* (TL →B)

* תל (TL) *<H8510>* translated as: *"mound, heap, heap of ruins"*

→ *<giving birth>* (B) *Plan(s)*

The idea of *plans* from a *heap of ruins* = [*bad planning*], but also the idea of *piling up plans* = [to make *overwhelming* or *in need of streamlining*].

3 - *Reflective Construct* (LBT)

* לב (LB) *<H3820-1>* as: *the heart, the feelings. the will, the intellect* | *the "inner man"*

+ (T) *Weaving together*

The idea of the *complexity of plans* [from *feelings/emotions*].

4 - *Meaning Construct*

> ### The Concept of *Control*
> [as having an *Earthly Leader*]

The idea of *making/planning.*
How to do or *How it will/should be done(s).*

Symbolically, as *"bad ideas"* [to let a person be in control of others].

The idea of *"Earthly" Leader [King].*

Note: This can also be *"unintentional"*
[what a *person believes* to be *true*].

Examples: When adding the human *senses, past beliefs, what feels likely to be true*, and *"make a snap judgment."* Especially when getting productive results, but for a limited number of people.

The idea of the phrase: *"A greater good."*

Daughter of Lamech & Zillah   [Sister to Tubal-cain]

Naamah, נעמה (NaMH) <5279>

Seed(Potential) + Observation + Life/Truth + Revealing

<Unseen/*Unrealized Potential* will *grow into/become realized.*>

1 - *Linear Construct* (NaMH)

* נע (Na) <*H5128*> as: *"vagrant"* [lives by begging], *"fugitive"* [lives on the run/without a home] |also translated as: *"to quiver, wave, tremble, unstable"*

+ * מה (MH) <*H4100*> as: *"what?"* [of *what kind?*]

The idea of *what will life/truth reveal?*

> Concept of [one's own] *Perception*

In addition, connected to *"Self-entitlement"* and *"Feeling sorry for oneself."*

2 - Dimensional Construct (NH →aM)

* נֹה (NH) <H5089> translated as: *"wailing, eminence, distinction"* | *a position of prominence or superiority | distinction*

→ <born within> * עַמ (aM) <H5971-5974> translated as: *"people, tribe, troops, flock"*

> Concept of *Self, high praise* towards *one's own people*

3 - Reflective Construct (HMaN)

* הַמ (HM) <H1990> as: *"hot"* or *"sun-burnt"*

* הַמ (HM) <H1991> as: *"abundance"*

> The idea of an *after position* of the *planted seed* or *the growing of the seed* [as the *seeing* of the *sprouting*].

+ <brings forth> * עַנ (aN)

> Other variants or words built from (TB):

** עַנֹב (aNB) <H6024> as: *"fruit"*

The idea of *the growth* of a *seed* into a *fruit* (*seed within itself*).

Symbolically, as a *path of completion* of a cycle of life>.

4 - Meaning Construct

> Concept of *"Feeling sorry for oneself* and *one's own people*

> In addition to *giving oneself high praise towards* [oneself] and/or *one's own people."*

Symbolically, this is the idea of *being like-minded* [aka: *echo chambers*].

The Overview

<The Path of Lamech>

It's the final review [analysis]

<What is the opportunity available, or where to take things from here?>

The idea of *personal experiences* and *analysis,* but through the *Path of Cain* [*Senses*] = *"Perspective and Perception."*

Symbolically, this is the "How our own *personal* or *selfish* behavior and way of *looking at others.*

Note: *Cain & Abel* = as the *can* or *will* lead to the *killing of "a brother."* Symbolically, *how* one's own *biases ["personal truths"]* will *reject* others' *biases ["personal truths"].*

Two Wives and Offspring of Lamech

1st wife - *Adah*

The Mother of *Perspective*

<but at a risk of *giving birth* [offspring] as: "a *reflection* of..."

Son - *Jabal* = *Arrogance*

To put into "Practice," as what a person believes

The Father of *Highly Valuing one's own belief* and *Walking a tight rope.*

Son - *Jubal* = *Ignorance*

the motivation behind what a person believes

The Father of *Charismatic* and *Faithful.*

2nd wife - *Zillah*

The Mother of *"Sin."*

<as the *personal benefit(s)* at the *harm of another.*>

Son - *Tubal-cain*

as "*Making and Planning the How to do(s) or How it will/ should be done(s)* but as a Bad/Forceful Boss(Leader).

Daughter - *Naamah*

"Feeling sorry for oneself and *one's own people.*

Generations of Adam/Eve
(version 2.0)

"A retelling of the Story of Adam [through Seth]"

Genesis 5:1-3
English translation (King James Version)

1 This is the book of the generations of Adam. In the day that God created man, in the likeness of God made he him;

2 Male and female created he them; and blessed them, and called their name Adam, in the day when they were created.

3 And Adam lived an hundred and thirty years, and begat a son in his own likeness, after his image; and called his name **Seth**:

Seth, שׁת (ShT) *<H8352> Sheth*

> **Glyph meaning - word formula:**
> *Aspects of Creation + Weaving [together]*

Creation's Matrix = the complexity of Creation

The name, **Seth,** is described as meaning *"appointed or placed"* – from the * שׁת (ShT) *<H7896>* translated as: *"appointed."*

1 - Linear Construct (ShT)

* שׁת (ShT) *<H8352>* as a Name: *Seth*

* שׁת (ShT) *<H8353>* translated as: *"six"*

* שׁת (ShT) *<H8351>* as a Name: *Sheth,* and also translated as: *"tumult"* <Defined as: *disorderly agitation, riot, hubbub,* or *violent agitation of mind or feelings.*>

— Also connected to meaning: *buttocks, hips.*

Note: The last 2 letters of the Hebrew Alphabet.

> ## Concept of *Creation*
> [Inferring the *last(end) stages* of it]

The idea of *creating [something* from *something else].*

2 - *Dimensional Construct* (Sh_T)

> **Note:** *2-letter words/roots can't have this function!?*

Other variants or words built from (Sh_T):

** שאת (ShAT) *<H7612>* as: *devastation, ruin*

** שבת (ShBT) *<H7673>* as: *rest, to cease, desist | to exterminate, destroy | to remove | to put an end to*

** שבת (ShBT) *<H7675>* as: *abode, session, locality | dwelling, seat*

** שבת (ShBT) *<H7676>* as: *Sabbath <the seventh day | day of atonement>*

** שחת (ShChT) *<H7843>* as: *to decay, ruin | to corrupt, spoil, pervert*

** שית (ShYT) *<H7896>* as: *to place | to dress <connection to BRAShYT>*

** שפת (ShPT) *<H8239>* as: *to locate, hang on, establish, reduce | to set, place, put, ordain*

** שרת (ShRT) *<H8334>* as: *to minister, serve | to attend as: a menial, worshiper, to contribute*

> Concept of *Destruction*

The idea of the *destruction* of *[something* in order to *create]*.

3 - *Reflective Construct* (TSh)

> **Note:** *the* (TSh) *is not a biblical Hebrew word!?*
>
> *Weaving together <brings forth> aspects of Creation*

The idea of the *visual image of a woven basket* having a *criss-crossed [crosshatched/checkered]* pattern.

Other variants or words built from (TSh):

** תשצב (TShTsB) *<H8665>* as: *checkered work, briodered*

> **Note:** The (T) represents the *outcome* state of how [something] plays out. The order of (ShT) is the idea of mankind's perspective *"of things to come"* versus (TSh) as *"that which has come"* or *"that which has played out."*

The interrelationship of the process = *making use of "what was destroyed from the creation process".* An example of this [as reflecting in mankind] would be the *"building [re-building] on top of ruins."*

> ## Concept of *Recycling*

The idea of *the duality* of *Destruction/Creation* has a *cycle* or a *repeating pattern* [*coming back together* and *finding balance*].

4 - Meaning Construct

> ### The Concept of *Creation,*
> as *reflected* in a *woven pattern*

The idea that *everything in the Universe* and *on Earth* is *reflecting* or has a *pattern* or *patterns.*

Note: The relationship to the (ShT) and its reflective nature (TSh) represents *a balance* and *getting the most out of* [something].

Symbolically, as a word and as the Name: *Seth* (ShT) represents, the idea on *living of the land,* and specifically *"the hardness of a land"* [like: the desert/wilderness — as: *"How to live when life is hard or under hardships"*].

Note: compare to the Egyptian deity *"Set"* or *"Seth,"* defined as the *"god* of *deserts, storms, disorder, violence,* and *foreigners."*

Generations of Seth

Genesis 5:6

English translation (King James Version)
And Seth lived an hundred and five years, and begat Enos:

Enos, אנוש (ANVSh) <H583> Enos/Enosh

> **Glyph meaning - word formula:**
> *Mind of God + Seed (Potential) + [held back] Interaction + Aspects of Creation*

The idea of *lacking God's Influence* within *Creation.*
<The Flaws within Creation>

The name **Enos** is described as meaning *"mortal man"* – from the other various or related words:

** אנושׁ (ANVSh) *<H582>* defined as: *Man, mankind, mortal,* but translated as: *another | men*

— used in Genesis 3:6, 4:23, 6:9 (AYSh) as: *another, husband*
— used in Genesis 18:16 (HANShYM) as: *the men*
— used in Genesis 19:4 as (ANShY) as: *men*

Note: Strong's intertwines with אישׁ (AYSh) *<H376>* as: *a man, husband.* — used in Genesis 2:24, 3:16

> (A) + (NV) *Seed(Potential) [held back]* versus the (Y) *Effort* as *Outcome*

** אנשׁ (ANSh) *<H605>* as: *to be weak, frail, feeble | sick (incurable)*
— used in 2 Samuel (VYANSh),   — used in Job (ANVSh),
— used in Isaiah (ANVSh)   — used in Jeremiah (ANVSh)/(ANSh)

** אנשׁ (ANSh) *<H606>* as: *man, human being*
— used in Ezra, Daniel

Note: This relates to the (A_Sh) as (ASh), which traces back to the Bereshit as *first spark/fire | origin* as the *center (core) of the aspect of beginning* = the "Concept of *Wisdom*" → (AYSH) *Effort <born within> Wisdom.*

The translation(s) of the word *<H605>* [*to be weak, frail, feeble*] connect to the "Concept of *Weak Wisdom*," or *Humanity's wisdom* is an evolving or growing process, and *<holding back> potential [within Wisdom]* is a *mortal flaw.* The idea of wisdom is that it: *"Grows beyond the single person or wise man."*

1 - Linear Construct (A+NVSh)

* (A) *Mind of God <brings forth>*

+ * נושׁ (NVSh) *<H5136>* as: *to be sick, distressed*
— used once in Psalm 69:20 [describing having a *"heavy heart"*], and actually is (VANVShH) translated as: *"and I am full of heaviness [sick]."*

The idea of the *primal* [uncontrollable] *feelings* or *being overwhelmed by feelings [losing control of...]*.

Another **Linear Construct** (AN+V+Sh)

* אן (AN) *<H575>* as: <a question> *where?* [of place] | *when?* [of time]

— the actual (AN) itself is used in Job 8:2 translated as: *long* [how *long* will you speak...}, and used in Job 7:8 as: *there is* (VAYNNY) *<H369>* as: *nothing*, but translated here as: *and I shall no longer/more [be]*.

> Concept of (AN) represents *Ancient Ways*

The idea of "*Primal nature*" or "*Animal impulses*," regarding *Intentions [*also as: "*urges*"].

Other variants or words built from (AN):

** אנה (ANH) *<H578>* as: *to groan* | *to mourn, lament*
  — in used twice in Isiah, but as (ANV) *<holding back>* of (AN)

Note: The (AN) *Potential from God* versus (AL) *the Lessons from God.*

The words built from (AL) of *similar* structure/meaning:

** אלה (ALH) *<H421>* as: *to bewail* | *to wail, lament*
** אלה (ALH) *<H422>* as: *to swear, curse* | *to take an oath* [before God]
** אלה (ALH) *<H423>* as: *oath, oath of covenant*

Note: The perception of the (A) and what was born from it
→ (N) *potential* = the Ancient Way of viewing God, or gods.

Specifically, the Sumerian god, "*An*" (AN)

The *Anunnaki*, or which means the offspring of *An*. Breakdown: (An) + (unna) + (Ki) is the *An* (Sky God) and *Ki* (Earth God), and the born from within the Father + Mother gods is the "*unna*" = *Nun* (Moon god), as: the daughter god.

-versus-

The Canaanite god, "*El*" (AL)

The *Supreme Father* god, usually represented as an elderly man with a long beard, and was believed to live on Mount Saphon. He was considered *all-knowing/powerful, and wise.*

---

2 - *Dimensional Construct* (ASh →NV)

* אש (ASh) *<H784>* as: *fire, flames* [supernatural fire]

→ *<born within>* (NV)

Symbolically as, *Potential [held back]* → *<born within> Wisdom (fire).*

The idea the *primal instincts [urges/senses]* of a *human*.
[the *Primitive* or "*Animal*" nature within *humans*]
is the *state* that will hold back "*Wisdom*."

Other variants or words built from (NV):

* נוא (NVA) <H5106> as: *to refuse, forbid* | *to hinder, hold back* | *restrain, disallow, frustrate* <the (A) as a suffix leads to the negative outcome>

3 - *Reflective Construct* (ShVNA)

Note: *the* (ShVNA) *is not a biblical Hebrew word!?*

Other variants or words built from (ShV):

** שוא (ShVA) <H7723> actually [LShVA] as: *evil, idolatry, uselessness*
<Actually translated as: *in vain* and as *a false [witness/report].*>

** שוא (ShVA) <H7722> as: *devastation, a tempest, ruin, waste*
— actually [ShVAH] = symbolizing, the *revealing/revelation* from *devastation.*

** שוא (ShVA) <H7721> as: *a rising, arise* [meaning to rise]
— actually [BShVA] = symbolizing the *plan/ beginning* of *devastation.* <as the *rising wave [tsunami]* bringing the "flood" [as a *"harbinger"* of the flood]>

** שוא (ShVA) <H7724> as a Name: *Sheva*
— meaning: to [be] *false,* and Jehovah *contends]*

→ <*born within*> is the (N) the *Seed* as: *the Potential born from [it].*

The idea of *having an ideology*
and the *potential* within it [can lead to *devastation*].

** שוב (ShVB) <H7725> as: *"to turn back, retreat, return"*

The idea of a *plan* to *head in a particular direction*
[with *devastation* invoking intent].

** שוד (ShVD) <H7736> as: *"to swell up, devastate | wasteth"*

The idea of a *path heading in a particular direction*
[with *devastating* intent].

+ * נא (NA) <H4994> as: *beseech (pray), now, Please*

* נא (NA) <H4995> as: *raw [uncooked]*

* נא (NA) <H4996> as Name: *No* <capital city/Upper Egypt> [*Thebes*]

The idea of *selfish/vanity* is an *underdeveloped* behavior/state.

Symbolically, "heading in the direction of becoming a
bad seed [having *bad/poor potential*]."

4 - Meaning Construct

> Concept of *Generalized Primal Impulses/Base Instincts*

Note: Like the correlation to the (RASh) as a watershed moment of *"Man making Fire"* and (Enoch) as watershed moment of *"Man walking on two feet"* / *"Man making and using tools,"* and (ANSh) would denote the watershed moment of *"Man recognizing mortality* [and the relationship of a *continuation of life*]."

Genesis 5:9

English translation (King James Version)
And Enos lived ninety years, and begat Cainan:

Kenan, קֵינָן (QYNN) *<H7018> Cainan, Qenan*

Past/Ancient Efforts + Seed(Potential) + Seed(Potential)
<Past/Ancient Efforts from Generations and Generations after>

1 - Linear Construct (QYNN)

Symbolically, the *"Seed from Cain"* represents *Holding on to the Past* and as: *The Generations of Cain = 5 Senses*, but *building off* from there.

The idea of the *outcome* from *living* on the *Path of "Cain"* = as *holding onto things one believes* versus *verifying factually* [in life and truth] = *"Blind Faith."*

Other variants or words built from (NN)/(NVN):

* אָנַן (ANN) *<H596>* as: *to mourn, complain, murmur*
* נוּן (NVN) *<H5125>* as: *to resprout, propagate by shouts, perpetual*

> Concept of *holding on to the past* to *build* or *bring forth* more *potential* from it.

2 - Dimensional Construct (QN →YN)

* קַן (QN) <H7064> as: *nest [bird] | room*

→ *<gives birth>* * יָר (YN) <H3238> as: *to rage, be violent,*
to suppress, to maltreat

The idea from *being "emotional" spoiled, entitled"*
[aka: *"Mama's Boy"* -to- *"becoming an adult* that is
violent and/or *rage(ful)."*

Note: In modern terms, as *being "woke."*
[*being "Karen" versus "Lashing out."*]

3 - Reflective Construct (NNYQ)

(NN) **Note:** *Is not a biblical Hebrew word!?*

Other variants or words built from (NN):

** אָנַן (ANN) <H596> as: *to mourn, complain, murmur*

+ (YQ) **Note:** *Is not a biblical Hebrew word!?*

Other variants or words built from (YQ):

** יָקֶב (YQB) <H3342> as: *trough, wine-vat*
** יָקֹד (YQD) <H3344> as: *to burn, be kindled*

The idea of a *very lacking perspective* of *what the past is* or *was*
[as the attempt to *influence* on what can *come from it*].

4 - Meaning Construct

> Concept of *"What we Believe"* or *"Having Faith"*
> (in the *"Lesser"*/Oneself (Man) vs. the *"Greater"*/ (God)

Symbolically, the idea of *holding* onto the *pain* of
the *past,* as the *motivation to build the future.*

The idea of the [*negative effects* of *"Faith"*] — Our senses can *deceive/*
trick us in *thinking something untrue.* <a warning to not just *leap,* but
look before you *leap!* [*"You may not like where you land"*]>

Note: The *wrong choice* or *path* a person can take and the *doubling down*
on the *"Path of Cain"* = [*"Blindly Following"* the *"old ways or gods"*].

Genesis 5:12

English translation (King James Version)
And Cainan lived seventy years, and begat Mahalaleel:

Mahalalel, מהללאל (MHLLAL) <*H4111*>

Life/Truth + Revealing + Learning/Teach + Learning/Teach
+ Mind of God + Learning/Teach [El = "Understanding"]

"the shining one of El" = "praise of God"
great-grandson of Seth, also a man of Judah

1 - Linear Construct (MHL+LAL)

* מהל (MHL) <*H4107*> as: *to cut down, reduce, to adulterate*
  | *to circumcise, weaken*
  — used in Isaiah 1:22 described as: *diluting* wine with water,
  but it uses (MHVL) as the <*holding back*> of (MH)+(V)+(L).

Other variants or words built from (MHL):

** מהלכ (MHLK) <*H4108*> as: *a place to walk*
  Note: The <*bringing forth*> (K) *flesh* [physical] place.

** מהלכ (MHLK) <*H4109*> as: *a journey, a going, a walk*

The idea of *putting yourself out in the world,* and *it may be*
tough going, but *you'll become better* by doing so.

* מהללו (MHLLV) <*H4110*> as: *praise*
  Note: The <*holding back*> (V) is *"praise"* — maybe inferring that
  one's journeys through life will be a *challenge/tough/difficult.*

  < * הל (HL) <*H1972*> as: *to remove, be remote* >

+ * לאל (LAL) <*H3815*> as a Name meaning: *"belonging to God"*

  Concept of a *"Balance of Understanding"*

< * לא (LA) <*H3808*> as: *not/No* ↔ * אל (AL) <*H410*> as: *God* >

God's Wrath ↔ God's Lessons

Note: A *fine line* between the *lack of understanding* and *having it.*

Another **Linear Construct** (MHLL+AL)

* מהלל (MHLL) *<H4110>* translated as: *"praise"* | meaning: *fame*

> Symbolically, the *path* of (HL) is *"wisdom to learning."* Inferring the *steps* to understanding the concept of *"Wisdom"* is learning from *one's mistakes/ failures*, which is connected symbolically to the *shine [metal]*, because it must be *worked hard* and *be forcefully rubbed "polished"* to have a *shine*.

> Additionally, it's the idea of *"Reflective Wisdom."*

Other variants or words built from (MHL):

** מהללמה (MHLMH) *<H4112>* translated as: *"Blow, strokes"*

> [Concept of *Experiences in Life*]

> The idea of the challenge of/from *Experiences in Life* (especially. Hardships) can bring a *balance of understanding*, as related to the *meaning to life* [but not quite *"wisdom"*].

2 - *Dimensional Construct* (MH+AL →LL)

* מה (MH) *<H4100>* as: *what?*   Life/Truth + Revealing

> The idea of "What *Life* or *Truth* can *Reveal*" [is the question].

+ * אל (AL) *<H410>* the singular [El] as: *"god, god-like one, mighty one"*

> *Mind of God + Learn/Teach = "Strong Understanding"*

→ * לל (LL) *Learning of Learning* | *Teaching of Teaching* | *Lessons of Lessons*

> [Concept of *Discovery of a Truth*]

> The idea of *this can elevate the lesson learned* [from it] to a *strong understanding* [but not quite *"wisdom"*].

3 - *Reflective Construct* (LAL+LH+M)

* לאל (LAL) *<H3815>* as a Name meaning: *"belonging to God"*

> [Concept of a *"Balance of Understanding"*]

> < * לא (LA) *<H3808>* as: *not/No* ↔ * אל (AL) *<H410>* as: *God* >

> *God's Wrath* ↔ *God's Lessons*

+ (LH) **Note:** *Is not a biblical Hebrew word!?*

Other variants or words built from (LH):

** לְהַב (LHB) *<H3851>* as: *a flash, sharply polished blade, point of a [weapon]*

** לְהַג (LHG) *<H3854>* as: *an intense mental application, study [a devotion to study]*

** לְהַד (LHD) *<H3855>* as a Name meaning: *"oppression"* <A feeling of being weighed down in mind or body> | also: *a man of Judah*

** לְהַהּ (LHH) *<H3856>* as: *to languished* <To exist or continue in miserable or disheartening conditions>, *to faint*

— used in Gen. 47:13 - described as languished/fainted (VT+LH)

+ (M) *Life/Truth*

> **Glyph meaning - word formula:**
>
> (LA) = [God's Wrath]/*"lack of understanding"* + *<brings forth>* (L) = Lessons + *<brings forth>* (LH) = [Hardships] *"lessons revealed"* + *<brings forth>* (M) *Life/Truth*
>
> (LAL) *"Balance of Understanding"* + *<brings forth>* (LH) = *"Lessons Revealed"* + (M) *Life/Truth*
>
> (as a *"Polished" Balanced Life*)

> Concept that *hardships* will bring a *value* of *having* or *needing* a *balanced life.*

4 - Meaning Construct

> The Concept of *Experiences*

The idea of *challenging experiences* [*Hardships (in Life)*] can bring *a balance of understanding,* and is connected to a *meaning to life* [Also, not quite *"wisdom"*].

Note: The (HL) *"departing from..."* is within (MHLLAL) versus (LH) [the reflective version] is within (ALHYM) *:Enlightenment:.*

Genesis 5:15

English translation (King James Version)
And Mahalaleel lived sixty and five years, and begat Jared:

Jared, ירד (YRD) *<H3382>*

Effort + Mind of Man + Path

1 - Linear Construct (YRD)

* ירד (YRD) *<H3381>* as: *to descend, bring down | to come* or *go down*

> Concept of *one's thoughts [in Life]* are what will *bring forth <are linked>* to the *way one* is *directed* in life.

2 - Dimensional Construct (YD →R)

* יד (YD) *<H3027>* as: *a hand*

→ (R) *<gives birth>* to *Mind of Man*

> Concept of *one's efforts [in Life]* leads to the *way one thinks.*

Note: The close relationship to *one's effort* and *thoughts,* and the link to how it plays out in both *Life and Truth* [One's Life is one's truth].

3 - Reflective Construct (DR+Y)

* דר (DR) *<H1858>* as: *a pearl, mother-of-pearl | white*
Note: The *"Pearl"* is that which is *"Hidden,"* inferring [something] *"Secret."*

+ (Y) *Effort <from it>*

Another *Reflective Construct* (D+RY)

* (D) *Path <to it>*

+ * רי (RY) *<H7377>* as: *a shower, irrigation | moisture/watering*

The idea of either *"Pearls* or *Droplets"* [of *Thoughts*]
in reference to *"Knowledge/Truth/Wisdom."*

4 - Meaning Construct

> ### The Concept of *One's Thoughts*
> *[in Life]* are what will *bring forth [One's Actions].*

The *outcome(s)* can be either *negative* or *positive:*

"Closed Minded" versus *"Open Minded"*

Genesis 5:18

English translation (King James Version)
And Jared lived an hundred sixty and two years, and he begat Enoch:

Enoch, חנוכ (ChNVK) <H2585>

** As noted with the earlier **Name** breakdown ** <see page 170>

The key concepts of the Name are:

The *"Sense of Touch"*
In relation to having two (2) hands and two (2) feet]

The Concept of *"Transition from Wild [to Domestic]"*
The idea of *"Unstructured to Structured."*

Concept of *"Establishing Guidance"*
The idea of *transitioning from "Chaos to Order."*

The concept is directly related to the *transitioning* and the *"attempt"* to **balance.** The idea of being on a tightrope, as the *shifting/swaying movements,* in order to stay balanced. Additionally, connecting to the *ebb and flow* of the sea and the relationship between *Chaos and Order.*

Note: The first use of *Enoch* or *how the namesake reacts* as coming from the *Path of Cain* is the connection to the physical world.

Whereas, the second use of **Enoch,** or *how the namesake* reacts as coming from the *Path of Seth,* is the connection to the spirit/mental world.

The idea of a *balanced mind.*

217

Like: two feet supporting and directing the body, as *mental feet*, which are the *Emotional and Intellectual aspects of the mind*, whereas the two hands are the *balance of the Mind and Body* (working together to perform the actions/efforts needed). **Note:** This leads to *"Walking the Path =* ד(D).

Symbolically, when [things] become *separated* or *split* from each other, there's the *potential* for *conflict* [like: the *splitting* of brothers, as *"branching"* = ח(Ch)].

Concept of *"Finding Balance"*

Note: There is an interesting relationship to the *name* Enoch, specifically to the four different characters with the name in Genesis. [aka: *The Four Israelites* — as the Sons of *Cain, Jered, Midian,* and *Reuben.*]

Enoch #2 of 4

The idea of *Finding Balance* is not a *stillness [stagnant]* or being *"level."* It's the *motion of the split of* and *into two* within oneself. [Like: *two arms* and *two legs,* specifically the movement of them when *"**walking**."*]

Genesis 5:22

English translation (King James Version)
And Enoch **walked** with God: and he was not; for God took him.

walked, ויתהלכ (VYTHLK) *<H1980>*

Tethering + Effort + Weaving + Revelation + Learn + Body/Flesh

1 - *Linear Construct* (VYTHLK)

* (VY) *<Tethering + Effort>* as: *"Conception-Birthing"*

   <As the "prelude and cause" to bring [something]>

+ (T) *Weaving* + * הלכ (HLK) *<H1980>* as: *to walk | "walked"*

Note: There are various aspects of the translated forms of this root word:

* הלכ (HLK) *<H1980>* as: *to walk | to flow [running along]*
— used in Genesis 2:14, actually word is (HHLK). It describes the river going out of the Garden of Eden and then branching into four heads, of which is specifically listed as: the Tigris river as *"it flows"* | *runs along* [toward the East side of Assyria].
— used in Genesis 3:8, actually word is (MTHLK) and translated as: *"walking"* [in the garden].

* הלכ (HLK) *<H1983>* as: *a toll [on goods at a road] |* as: *customs*
The idea of a *journey with tolls.*

> Concept of *"Movement,"*
> but with *Intention* and *Complexity.*

The idea of *having direction* and *purpose.*

Note: The moving from (H) to (L) to (K) = going away from *God* as: from the *Spirit/Divine <realm>* to the *Physical/Flesh <realm>*.

Another *Linear Construct* (VY+THL+K)

* (VY) *<Tethering + Effort>* as: *"Conception-Birthing"*
As the *"prelude and cause"* to *bring* [something]>.

+ * (THL) **Note:** *Is not a biblical Hebrew word!?*

Other variants or words built from (THL):

** תהלה (THLH) *<H8416>* as: *laudation, a hymn | praise, song | thanksgiving* [paid to God]

+ (K) *Flesh/Body = "Made Flesh",* as: *output into the Physical realm*

The idea of the *pre-stage* (VY) = *"Dance" (as joyous movement of the feet)* + (THL) = *Singing <Praising [God]>* + (K) *<in the Physical/Earthly realm>.*

> Concept of *"Joyous Journey"*

— The idea of *having an interaction, connection with,* or a *relationship* [with God].

Symbolically, as *"Having Freedom"* – as: *the rule under "one" king* — Specifically, the *Idea of God, as "King."*

In other words, *to walk with God* is to *have* or *serve* only one master/king [*"God"* alone].

2 - *Dimensional Construct* (VY+LK →TH)

* (VY) *<Tethering + Effort>* as: *"Conception-Birthing"*

As the *"prelude and cause"* to *bring* [something]>

+ * (LK) **Note:** *Is not a biblical Hebrew word!?*

Other variants or words built from (LK):

** לכד (LKD) *<H3920>* as: *"to catch, to capture, occupy, to choose, to cohere"*

** לכה (LKH) *<H3922>* as a Name meaning: *"a journey"*

→ *<giving birth>* * (TH) **Note:** *Is not a biblical Hebrew word!?*

Other variants or words built from (TH):

** תהו (THV) *<H8414>* translated as: *"formless."*

(TH) As the ***not*** *[held back]* version:
The idea of the *capacity of having "Form."*

Concept of *"Having Form"*

The idea of *making a journey* or *the attempt to capture* the *"Form"* or the idea of the *"Essence"* [of something].

Symbolically, as *"Patterns, not yet observed"* or *How things are [all] connected.*

Another *Dimensional Construct* (T+K →HL)

* הכ (TK) *<H8496>* as: *oppression, injury*

Note: The *[held back]* is * הכו (TKV) *<H8497>* *sit down [at your feet]* or *followed [in your steps]>*

→ * (HL) **Note:** *Is not a biblical Hebrew word!?*

Revealing/Revelation + Learning/Lessons

Note: The moving from (H) to (L) = going away from *God* as: from the *Spirit/Divine <realm>.*

Other variants or words built from (HL):

* הלא (HLA) *<H1972>* as: *to remove, to remote*

> Concept of *being lured off* [to a distant place]
> <as being *oppressed* or *injured*>

The idea of *being in Exile.*

3 - Reflective Construct (KLHT)

* כל (KL) *<H3605>* as: *the whole, all, any, every*

Other variants or words built from (KL):

** כלה (KLT) *<H3615>* as: *the end, to be completed*
— used in Genesis 2:2: "And God *ended/completed* (VYKL)
...His work on the seventh day.... <The word is not a (KLT)>

Note: The variation of the (KL) by strong concordance, and
by translation in regard to function.

+ * (HT) **Note:** *Is not a biblical Hebrew word!?*

Other variants or words built from (HT):

** התוכ (HTVK) *<H2046>* as: *melted*
— used in Ezekiel 22:22 as describing *"Silver being melted."*

(HT) As the **not** *[held back]* version:
The idea of *being* in a *solid/frozen state* [versus a *liquid* state].

> Concept of "Everything being in a *Solid State* or *Form*"

The opposite idea of *being ruled under an Earthly/Physical/
Human King/Leader, as "Not having God"* as *King.*

Symbolically, connected to *"Conquering," "Creating an Empire,"* and
*"**Not** Having Freedom"* — the idea *this may/can/will lead to
oppression/being frozen,* and *"not free to be whom your are."*

4 - Meaning Construct

> Concept of *being caught up* or *dazzled* by *[something]*

The idea of *"feeling joyous,"* but there is an *unseen danger* to it.

Note: Symbolically, *"Walking with God"* [regarding *Enoch*] is the *finding a balance in Life* versus the idea of *"Wrestling with God"* [regarding *Jacob*] as the *struggle to do so.*

Genesis 5:21

English translation (King James Version)
And Enoch lived sixty and five years, and begat Methuselah:

Methuselah, מתושלח (MTVShLCh) <H4968>

Life/Truth+Weaving+Tethered+Aspect of Creation+Teach/Learn (type of Understanding)+Branching

> **Note:** The similarity to the generations from Cain.
> *Methushael,* מתושאל (MTVShAL) <H4967>
> [The Duality of the *Mouth* = *Eating* and *Speaking* <as a *Necessity*]
> The Sense of Taste

1 - Linear Construct (MTV+ShL+Ch)

* מת (MT) <H4962> as: *"an adult, a man"*

> Concept of *"un/under-developed maturity"*
> [versus *"developed maturity"*]

Symbolically, as *"eating like an animal"* versus *"the refined table manners"* <Also as a comparison of *"lesser to greater"*>.

+ (V) *[held back]*

+ * של (ShL) <H7944> as: *error, fault, irreverence*
— used once in 2 Samuel 6:7 ... *error* (HShL) and he died (VYMT).

Note: Described as *being/acting disrespectful towards [God]* and then being struck *dead* versus the Name (MTV+ShL+Ch) as <*holding back*> (MT) then (ShL) – a reversed order placement.

+ * של (ShL) <H7945> as: *on account of, whatsoever, whichsoever | who, which | cause/sake [of]*
— used 4 times in 2 Kings 6:11 (MShLNV), Ecclesiastes 8:17 (BShL), Jonah 1:7 (BShLMY), Jonah 1:12 (BShL))

+ * (Ch) *branching/diversity*

Symbolically, as *a child* [or *immature adult*] *starting off trying to be well-behaved,* then *inevitably becoming ill-behaved,* and the *various ways in which this can play out.*

Concept of *becoming a "Bratty Child"*

The idea of *"Feeling Entitled."*

—*thinking oneself is owed something* that *was not earned,* or just *doing whatever you want* and *when you want to do it.*

Concept of *becoming a "Restless Child"*

The idea of *"Feeling Impatient."*

— *Thinking oneself has to do something* which may not be appropriate in timing or at all. Again, [a type of *"Entitlement"*] just *doing whatever you want* and *when you want to do it.*

The generalized idea of *realizing* [something] *may have gone too far,* or *the moment of crossing the line.*

Note: There's a relationship to the words:

* מת (MVT) *<H4191>* as: [*from it you will*] *surely* (MVT) *die* (TMVT) — used in Genesis 2:17 describing *eating the fruit from the Tree of Knowledge of Good & Evil.*

* שאול (ShAVL) *<H7585> Sheol* / as: *underworld, grave* (place: people descend at death) — used in Genesis 37:35 actually (ShALH).

2 - *Dimensional Construct* (M+Ch →TL →VSh)

* מח (MCh) *<H4220>* as: *fat, rich* | *<H4221>* as: *fat, marrow*

→ * תל (TL) *<H8510>* as: *mound, hill*

→ * (VSh) **Note:** *Is not a biblical Hebrew word!?*

Other variants or words built from (VSh):

** נוש (NVSh) *<H5136>* as: *sick, distressed [to be full of heaviness]*

** ושני (VShNY) *<H2059>* Name: *Vashni* [*strong*] | meaning: *weak*

** ושתי (VShTY) *<H2060>* Name: *Vashti* | meaning: *beautiful*

> ## Concept of the *"being on High ground"*

The idea of *one who lives at the "Top of the Hill,"*
"being fat or rich," and *"being sick or weak."*

Symbolically, to behave as if *having the attitude* of *Moral Superiority.*

Note: Also similar to the visual of the *"Humpty Dumpty"* nursery rhyme.

3 - *Reflective Construct* (ChL+ShV+TM)

* חל (ChL) *<H2455>* as: *"though it was an ordinary,"* *"common"*

— used as in 1 Samuel 21:5 *"common"* (ChL) describing *"bread"* →
which is a *reflected* variant version of the word: לחם (LChM) *<H3899>*
from the root * לח (LCh) *<H3892>* as: *fresh, unused, un-dried, moist,*
vigor. Also, as the *fresh/new plant growth*, but also associated with
the *"vigor"* [has in a person who is *young*.]

Note: * חל (ChL) *<H2455>* also translated as: *"unholy"*
— used in Leviticus as (HChL) *revealing + <brings forth> +* *"common"*
— used in Ezekiel as (LChL) *learning + <brings forth> +* *"common"*
along with (VYChLLV) as: *"and profaned."*

+ * (ShV) **Note:** *Is not a biblical Hebrew word!?*

Other variants or words built from (ShV):

** שוב (ShVB) *<H7725>* as: *"to turn back, to retreat, return"*

** שוא (ShVA) *<H7723>* as: *"false, vain, evil, idolatry, uselessness"*

** שוא (ShVA) *<H7721>* as: *a rising, arise*

— used once in Psalm 89:9 actually [BShVA] → symbolizing (B)
plan [the beginning of ...] as the *rising wave* [a tsunami] *bringing*
the *"flood"* = as a *"harbinger"* of the *flood.*

+ * תם (TM) *<H8535>* as: *"complete, pious, gentle, dear"* | *"peaceful"*
* תם (TM) *<H8537>* as: *"innocence"*

The idea of *"just being ordinary"* can lead to becoming *"closed or narrow-*
minded" | a *turning back* or *away* from *knowledge/understanding/wisdom.*

> ## Concept of the *"Opposite of improving oneself"*

The idea of *Not improving oneself.*

Symbolically, this is the *reflected* condition of *"bread"* [as: *Food of*
Life] = *transitioning* from the *seed* to *flour* to *bread* <as a *Path*>.

4 - Meaning Construct

> Concept of *Outward Expressions [from the Mouth]*
> *Duality of the Mouth (Inward - taste | outward - speech)*, but also the symbolic idea *of many flavors [of taste].*

The idea of *many diverse experiences/ideas.* In addition, connects to *conversions/expressions* from them, as well.

Symbolically, to *take in food* [into the mouth] is necessary to live, versus *"what comes out of the mouth"* [*vomiting*] and *words* <having potential for evil [relationship to *vomiting*].

Note: The *Jesus* quote: *It is not what goes into the mouth that defiles [a man], but what comes out of it* [Matthew 15:11].

Additionally, the idea of *Life's Experiences* becoming *merged* or *mixed* with *Knowledge/Education* can generate *division.* The internal expression represents the difference between becoming the *wise old man* versus the *angry, bitter one,* and then what is *passed on [taken in]* is the perception of *knowledge, wisdom, etc...*

Symbolically, relating the idea of *passing on [knowledge and wisdom from Life experiences] through spoken words* (the term is associated with death as to *"pass on"*).

> Concept of *"What we are* and *how we act* will *pass on* or *reflect in others"*

<Violence begets Violence versus Smiles are Contagious>

The idea of two functions of the *mouth*: to *eat food* that was prepared (from ingredients), and the *mouth:* to *speak* from the prepared thoughts (as ingredients of the mind).

Genesis 5:25
English translation (King James Version)
And Methuselah lived an hundred eighty and seven years, and begat Lamech:

Lamech, למכ (LMK) <H3929>

Learn/Teach + Life/Truth + Flesh/Body

** As noted with the 1st Lamech breakdown ** <see page 183>

The key concepts of the Name are the *"Sense of Smell."*

The Concept of *"What is made Flesh"*
The idea of [something] *created in the Physical world,"*
but what comes from *Life Lessons.*

Concept of *"Hubris."*

The idea of a *person who thinks they know so much [or everything]* that
they think they *have everything all figured out* or *can predict the future.*

The concept is directly related to the *transitioning* and the *"attempt"*
to *seek the opportunity* for one's *own truths* and *life experiences.*

Note: The first use of *Enoch* or *how the namesake* reacts as
coming from the *Path of Cain* is the connection to the physical world.

Whereas, the second use of **Lamech**, or *how the namesake*
reacts as coming from the *Path of Seth,* is the connection to
the spirit/mental world.

The idea of a *being on a "precipice," "edge,"* or *"limits of
learning"* [via: *self-life experiences*]. Thus, *needing a revelation* to
get over the hump [symbolizing an *"End"*].

Symbolically, to *get the scent* of *something coming* or *as food cooking.*

Additionally, the relationship of phrases like: *"Seize the moment* or
Seize the day," or the extreme version: *"Grab the bull by the horns."*

The common idea of *Life Experiences* and *Lessons,* and
from a perspective as a *"Journey"* (as: *The Sacrifice of Time*).

Note: The function of (LM) to (D) *Path* as the *"Life Lessons Journey"*
למד (LMD) <H3925> translated as: *"to goad, to teach"*

-versus-

The (LM+K) *Flesh/Body* as *"Life Lessons applied to the Physical world"*

Another *Linear Construct* (L+MK)

* (L) *Life/Truth*

> + * (MK) **Note:** *Is not a biblical Hebrew word!?*

Other variants or words built from (MK):

** מכאב (MKAB) ‹H4341› as: *anguish, affliction, sufferings, sorrows*

** מכה (MKH) ‹H4347› as: *a wound, carnage, pestilence*

Note: The (MK) *Life/Truth + Flesh/Body (Physical)* inferring a function of *Life* is about *suffering* or *the struggle to live* [the idea of the *Survival of the Fittest*], but also connects to the birthing process as being a *painful struggle.*

> Concept of *living life,* and *finding truth*
> as the *struggle,* and is necessary for *survival.*

Another *Meaning Construct*

> Concept of *being "educated" [being taught]* is
> connected to *"a struggle"* in the physical world.

The idea of the *"Suffering Servant" and "making sacrifices."*

The Overview

The complexity of *output(s)* or *choices* [in order to understand the world mankind lives in].

Formatted as the perspective of *"The Path of Adam* [Rational thought] *and Eve* [Emotional thought] *through Seth* [a *Comfort/Desire* condition] *to the offspring generations of Seth as:* the **Seven (7) Virtues/Sin** ‹*from the Catholic perspective›.*

Seth represents the *"Self"* [as: *Body/Mind Union*], and infers an idea of *self-regulating,* defined as: *"appointed, placed."* In addition, there's an implied *ability to elevate* above the *animal instinct* [the idea of the 5 senses as: *"sensory abilities"* = Path of Cain].

Note: This is the *"How our own personal* or *selfish behavior,* and the *way of looking at others.* In addition, this will lead to *Noah* and the *Flood* (symbolically a type of a *big change*).

\<The Path of Seth\>

Seth
Living in [or *building off*] of *hardship*, as a way of interacting with the physical world [*"Earthly"* realm], but also *with others.* In addition, on the surface level of interaction [including *scripture*] as *"Digging Deeper."*

1 Enos
The attempt to *handle the primal nature/urges* [animal instinct] *of man.*
[The Virtue/Vice(Sin) of *Chastity* vs. *Lust*]

2 Kenan
The attempt to *believe or have faith in* [something].
[The Virtue/Vice of *Faith* vs. *Idolatry*]
\<the positive and negative versions *of worship methods*\>
[The Virtue/Sin of *Temperance* (Self-control/restraint) vs. *Gluttony*]
\<the positive and negative versions *"of personal behavior"*]

3 Mahalalel
The attempt to *find value in experiences* [both good and bad ones].
[The Virtue/Vice of *Good Works* vs. *Greed*]
[The Virtue/Sin of *Charity* vs. *Greed*]

4 Jared
The attempt to *be aware of one's thoughts* and *way of thinking.*
[The Virtue/Vice of *Concord* vs. *Discord*]
[The Virtue/Sin of *Diligence* vs. *Sloth*]

5 Enoch
The attempt to *find balance in one's life.*
[The Virtue/Vice of *Sobriety* vs. *Indulgence*]
[The Virtue/Sin of *Kindness* vs. *Envy*]

6 Methuselah
The attempt to *find* or *take the "High Ground."*
The choice of *"being"* or *"becoming"* the negative version: *having the attitude [thinking] as having a Moral Superiority* or *"being" through [actions]* of the positive version: *do the morally right thing.*
[The Virtue/Vice(Sin) of *Patience* vs. *Wrath*]

7 Lamech
The attempt to *evaluate oneself* and *one's thoughts and actions.*
Note: It's the *final review* [analysis] \<At the *"precipice"*\>.
[The Virtue/Vice(Sin) of *Humility* vs. *Pride*]

Note: The concept of the Seven (7) Virtues/Sins was first introduced in the [late 4th - early 5th century AD/CE] by a Roman Christian poet: *Aurelius Prudentius Clemens,* as an allegorical poem representing Christian morality. His poem _Psychomachia_ *(Battle of Spirits* or *Soul War / as the battle between good and evil)* depicts a battle between *female personifications of virtues and vices,* with each of the seven (7) virtues confronting and defeating a particular [opposing] vice.

Virtues *[Latin]* | **Vice** *[Latin]*
1 Chastity *[Pudicitia]* | Lust *[Sodomita Libido]*
2 Faith *[Fides]* | Idolatry *[Veterum Cultura Deorum]*
3 Good Works *[Operatio]* | Greed *[Avaritia]*
4 Concord *[Concordia]* | Discord *[Discordia]*
5 Sobriety *[Sobrietas]* | Indulgence *[Luxuria]*
6 Patience *[Patientia]* | Wrath *[Ira]*
7 Humility *[Mens Humilis]* | Pride *[Superbia]*

Later in 590 AD/CE, the seven capital vices (sins) were revised by *Pope Gregory I.*

Virtues *[Latin]* | **Vice/Sin** *[Latin]*
1 Chastity *[Castitas]* | Lust *[Luxuria]*
2 Temperance *[Temperantia]* | Gluttony *[Gula]*
3 Charity *[Caritas]* | Greed *[Avaritia]*
4 Diligence *[Diligentia]* | Sloth *[Acedia]*
5 Kindness *[Humanitas]* | Envy *[Invidia]*
6 Patience *[Patientia]* | Wrath *[Ira]*
7 Humility *[Humilitas]* | Pride *[Superbia]*

Genesis 5:28-29

English translation (King James Version)
28 And Lamech lived an hundred eighty and two years, and begat a son:
29 And he called his name Noah, saying, This same shall comfort us concerning our work and toil of our hands, because of the ground which the LORD hath cursed.

Noah, נֹחַ (NCh) <H5146> *Noach*

The Seed + Branching/Diversity

Note: There is a reflective nature and relation to the name Enoch = (ChNVK)

1 - *Linear Construct* (NCh)

* נֹחַ (NCh) <H5146> as the Name: *Noach/"Noah"*
   Note: Associated with meaning: *"rest"* or *"consolation"* | *"comfort"*

Other variants or words built from (NCh):

** נחה (NChH) <H5148> as: *"to guide, transport"*
— used as Genesis 24:27 actually (NChNY) as: *"has guided"* and *"led me"*

As the what was Revealed from the Seed(s)/[Potential]
*What will **Sprout** = "Sprouting Seed"*

> Concept of *"Establishing Guidance"*

The idea of going from *"Chaos to Order."*

Symbolically, a process going from a *variety of* [or *potential from*]
Seed(s) to Sprouting Seed(s) to become the Plant [Crop]"

** נחם (NChM) <H5162> as: *to sigh, breathe strongly, to be sorry,*
console oneself, repent, regret, comfort, be comforted, be moved to pity,
have compassion | rue, suffer grief, repent | to comfort oneself'

— used in Genesis 5:29 And he called his name *Noah* [NCh], saying, This
same *shall comfort us* (YNChMNV) concerning our work and toil of our
hands, because of the ground which the LORD hath cursed.

*"Seed"/Potential + "Branching"/Diversity = **(Noah)** + "Water"/Life/Truth*

The idea of *Comfort* that *brings the tears* [of joy], and the
idea of the *"Flood"* [comes after the introduction of *Noah*].

** נחיר (NChYR) <H5156> as: *nostrils*
— used once in Job 41:20 as (MNChYRYV)

Symbolically, as having a *"Runny Nose."*

2 - Dimensional Construct (N_Ch)

Note: 2-letter words/roots can't have this function!?

Other variants or words built from (N_Ch):

** נוח (NVCh) <H5117> as: *to rest, to settle down*

** נבח (NBCh) <H5024> as: *to bark*
— used once in Isaiah 56:10 (LNBCh) describes *"watchman"* [of
Israel's Sinful Leaders] as: being *blind, mute,* and *[dumb] dogs* which
can not *bark.* Additionally, as *sleeping* and *lying* down on the job.

> Concept of a *"Dog guiding [his master]"*

The idea of a *hunting dog tracking down [something],*
then making it known by *barking.*

Symbolically, connecting *barking* to a *loud vocalization.*

The idea of *speaking up [loudly]* to bring about *guidance* or the *need for change*, like: *"Protesting"* | Origin point of a *Revolution.*

** נסח (NSCh) *<H5255>* as: *to pull* or *tear away* | *plucked*

"Seed"/Potential + "Branching"/Diversity →"Thorn" <born within>

Symbolically, as a *"painful* or *harmful" guidance* = as the connection to *thorns* on a plant, or as a *thistle [thorny weeds]* get *uprooted* or *plunked* from the garden.

3 - Reflective Construct (ChN)

* חן (ChN) *<H2580>* as: *grace, favor, charm, pleases*

— used in Genesis 6:8 But *Noah* (NCh) *found grace* (ChN) in the eyes of the LORD (YHVH) = [in regard reflecting *the "guidance"* to *Revelation*]

Note: The phrase: *"finding favor in the eyes* [sight]" is used many times with the Genesis characters ... Noah, Abraham/Lot, Jacob/Laban.

4 - Meaning Construct

> Concept of *establishing guidance* or *the guiding principles*

The idea of *"foundation"* [or the *beginning stage*] of *"building" morals* [as the *building of the Ark*].

Note: denotes the watershed moment of *"Man recognizing morality."*

Genesis 6:9

English translation (King James Version)
These are the generations of Noah: Noah was a just man and perfect in his generations, and Noah **walked** with God.

walked, התהלכ (HTHLK) *<H1980>*

Revealing + Weaving + Revelation + Learn + Body/Flesh

> Concept of *"Movement,"*
> but with *Intention* and *Complexity.*

The idea of *having direction* and *purpose.*

The difference between *Enoch walked,* ויתהלכ (VYTHLK) *<H1980>*
[conceived/birthing] version – as an earlier state of being on a *"Joyous Journey."*

> The idea of (ChNVK) is *"what brings balance to us [as humans]"* but
> inferring the idea of *focusing on [one's own] potential,* and when *aligned
> with an "elevated nature" [walking alongside of God]* = a *joyous state of
> being and experience with life.*

And with *Noah walked,* התהלכ (HTHLK) *<H1980>* version – as the
revealing or *revelation* that *<brought forth>* a *"Joyous Journey."*

> The idea of (NCh) is *"what guides us [as humans]"* but implies the idea of
> *many potentials,* and when *aligned with an "elevated nature" [walking
> alongside of God]* = a *joyous state of being and experience with life.*

Genesis 5:32

English translation (King James Version)
And Noah was five hundred years old: and Noah begat et **Shem**, et **Ham**, and **Japheth**.

Genesis 6:10

English translation (King James Version)
And Noah begat three sons, **Shem**, **Ham**, and **Japheth**.

The (3) Sons of Noah

Shem, שׁמ (ShM) *<H8035>*

Aspects of Creation + <brings forth> Life/Truth

Described as the *"Father of all the children of Eber,"* * יבר (aBR) *<H5677>*

Observations (a) + (BR) *Son [firstborn] Plan + Mind of Man*

The idea of referring to *when/whom* was making *observations* that
<brought forth> the development of (BRA) and (BRAShYT).

Note: The implication is the *"Creation (Sh) & Life/Truth (M)* is the
format and *key* to *Everything,* and when *Revelation (H) <brings it
forward>* it's the *HaSheM, (HShM) as it's knowledge* from *God (A).*

1 - Linear Construct (ShM)

*שֵׁם (ShM) <H8035> as a Name: *Shem* | meaning: *to be **"put"** [by God]*

*שָׁם (ShM) <H8033> translated as: *there, then, thither*
— used in Gen. 2:8 ..."and He put (VYShM) <H7760> there (ShM) <H8033>

*שֵׁם (ShM) <H8034> translated as: *"Name [of the...]*
— used in Gen. 2:11,13,14 as an introduction to/of the rivers of Eden.
versus
— used in Gen. 2:19,20 (ShMV) the *[held back]* version | translated as:
"that was *[its] name.*" [Adam *naming* [each] creature],

*שֻׁם (ShM) <H8036> as, *the name(s), in the name*
— used in Ezra, Daniel [also: as a variant of is the (ShVM) <H7761>
translated as: *issued, commanded*]

> ## Concept of *"the assignment"*

The purpose of what *something is/does* [both as *"a label and a duty"*].

The idea that *one's name is* and *should* represent the *character*
or *acts one does/going to do [accomplish].*

2 - Dimensional Construct (Sh_M)

Note: *2-letter words/roots can't have this function!?*

Other variants or words built from (Sh_M):

**שֹׁהַם (ShHM) <H7718> used when reference *stones(precious stone)* |
translated as: *onyx* <colors are black & also, greenish> | also connected to
chrysoprasus, beryl, malachite <common thread is *greenish* coloring> [maybe
as a linking symbolically to *plants/grass*, as a relationship to *life* or *new life*]
— used in Genesis 2:12, Exodus (multiple times), and Job 28:16 (BShHM)

**שֹׁהַם (ShHM) <H7719> as a Name: *Shoham* [a "Levite"]
— used in 1 Chronicles 24:27

**שׂוּם (ShVM) <H7760> as: *to put, place, set, appoint, make* |
to lay hands on (violently)

**שׂוּם (ShVM) <H7761> as: *to issue / commanded*

**שׂוּם (ShVM) <H7762> as: *garlic* [from: unused root meaning: *to exhale*]

**שָׁכַם (ShKM) <H7925> as: *to rise or early start*

**שֶׁכֶם (ShKM) <H7926> as: *the neck* [a *place* of *burdens (shoulders/back)*]

**שָׁלַם (ShLM) <H7999> as: *to be safe/friendly/to reciprocate/at peace*

** שׁלם (ShLM) *<H8000>* as: *to complete/restore/be finished/bring to an end*

** שׁלם (ShLM) *<H8001>* as: *prosperity, welfare, well-being, peace*

** שׁמם (ShMM)*<H8074>* as: *to be desolate, be appalled, stun, stupefy*

** שׁפם (ShPM) *<H8221>* as: *a beard, mustache / (upper) lip*

> Concept of *"giving [something or someone] a Name"*

The idea of *"Personifying [something or someone]."*

3 - *Reflective Construct* (MSh)

* משׁ (MSh) *<H4851>* meaning: *"drawn out"*

> Concept of *"What we can draw from"*

The idea of *"making conclusions [from]/connections [to]."*

Note: The reflected relationship is the *"Give* (ShM) and *Take* (MSh)*"* — and together both are the Balance (or *finding it*) as the idea of *Enoch*, but also has *the building something* concept [perhaps as a *great building* notion, like the *Tower of Babel*].

The idea of the *Reflection* of the *way to* or *how to Live* or *Living off the Land.*

(Actually, how the people are doing this.)

4 - *Meaning Construct*

> Concept of the *"How to Live* or *Living off the Land"* (as the *Way* or *Path*)
>
> *(Actually, how the people are doing this.)*

Note: The How to *"Walk the Path"* is to be *"Giving"*: <the reflected relationship is The *"Give* (ShM) and *Take* (MSh)," together with *"The Finding Balance"* = the *Path* (D) to *"Walk with God".*

Additionally, it's the watershed moment of *"Man recognizing the key* or *critical importance* of the *balance* of *Living off the land."*

Ham, חַם (ChM) <H2526> Cham

Branching(Diversity) + Life/Truth
(Also: *Branching Rivers*)

> *The Diversity of Life/Truth* | *"Dividing up"* | *"Branching from..."*
> like: *Evolution* or *"Evolving from..."* as: *"Dividing/Division from"*
> or *"Giving away* or *Portioning out".*

In Genesis 9:22, it states that Ham *saw the nakedness of his father* [after his father, Noah, got *drunk* on wine] — this seems to imply the idea of *exploiting/taking advantage of the vulnerabilities of others.* When Noah woke up and realized what Ham had done, and then said: *"Cursed be Canaan..."* [the fourth and youngest son of Ham].

1 - Linear Construct (ChM)

* חַם (ChM) <H2526> as a Name: *"Cham"* | translated as: *"Ham"*

* חָם (ChM) <H2524> as: *"father-in-law"*
  — used in Gen. 38:13 ...*"your father-in-law"* (ChMYK)
  — used in Gen. 38:25 ... *"her father-in-law"* (ChMYH)

* חַם (ChM) <H2525> as: *"hot, warm"*
  — used in Joshua 9:12 *This bread of ours is "warm/hot"* (ChM)
  — used in Job 37:17 ... *why [are] your garments "hot / warm"* (ChMYM)

* חַם (ChM) <H2526> as: *"heat, hot"*
  — used as the idea that [being hot/heat] → *"will lead to anger."*

* חֹם (ChM) <H2527> as: *"heat, hot"* [in the day – from the sun]
  — used in Genesis and 1 Samuel

> ### Concept of *"Results from External Influences"*

The idea of *"external efforts"* which *affect others,* which *leads to a different state* or *condition* [as: *being warm/hot*].

Other variants or words built from (ChM):

** חֱמָא (ChMA) <H2528> as: *rage, anger, wrath, fury*
  — used in Daniel 3:13 as: *anger/fury* (VChMH)
  — used in Daniel 3:19 as: *wrath/fury* (VChMA)

Note: Symbolically, the relationship connecting *anger/rage* to *heat.*

** חמא (ChMA) <H2529> translated as: *curds | butter*
— used in Genesis 18:8 (ChMAH)
— used is Deuteronomy 32:14 (ChMAT)

Note: The process of making curds is to *heat up* and dry out, and the base *milk* will *clump into parts* [aka: *"Dividing up"*].

Also, a similar process of butter going bad (spoiling) involves *separation* of the milk fat, which is increased by *heat,* and the taste becomes *bitter.*

The idea of duality of *separation/diversity.*

Symbolically, sometimes leads to a *good state (tasty morsels: curds),* but also can lead to *bitterness* and *anger (spoiled, rancid butter).*

> Concept of *"Anger"/being angry/"Bitter"*
> The *result* from *external influence: Emotion/"Emotional state."*

The idea of *"Not putting in an effort,* which *leads to bitterness* or *anger towards those who do.*

2 - *Dimensional Construct* (Ch_M)

Note: *2-letter words/roots can't have this function!?*

Other variants or words built from (Ch_M):

** חרם (ChVM) <H2345> as: *sun-burnt, swarthy*
— used four times in Genesis 30:32-40 translated as: *brown ones, black ones, dark-colored ones* [when describing which of the *"lambs"* that Jacob removed from Laban to keep for himself as a payment].

Note: As the interaction with the *heat of the day* and from the *"Sun,"* | and is the *<holding back>* the (Ch) *dividing/diversity* [as though the *tanning/pigmentation* of the skin from the sun, rather than the sun burning it to a *"red"* color].

** חכם (ChKM) <H2449> as: *wise | to be* or *become wise, act wisely | to make wise, teach wisdom, instruct | deal with wisely*
— used in Exodus 1:10 translated as: *let us deal wisely* [but also as: *let us deal "shrewdly"* (NTChKMH)]

As the *body/flesh* (K) *<born within>* the (ChM) *"anger/bitterness"* [*dividing/diversity <bringing forth Life(Living together)>*]

The idea of *Street Smarts* as a type of *Wisdom.* *<a dividing/diversity* from this would lead to... the ideas of *Street Gangs/Tribal behavior.>*

3 - *Reflective Construct* (MCh)

* חם (MCh) <H4220> as: *fat* [of animals], *marrow* [of the bone] |
  also translated as: *wealthy* <fat ones>

* חם (MCh) <H4221> as: *marrow* [of bones] used in Job 21:24

* חם (MCh) <H4220> as: *"fat, rich"* | <H4221> as: *fat, marrow* [from
  the kill of the Hunt]" <*snapping/breaking the bone open*>

Other variants or words built from (ChM):

** חמא (MChA) <H4222> as: *"to rub, strike hands together"*

> Concept of *"Clapping"*

The idea of *making sound* (*to push prey*, later to *"herd to flock"*).

> Concept of *Hunting*

The idea of *"to smite, kill, impale."*

4 - *Meaning Construct*

> Concept of *"When people become Divided"*

The idea of *coming from* the previous states of *hardships*
and then *the how* as the *rebuilding* from it is handled, and
"the anger (and *frustration*) that comes from it.

In addition to comparing the *diversity* of nature (evolution) to the
diversity of people (culture) as: *Tribes* and *Nations*, etc…

Note: This is both the *Nature's way of things,* and such diversity can
lead to negative or positive outcomes, like the *"Road to Hell"* versus the
"Road to Heaven."

The idea that *diversity* can bring a *revitalizing of the stagnant,*
but also a *division* [usually because of a *forced conformity* to
the *new "ways,"* which ironically is when this goes too far, and
it can attempt to eliminate *diversity* as well].

Japheth, יפת (YPT) <H3315> Yepheth

Effort + Spoken + Weaving together

> The idea of making an *effort* to develop more *advanced*
> or *complex* oral *tradition(s)* or *language* itself.
>
> Inferring the goal is to *achieve* a *complexity* of *togetherness*
> "Like a woven basket of a [one] world people."

1 - Linear Construct (YPT)

* יפת (YPT) <H6601> as: *"enlarge"* <to be spacious, wide or open | roomy>
  — used in Genesis 9:27 *May* God *enlarge* (YPT) Japheth (LYPT)

  ** (Variants translated) as words: *seduce, enlarge, entice, persuade, allure | to be simple, delude | to entice, deceive* <usually as (YPTH), (PTY), or adding (N) potential>

  <The idea of *"opening Pandora's box."*>

Other variants or words built from (YPT):

** יפתח (YPTCh) <H3316> as Name: *Yiphtach* | meaning: *"he opens"*
  — used in Joshua 15, 19 and Judges 11

Other variants or words built from (YPT):

** יפה (YPH) <H3302> translated as: *"to be fair or beautiful"*

> Concept of *"Bright Shiny Object"*

The idea of *"being vain."*

Symbolically, *"Wearing Bling"* or the phrase: *"Putting lipstick on a pig."*

> Concept of *"Being Superficial"*

The idea of being *"attention-grabbing"* or *"widely appealing,"* but this is *usually not useful, substantial,* or *long lasting.*

Note: (Y) *"Effort"* to <bring forth> → (PT)

** פת (PT) <H6595> as: *piece/bits [of bread] | morsels, fragments*

The idea of the *"Effort to get Scraps"* or the phrase: *"Let them eat cake."*

2 - *Dimensional Construct* (YT →P)

<Making it the (YT) <the feminine ending> that *<gives birth>* to the *spoken*>

* **יֹת** (YT) *"Effort of the Weaving together."*

— The visual imagery of weaving together a basket is the interwoven assembly of parts of a solid fixture to create another. Also, it symbolizes the act or process of *giving birth.*

Other variants or words built from (YPT):

** **יֹתֵב** (YTB) *<H3488>* as: *"to sit, dwell"* <pre-state to moving/*effort*>

The idea of *planning* [something] *to be developed* [into something].

** **יֹתֵד** (YTD) *<H3489>* as: *a peg, pin, stake, nail*

The idea of an *effort to* (Y), and as *a path/way* (D) of *holding together* [something] to be *developed* [into something] = *weaving together* (T)

versus *<giving birth>* → (P) *mouth* = that which is *spoken.*

> Concept of *"Speaking with Passion [emotion]"*

The idea of connecting to how this can *influence* and *be used* to *develop/build* [something].

3 - *Reflective Construct* (TPY)

* **תֹם** (TP) *<H8596>* as: *a timbrel, tambourine*

— used in Genesis 31:27 (BTP) describing a *musical instrument*, and implying the *potential outcome being pleasant* <when Laban spoke to Jacob - after Jacob fled away secretly and Laban caught up and confronted him.>

+ * (Y) *as to make the effort of having a "pleasant outcome"*

Other variants or words built from (YPT):

** **תֹפִין** (TPYN) *<H8601>* as: *"baked"* / perhaps *baked pieces*
— used in Leviticus 6:21 (TPYNY) as: *"the baked"*

> **Note:** The plural (YN), which symbolizes the *Efforts of the Seeds* = as the idea of *"Ingredients."*

4 - Meaning Construct

> Concept of the *Effort to Communicate* and
> to *intertwine* people *together* [as *"One"* Group].

The idea of *Motivational Speaker/Speaking.*

Note: This comes with *potential consequences*
(*Good* or *Bad*)| (*Positive* or *Negative* or *Both*).

Symbolically, the *"Casting of the Net"* and the *"Net* as it *opens."*
The real question is: *"How big is the reach of [the opened net]?"*

The idea of the *"Sphere of Influence."*

The Overview

<The Path of Noah>

The symbolic idea of getting *guidance* [as a *proper foundation*] <Noah>
and *"building"* morals [as the *building of the Ark*]; the flood represents the
fluid nature and as *"testing the waters"* [analysis/critique their value];
then landing ashore is *how to "Live off the land"* **<Shem>**.

After leaving the ark, Noah gives a blessing ...

Genesis 9:27

English translation (King James Version)
God shall enlarge Japheth, and he shall dwell in the tents of Shem; and
Canaan shall be his servant.

> Concept of *communicating togetherness* <Japheth>
> and *a way of living together* <Shem>.

1 *Shem*

The How to *"Walk the Path"* is to be *"Giving"*: <the reflected relationship is
The *"Give* (ShM)* and *Take* (MSh),"* together with *"The Finding Balance"*
<Enoch> = the *Path* (D) to *"Walk with God."*

The watershed moment of *"Man recognizing the key* or *critical
importance* of the *balance* of *Living off the land."*

2 *Ham*

The How and When people become *divided* is usually *coming from* the past or experienced states of *hardships,* and then the how the *rebuilding* from it is handled, and *"the anger* (and *frustration*) that comes from it.

The consequences of *diversity* of people (culture) lead to *Tribes* and *Nations, etc..,* and when *imbalances* occur: *war, civil war, coups, revolutions, genocides, etc...* are attempted or even *inevitable.*

The idea that *diversity* can bring a *revitalizing of the stagnant,* but also a *division* [usually because of a *forced conformity* to the new *"ways,"* which ironically, when this goes too far, it tends to attempt to eliminate *diversity* as well]].

Both *"Cursed by Noah and servant to Japheth"*

Canaan, כנען (KNVN) *<H3667>* [Ham's 4th son]

The *"NOT"* being honest or *upright* and *what will/can be potentially gained* from it: *"being a Liar/Manipulator/[even Narcissist],* but also the idea of *flattering oneself* or *not giving praise to others,* as well as: *"not having"* original (new) thoughts.

Concept of *"what a person does"* affects their way of existing in the world [but also affects others]. The idea of *one's position/status/role* in life *affects the ability* to *"Adapt,"* especially *"at a precipice." <The idea of at the end/last moment* or *when the pressure is on,* which also connects to *going along with the crowd* and *"blindly following."*

---

3 *Japheth*

The necessity to make the *Effort to Communicate* and to *intertwine* people *together* [as *"One"* Group]. The idea of *Motivational Speaker/Speaking.*

Concept of *"Speaking with Passion [emotion]"*

The idea of connecting to how this can *influence* and *be used* to *develop/build [something].*

Communication isn't just words, it's *actions* and *presentations:* Are you going to *show off [be flashy]* or *be modest [humble]*? Is the intent *selfish* or *selfish*? How do one's *actions* or *words motivate* others? Is it for your *glory* or *God's* = *(selfish leads to evil)* or *(all-inclusive leads to good).*

The idea of *communicating togetherness [oneness]* as a *way of living [together]* <is the symbolism of *Japheth dwelling in the tent of Shem*>.

The connection of meaning to Names and the groupings, as the listing of Ancient knowledge and Wisdom, continues throughout the Genesis narrations.

Note: At different times in Human history, people have extracted concepts from these groupings. The question is whether these people were attempting to capture the original intention of the author of Genesis, or if it was merely an extraction of meaning, such as the concepts of *Virtues* and *Vices/Sins*.

Nevertheless, another example of extraction can be observed, as seen in the names of *Cush* and *his generations* (Genesis 10:7-8).

Regarding what is seemingly the influence on the Italian writer *Dante Alighieri's* poem [aka: *Dante's Inferno*], and the relationship to the format of the *nine (9) "circles of Hell."*

Specifically, the format in relation to *Cush, six (6) Sons, and two (2) Grandsons,* but in the negative version of meaning, as: Symbolically, as *the "Road to Hell"* and its *eight (8) stepping stones.*

Genesis 10:7-8
English translation (King James Version)

7 And the sons of Cush; Seba, and Havilah, and Sabtah, and Raamah, and Sabtecha: and the sons of Raamah; Sheba, and Dedan.
8 And Cush begat Nimrod: he began to be a mighty one in the earth.

The Hamites via Cush

1) *Dante's Circles of Hell* — Idea of *Limbo*

Cush, כוש (KVSh) <H3568> Kus/Kuwsh

Flesh/Body + [held back] Interaction + Aspect of Creation

1 - Linear Construct (KV+Sh)

כו (KV) <H3551> as: "a window" *Flesh/Body + [held back]*

The idea of *piercing [through the wall]*

+ (Sh) *<bringing forth> Aspect of Creation*

Concept of *"destroying in order to create"*

2 - Dimensional Construct (KSh →V) <interaction (V) within (KSh)>

* כש (KSh)   **Note:** *Is not a biblical Hebrew word!?*

The generalized idea of (KSh) is to *increase one's own property.*
Especially via *sheep* [food=meat and fabrics=wool, and the *interaction
within* is a relationship to the *self* [as *doing the work oneself*] and
<*holding back*> the (K) *physical* is isolating a property <maybe
building up or *possession* of land *[for the raising of sheep]* for a nation's
sake>.

Symbolically, *the <gives birth> to <holding back>* as the idea of
leaving/saving [some(thing)] *for the next year,* to *rebuild the herd* or
grassland for the next generation *of the herd.*

Other variants or words built from (KSh):

** כשב (KShB) <H3775> as: *"a young sheep"*

Note: As an example of *destroying in order to create* [as the
necessity to maintain life]. In regard to a *"sheep"* (in order to get
ready to be *slaughtered* or *flocked*), the necessity the sheep have
to *eat the grass,* which is *clearing* or *using up the grass.*

The idea of *"making a sacrifice (in order to benefit Life)"*

> Concept of *"Charity"* or *"Forced Charity"*

The idea of *giving up [something]* that belonged to *oneself* or *others.*

Symbolically, like: *a double-edged sword* or even the
phrase: *"Damned if you do* or *damned if you don't."*

Other variants or words built from (KV):

** כוכב (KVKB) <H3556> as: *"Star(s)"*

Note: *"Star [out of Jacob]"* → <*as a Messiah,* and the idea that he
will be a *"warrior who/then bring peace,"* also a connection to
sheep and the idea of a *"good" shepherd.*>

Other variants or words built from (KV_Sh):

** כורש (KVRSh) <H3566> as: *"Cyrus"* [the king of Persia and
conqueror of Babylon; first ruler of Persia to make a decree
allowing the Israelite exiles to return to Jerusalem.]

Note: *"Cyrus"* and the connection to *"Star"* → <*as a Messiah-type,*
and the idea that he was a *"warrior[King] who freed Jews from
Babylon and brought a type of "peace."* | Although maybe even as
a type of *"False Messiah."*> The idea of a *falling star,* which
shines bright at first, but then fades away (burns out).

3 - *Reflective Construct* (ShVK)

Aspects of Creation [held back] + <bring forth> Flesh/Body/physical

* שׂוּךְ (ShVK) *<H7753>* as: *to entwine, shut in* | translated as: *a hedge*
— used in Job 1:10 (ShKT) and Hosea 2:6 (ShK)

Note: There is not a (V) *within* the (ShK) – Inferring the not *holding back* of *creation* [as a process of the growing of a *live plant/bush*].

The idea to *fence up* or to *shut in* with a *hedge* [*living* plant/bushes].

* שׂוֹב (ShVK) *<H7754>* as: *branch, brushwood, bough*
— used in Judges 9:48 (ShVKT) and Judges 9:49 (ShVKH)

Note: There is a (V) *within* the (ShK) – Inferring the *holding back* of *creation* [as a process of the *cutting* off from a *live plant/bush*].

The idea of *a cut branch* or the *cutting of a branch.*

Symbolically, as a *destructive version* compared to the *flocking of wool*, which can be *regrown*.

> Concept of *Destruction held back* in order for the *physical world/nature/people (Life) to exist.*

Other variants or words built from (ShV):

** שׁוְא (ShVA) *<H7723>* [LShVA] as: *evil, idolatry, uselessness*
— actually translated as: *in vain* and *false* [witness/report].

** שׁוֹא (ShVA) *<H7722>* [ShVAH] as: *devastation, tempest, ruin, waste*
Note: The result of *<bringing forth>* the *revealing* (H) *from* (ShVA)

** שׁוֹא (ShVA) *<H7721>* [BShVA] as: *a rising, arise*
— used once in Psalm 89:9 actually [BShVA] → symbolizing (B) *plan* [the beginning of ...] as the *rising wave* [a tsunami] *bringing the "flood"* = as a *"harbinger" of the flood.*

** שׁוֹא (ShVA) *<H7724>* as a Name: *Sheva*
— meaning: to [be] *false*, and Jehovah *contends*

** שׁוּב (ShVB) *<H7725>* as: *"to turn back, retreat, return"* | translated as: *returned, receded, there/fro, brought back, surely, certainly, restore, again, take, needs bring, again, put, bring, drew back*
— used in Genesis 3:19 In the sweat of thy face shalt thou eat bread, till thou *return* (ShVBK) unto the ground; for out of it wast thou taken: for dust thou art, and unto dust shalt thou *return* (TShVB).

4 - Meaning Construct

> Concept of *"Some act* of the *Destruction before* or *as part of Creation"*

The idea of *"maybe building* or *possession of land.* Symbolically, [for the *raising of sheep*] for a *nation's sake.*

> 1) *Dante's Circles of Hell* — Idea of *Limbo*

---

2) *Dante's Circles of Hell* — Idea of *Lust*

Cush's son #1

Seba, סְבָא (SBA) <H5434>

Thorns + Blueprint/Plan + Mind of God

1 - Linear Construct (SBA)

* שָׂבָא (SBA) <H5433> as: *drink heavily, become tipsy*

The idea of a *condition* of *being full* or *gratified beyond the point of satisfaction.*

Note: The connection to the (A) in the suffix position, as with (LA) meaning: *"God's wrath,"* infers the idea of being a *"belligerent drunk,"* and coming from the (SB) as: *"Thorny Plans,"* infers the idea of having an *unpredictable outcome [could go either way].* The idea of *"being blurred"* or symbolically and actually having *blurred vision.*

> Concept of being *"Irresponsible"*

The idea that there's a *fine line* between being *irresponsible* and *responsible.* | Also, between a *controlled* and *uncontrolled* behavior.

2 - *Dimensional Construct* (SA →B)

(SA) **Note:** *Is not a biblical Hebrew word!?*

Other variants or words built from (SA):

** סאה (SAH) *<H5429>* as: a *"seah" [a measure of flour/grain]*

The idea of that which was *plucked/removed* from the *grass* and *crushed [from the grass]* *<to be a benefit [as food]>*

** סאון (SAVN) *<H5430>* as: *a boot/sandal [of a soldier]*

Symbolically, the idea of *crushing* or *trampling* the *grass.*

The idea of *<to not be a benefit [as food]>*

Symbolically, *a very fine [or pinch] of the grain* [as a *fine-line* of *measurement*] and as the *moment of the crossing over the line* or *going too far.*

[Maybe, even like: *a crossroads being passed by*] as the *moment of realization* that *it's too late*] | *"the what's do is done"* or *"the damage is done."*

** סאן (SAN) *<H5431>* translated as: *a booted warrior*

— used in Isaiah 9:5 *<KJV>* For every *battle* (SAVN) of the *warrior* (SAN) is with confused noise, and garments rolled in blood; but this shall be with burning and fuel of fire. [-versus- Other translations: *"scandal of warrior"* | *"trampling boot of battle"* | *"warrior's boot in battle"*] .

Note: The seemingly better translation would be:
the boots of the "crushed" or the "fallen" warrior.

> Concept of the *lack* of *taking responsibility* and
> the *consequences* of *irresponsible actions.*

3 - *Reflective Construct* (AB+S)

Note: *Is not a biblical Hebrew word!?*

* אב (AB) *<H1>* translated as: *"Father"*

+ (S) *"Thorn" (protect/hate)*

Symbolically, as: *The Father of the Thorn(s)* or *"Thorny Father."*

The idea of the *protective* or *over-protective Father.*

> Concept of the *fine-line* between *Responsible* and *Irresponsible*

The idea of *Controlled(ing) behavior* [*Methodical* versus *Obsessive*].

Another **Reflective Construct** (A+BS)

* **(A)** *"Mind of God"*

+ **(BS)** *Plan + "Thorn" (protect/hate)*

Other variants or words built from (BS):

** בסר (BSR) *<H1155>* as: *an immature grape, unripe fruit, sour grapes*

The idea of the *moment* just *before [a fruit]* is *ripe [ready to eat]*.

> Concept of *"Not quite ready."*

Symbolically, the *plan* or *purpose* of the *thorns* is to protect the *flower* or *fruit*.

> Concept of *Discipline*

The idea of the *Father's responsibility* to *discipline*.

Symbolically, [the rose thorn] as: *harsher discipline: draws blood/pain* versus [the lily thorn] as: *softer discipline = without drawing blood/pain.*

4 - Meaning Construct

> Concept of *"Over-indulgence* or *Self-gratification"*

The idea is like: *Lust, Greed, Drunkard/Gluttony*

Symbolically, the idea of *"flowing excessively,"* like a *river flowing,* but as *"wild rapids"* versus the just *"flowing"* — used in Gen 2:11 with river: *Pishon,* it *"flows through/winds around"* (HSBB).

Note: The Sebeans [*"People of Seba"*] are known as *"drunkards."* Also: a connection to the idea of *"Sea Peoples"* — a behavior linked to *Pirates/Vikings* [aka: *Heathens*] = <*"Sea Peoples"*>.

> 2) *Dante's Circles of Hell* — Idea of *Lust*

3) *Dante's Circles of Hell* — Idea of *Gluttony* (but also a type of *greed*)

Cush's son #2

Havilah, חוילה (ChVYLH) <H2341>

Branching/Diversity + [held back] Interaction
+ Effort + Learn/Teach + Revealing

1 - Linear Construct (ChVYLH)

* (ChV)   **Note:** *Is not a biblical Hebrew word!?*

Branching/Diversity <holding back>

Symbolically, used to denote a *"focusing in"* on a *thing* [but could also represent a *lacking* or *at the lose of other things*].

The idea of *limited choice* or *options [even reduced to a single thing]*.

Other variants or words built from (ChV):

** חוא (ChVA) <H2324> as: *to show, interpret, explain, inform*
— used in Daniel with a variety of variants (NChVA), (THChVN), (HChVNY)

** חוב (ChVB) <H2325> as: *forfeit, endanger | to tie, owe, guilty*
— used once in Daniel 1:10 <*KJV*> *then shall ye make [me] endanger* (ChYBTM) *my head...*

** חוב (ChVB) <H2326> as: *debt, debtor*

** חוג (ChVG) <H2329> as: *compass, inscribed/drew* [a circle]
— used once in Job 26:10 *He hath compassed* (ChB) *the waters...*

+ * (VY) *"Conception-Birthing"* <to initially get the *inspiration* for... >

+ * (LH) *learning/teaching <brings forth> revealing/revelation*

Note: (LH) as: *special lessons/learning* that *<brings forth> Revelation* -versus- the reflective (HL) as: *departing from [to move/go away].*

The idea of *"leading to [something]."*
— as a *"type of learning, understanding(s) or wisdom."*

Note: Depending on where the lessons are coming from, it could represent a *lacking/weak "ignorant" developing/development.*

Other variants or words built from (LH):

** להב (LHB) <H3851> as: *"flash of, a sharply polished blade, point of a weapon"* | *flame, bright*

> The idea of *"Hard"* or *"Sharp"* Lessons.

2 - *Dimensional Construct* (ChH →VYL)

* (ChH) **Note:** *Is not a biblical Hebrew word!?*

> *Diversity/Branching + Revealing/Revelation*

Other variants or words built from (ChH):

** חוה (ChVH) <H2332> as the Name: *Eve*

Note: The (V) *<holding back>* and *Interaction within* (ChH).

Symbolically, represents *focusing on one child at a time* [or *even giving birth to one at a time*].

Whereas, the (ChH) is the *process* of *having(birthing)* or *bringing forth* many/multiple [children] at a time.

Other variants or words built from (Ch_H):

** חוה (ChVH) <H2331> as: *to live, declare* | *"I will tell"*

** חוה (NChH) <H5148> as: *to guide, to transport*

→ * (VYL) *"Conception-Birthing"* + *Lessons/Learning*

> — but also as: *The "Tethering"* to (YL)

Other variants or words built from (YL):

** ילד (YLD) <H3205-6> as: *to bear young, act as a midwife*

> Concept of having *"Concepts"* or *"Ideas."*

The idea of *many variations of concepts coming about [emerging].*

Note: Symbolically, the (ChH) is like having many *[Human] offspring*, and the (LH) is like *nursing* them -versus- having a *litter,* and the *suckling of a litter [of animals]* is the idea of (LYLYH) *"night"* or (LYLYT) *"Lithith"* [*female night monster*]. <Maybe the origins of the story of being *Adam's* other wife, and giving birth to the *"Night Monsters."*>

---

3 - Reflective Construct (HLYVCh)

Note: *Is not a biblical Hebrew word!?*
Other variants or words built from (HL):

** הלא (HLA) *<H1972>* as: *to be removed [cast] far off, outcasts*

** הליך (HLYK) *<H1978>* as: *a step [taken steps] | walk*

** הלכ (HLK) *<H1980>* as: *flowing*

The idea of (HL) is a *"departing from [to move/go away]."*

+ * (VY) *"Conception-Birthing"* <to initially get the *inspiration* for... >

+ *(Ch) *Diversity/Branching*

> Concept of *creating "Divisive Diversity"*

The idea of *tearing down [something]* or *being "cast out."*

4 - Meaning Construct

> Concept of *"building up to [something]*

The idea of *"Possessing/Hoarding"* for Oneself.

Symbolically, as "the *Coming out <brought forth>* from the *Dark(ness) [pre-Night]*," like the *"Star"* [relationship of Cush].

Note: The letters [*Efforts* (Y) + *Learn/Teach* (L) + *Revealing* (H)] are used in words like: *Elohim* (ALHYM), placed as prefixes (L) or (H) to describe the *level of understanding as mankind flowing/heads to God.*

Note: The land of *Havilah* (HChVYLH) *<H2341>*

— used in Genesis 2:11 ...river *Pishon*, as "it *flows around"* (HSBB) the land of *Havilah* (HChVYLH) where there is gold;

The idea of *building up of sediment of the land* = *gluttony/greed* of the river is like its *"over-indulgence"*). In addition, the comparison of Seba [as *over drinking*] and the river, *Pishon* [as: *having a similar trait*].

---

3) *Dante's Circles of Hell* — Idea of *Gluttony* (but also a type of *greed*)

---

4) *Dante's Circles of Hell* — Idea of *Greed*, (but also a type of *gluttony*)

Cush's son #3

Sabtah, סבתה (SBTH) <H5454>

Thorns + Blueprint/Plan + Weaving [together] + Revealing

1 - *Linear Construct* (SBTH)

* (SB) **Note:** *Is not a biblical Hebrew word!?*   *"Thorny Plans"*

The idea of an *unpredictable outcome* [could go either way]
Symbolically, to *"have blurred vision."*

Note: like his brother: *Seba,* סבא (SBA).

+ * (TH) **Note:** *Is not a biblical Hebrew word!?*

Other variants or words built from (TH):

** תהו (THV) <H8414> translated as: *"formless."*

(TH) As the **not** *[held back]* version:
The idea of the *capacity of having:* "Form."

> Concept of *having a "Blurred Form"*

The idea of *"having a blurred vision while making observations of patterns."*

Another *Linear Construct* (S+BTH)

* (S) *"Thorny" (protect/hate)*

+ * בתה (BTH) <H1326> as: *"desolation, end, waste[land]"*

* בתה (BTH) <H1327> as: *cliff, precipice*

The idea of an *unpredictable outcome [could go either way]*, but is leading to a *"desolation, end, cliff, precipice."*

Symbolically, *having blurred vision* while *heading towards a cliff.*

> Concept of *Not paying attention to what is in front [oneself]* or *not wanting to see [that which should be obvious].*

2 - *Dimensional Construct* (SH →BT)

* (SH) **Note:** *Is not a biblical Hebrew word!?*

> *"Thorny Revealing/Revelation(s)"*

> The idea of *fuzzy/harsh revelations [of things]*, and as being an *unpredictable outcome* [could go either way].

> Other variants or words built from (SH):

** סהר (SHR) *<H5469>* as: *roundness, [like a circle, enclosure]*

** סהר (SHR) *<H5470>* as: *"prison" | house of roundness, dungeon"*

> Symbolically, similar to the *"thorned crown put on Jesus' head"*

** נסה (NSH) *<H5254>* as: *to test, to attempt, to try | "did tempt"*

** הסה (HSH) *<H2013>* as: *to hush, keep/be silent, hold peace/tongue*

→ * בת (BT) *<H1323>* as: *daughter*

* בת (BT) *<H1324-5>* as: *a unit of measure [of liquids]*

Symbolically, the (BT) is a *daughter* within (SH) = (SHBT), which is *"being in or resting in prison"* -versus- the similar (ShBT) *<H7676>* *Shabbath,* which is *"God's day of Rest."*

> Concept of *being locked in one's own mind(thoughts)*

The idea of being *stuck* or *stubborn* in what one believes, and the connection this has to *being in a prison of one's own mind.*

3 - *Reflective Construct* (HTBS)

* (HT) **Note:** *Is not a biblical Hebrew word!?*

> *"Revealing/Revelation(s) + Weaved [together]"*

> <infers, to be in a *solid state* or *frozen state*>

> Other variants or words built from (HT):

** התוכ (HTVK) *<H2046>* as: *is melted*

— used once in Ezekiel 22:22, describing *"Silver being melted"*

(HTV) is the (HT) + (V) being *[held back]*, but <bringing forth> (K) made *flesh/body* as being still in a *Physical state.*

** התל (HTL) *<H2048>* as: *to mock, deceive, to deride, to cheat*

+ * (BS) *Plan <bring forth> "Thorny" (protect/hate)*

> <infers: *to be not ready* or a *pre-state of [something]*>

Other variants or words built from (BS):

** בסר (BSR) <H1153> as: *temple slave* (or *group of slaves*)

** בסר (BSR) <H1154-5> as: *unripe grapes, sour grapes*
<the pre-stage of *being fruit* /or *becoming wine*>

> Concept of *"Something is not quite right."*

The idea of *being unsure* or *not being honest* [both with *oneself* or *others*].

Symbolically, the *frozen/rigid, **sour** grape.*

4 - Meaning Construct

> Concept of *"taking in [inward]* and *imprisoning [within]"*

The idea of *"Selfish behaviors"* [also: connection to the *Ego*].

> 4) *Dante's Circles of Hell* — Idea of *Greed,* (but also a type of *gluttony*)

---

5) *Dante's Circles of Hell* — Idea of *Anger*

Cush's son #4

Raamah, רעמה (RaMH) <H7484>

Mind of Man + Observation + Life/Truth + Revealing

1 - Linear Construct (Ra+MH)

* רע (Ra) <H7451> translated as: *"bad, evil, wicked"*
— used in Genesis 2:9 ...of the tree of the knowledge of good and *evil."*

* רע (Ra) <H7452> as: *"a crash [of thunder], noise, a shout [of joy]"*

* ‏רע‎ (Ra) <H7453> as: "another, friend, companion, neighbor"

Note: actually (RaHV), which is the (Ra) as: Evil/Wicked (Concept of *Selfishness*) + *Revealing* + *[held back]*.

The idea of *"Revealing <Ones selfishness> as being held back."*

* ‏רע‎ (Ra) <H7454> as: "[my/your] thoughts"

+ * ‏מה‎ (MH) <H4100> translated as: "what?" [more like: "What!"]

The idea of *questioning one's internal thoughts,* but as the *anger/agitation(annoyance)* of being questioned (as though one is *right/correct*).

The stage before the *revealing/revelation* from...

** ‏רעמ‎ (RaM) <H7482> as: "to tumble, be violently agitated, to crash, to irritate" and "a peal of thunder"

** ‏רעמיה‎ (RaMYH) <H7485> Name meaning: "Thunder of Jehovah"

Another use of the word, but not as the Name:

* ‏רעמה‎ (RaMH) <H7483> described as a "Horse's Mane (as quivering in the wind)" | vibration, quivering, waving.

Symbolically, like: a "mane [of horse]."

The idea of *what we need to hold on to.*

Symbolically, the *need* to *hold onto [the mane]* while *riding bareback on a horse.*

<The *Horse* = Ancient symbolic representation of *"Ideas"*>

> Concept of a *human seeing their version* of *Life* or *Truth* and what it *Reveals* = **Perceptions.**

Note: The negative version leads to *"What is Evil"* or *"What is Selfish."*

2 - *Dimensional Construct* (RH →aM)

* (RH) **Note:** *Is not a biblical Hebrew word!?*

Mind of Man + Revealing/Revelation

The idea of *Mankind's outcome of understanding knowledge [wisdom] (or lack of it).*

Other variants or words built from (RH):

** רהב (RHB) <H7492> as: *to act stormily, boisterously* or *arrogantly* | translated as: *"You made me bold or confused"*

** רהה (RHH) <H7297> as: *fear, be afraid*

→ * עמ (aM) <H5971-2> as: *tribe, nation, people | compatriots, country-men [members of one's own]*

* עמ (aM) <H5973-4> as: *with, against, toward, equally, like, beside*

> Concept of *"confusing"* one's own people

3 - Reflective Construct (HMaR)

* המ (HM) <H1990> as: *hot, sun-burnt*
* המ (HM) <H1991> as: *abundance, wealth*

+ * ער (aR) <H6145-6> as: *a foe, enemy, adversary*
— actually used as (aRK) or the idea of *"making flesh (Physical)."*

> Concept of *building up enemies*

Symbolically, *sun-burning [others]* to *generate foes [enemies].*

4 - Meaning Construct

> Concept of a *"Personal"* or One's own *"Perceptions"*

The idea of a *"Personal Truth."*

[Mankind's Truth, as a Lesser Truth that Reveals]

> 5) *Dante's Circles of Hell* — Idea of *Anger*

Sons of Raamah

This is the escalation of *[personal] perception*
<to the *Negative → Levels of Violence*]

6) *Dante's Circles of Hell* — Idea of *Heresy*
The idea of *[breaking/tearing down "God's" Spirit]*

Raamah's son #1

Sheba, שׁבא (ShBA) <H7614>

Aspect of Creation + Blueprint/Plan + Mind of God

The idea of *Creation/Destruction <brings forth>* a
Plan, which *<brings forth>* the *Mind of God.*

Note: The connection to the (A) in the suffix position, as with
(LA) meaning: *"God's wrath,"* infers the idea of *"destruction,"*
rather than *"creation."*

> Concept of *having something taken
> away, apart,* and *leaving pieces behind.*

The idea of *"creating in order to destroy"* -or-
the reverse as *"destroying in order to create."*

1 - Linear Construct (ShBA)

* שׁבא (ShBA) *<H7614>* as a Name: *"Sheba"* | meaning: *"seven"/"an oath"*

> **Note:** There are three (3) people that have this Name:
> 1) son of *Raamah,* grandson of *Cush,* and a descendant of *Ham*
> 2) son of *Joktan* and a descendant of *Seth–Noah–Shem*
> 3) son of *Jokshan,* the son of *Abraham* by *Keturah*

Other variants or words built from (ShBA):

** שׁבאי (ShBAY) *<H7615>* *"Sabeans"* | *People of the nation of Sheba* |
Meaning: *"people coming from a nation far away"* or *"he who is coming."*

> **Note:** Similar to *1000-year reign of the Lamb* [in Revelations] in
> the relationship to: *"he who is coming."* — describes as the *"End
> of Days"* [aka: *a seventh day*] and the *coming of the Messiah.*

Other variants or words built from (ShB):

** שבב (ShBB) <H7616> as: *"fragment, ruin"*

** שבה (ShBH) <H7617> as: *"to transport into captivity"*

** שבו (ShBV) <H7618> as: *"a gem, the agate"*

> The idea of <holding back> the <ShB>.

Symbolically, *chipping away* at the *gemstones* in order to create *"Gems."*

** שבת (ShBT) <H7676> as: *"Shabbath"* | *"God's day of Rest [7th day]"*

> ┌─────────────────────────────────────┐
> │ Concept of a *"Subdivision."* │
> └─────────────────────────────────────┘

The idea of *creating [something]* that will *separate* into *smaller sections.*

> Symbolically, *being* in one *"temporary"* [state or existence]
> and then *becoming many other parts.*

> **Note:** In other words, the positive version is *breaking
> into pieces* or *smaller sections* in *order to create.*
>
> <**Examples**: Like: *Gems;* including the idea of simple party
> gadgets: *Strobing lights* or *Pop-out streamers*>.
>
> — versus the negative version as creating [something]
> that *will be destroyed* or *used to destroy.*
>
> <**Examples**: Like: the *extreme* negative version is
> the idea of *"a bomb/grenade/explosives."*>

2 - Dimensional Construct (ShA →B)

** שאב (ShAB) <H7579> as: *to bale up [to draw] water*

> — the Negative version is the idea of [*a cause from*] *"a flood"*

* (ShA) **Note:** *Is not a biblical Hebrew word!?*

> *Aspect of Creation + Mind of God* <The (A) is at the end is the
> idea of *"wrath"* as: *Creation's Wrath* — the idea of a *"Storm."*

The idea of *creating* or *bringing* a *"Storm."*

Note: The Negative version is a *destructive storm.*

Other variants or words built from (ShA):

** שאג (ShAG) <H7580> as: *a rumble, moan* | *roar mightily*

> Symbolically, the *roar, roaring [of a lion]*

** שאגה (ShAGH) <H7581> as: *roaring, cries* | *distress cry*

3 - Reflective Construct (AB+Sh)

Mind of God + Plan + Aspect of Creation

* אָב (AB) *<H1-2>* translated as: *"Father"*

+ * (Sh) *Aspect(s) of Creation*

The idea of *"God's Plan"* was to make *Creation."*

Symbolically, as *"Father"* of *Creation"* or the *"Creator Father."*

4 - Meaning Construct

> Concept of *"Intentional tearing down* of *one thing* in order to make *another.*

Note: The Negative version is *"to break another's spirit."*

> 6) *Dante's Circles of Hell* — Idea of *Heresy*
> The idea of *[breaking/tearing down "God's" Spirit]*

---

7) *Dante's Circles of Hell* — Idea of *Violence*

Raamah's son #2

Dedan, דְּדָן (DDN) *<H1719>*

Path + Path + Seed{Potential}

> Concept of the *Path to "Dan"* [to *"Judge"*]

Note: A belief in *oneself* to be *worthy* of *judging others*, but often *fails to judge oneself.*

1 - Linear Construct (DDN)

* דדן (DDN) <H1719-20> meaning: *"the low country."*

* דד (DD) <H1717> as: *the breast | breast, nipple, teat (bosom)*
— used four times, but actually with (DDY).

+ * (N) *The Seed (Potential)*

Symbolically, the *young suckling* on for *nourishment/comfort* | but also *"the baby state"* [the *neediness/dependence* a baby has to its *Mother*].

Other variants or words built from (DD):

** דדה (DDH) <H1718> as: *"to walk gently [deliberately], to move slowly"* — [Symbolically, like: *stalking a prey*]
— used in Psalms 42:4 *"lead them in procession"* is actually (ADDM).
— used in Isaiah 38:15 *"I will wander"* or *"I shall go softly"* is (ADDH).

Note: Both use (A) *Mind of God* + *<bringing forth>* (DD) as a *"Path of Paths,"* but also as *two paths* or *a choice of paths.*

> Concept of *narrowing in* or *focusing in on a task* or *way.*

The idea of making a *decision* or an *action* to *take.*

Note: Maybe even the idea of *Doubling Down,* but also of being *narrow-minded* or just having a *lack of open-mindedness.*

2 - Dimensional Construct (DN →D)

* דן (DN) <H1835> as a Name: *"Dan"* | [*"to judge"*] <see page 292>

The idea of (DN) *"Paths"* and *"Potentials"* — as *many ways* to *go through life* and *many things* to *build off of* or *from,* then to choose (D) a *path* or direction to go.

> *"The two potentials"* - as the *fork in the road* and symbolically as: *un-sprouted seed* (pre-branching) versus *a crossroads* versus *a two-way road.*

Note: Potentially the origin of the idea of *two witnesses,* and of the two choices of *Good versus Bad(Evil).*

Symbolic of the *Scale(s) [of Judgment]* = "The *Balance* of the *Scales.*"

> Concept of *"Pushing"* (as *"Directing"*) an *Intention* [or *even a "Narrative"*].

3 - Reflective Construct (NDD)

* (NDD) <H5074> as: *to wave to* and *fro, to rove, flee, to drive away | retreat, depart, to wander, stray | to flutter (of birds)*

* (ND) <H5067> as: *a mound, wave | heap*

+ (D) *path*

> Concept of *NOT "pushing (directing) an intention/direction/[or even a narrative]"*

4 - Meaning Construct

> Concept of *narrowing in on a task* or *focusing in* [on a *decision* or *action* to *take*], but as *being judgmental.*

The idea of having a *lack of open-mindedness.*

Note: The fine line between going *too far* with either the *conservative/old ways* or the *liberal/progressive/new ways.*

<Specially in regard to: *"violence"*>

7) *Dante's Circles of Hell* — Idea of *Violence*

---

8) *Dante's Circles of Hell* — Idea of *Fraud*

Cush's son # 5

Sabtecha, סבתכא (SBTKA) <H5434>

Thorns + Blueprint/Plan + Weaving [together] + Flesh/Body + Mind of God

1 - Linear Construct (SBTKA)

* (SB) **Note:** *Is not a biblical Hebrew word!?* "Thorny Plans"

The idea of an *unpredictable outcome* [could go either way].

Symbolically, to *"have blurred vision."*

+ * תכ (TK) <H8496> as: *oppression | injury, fraud, deceit*

+ * (A) <bringing forth> wrath [of God] <as suffix of the (A)

> Concept of *"acts against another"*

The idea of some type of *forced [bad, wrongful] actions.*

Example: *Vengeance/Revenge* or *Theft/Fraud* <The idea of a *"Conman"*>

2 - Dimensional Construct (SBA →TK)

* שבא (SBA) <see page 245 for details>
[The name *Seba* and the word as: *drink heavily, become tipsy.*]

→ * תכ (TK) <H8496> as: *oppression, oppressor, injury | fraud, deceit*

> Concept of being an *"Irresponsibly Violent"*

The idea of being *"belligerent drunk."*

Another *Dimensional Construct* (SA →BK →T)

(SA) **Note:** *Is not a biblical Hebrew word!?*

Other variants or words built from (SA): <see page 246 *for details*>

> Concept of the *lack* of *taking responsibility,*
> and the *consequences* of *irresponsible actions.*

→ * (BK) **Note:** *Is not a biblical Hebrew word!?*

Other variants or words built from (BK):

** בכא (BKA) <H1056> a Place Name, meaning: *"weeping"*

** בכא (BKA) <H1057> as: *the weeping tree | translated as:*
    balsam tree or *mulberry tree* [both *drips sap* when it is *cut*].

> Concept of an *"Act of Intention"*
> of a *benefit* that *brings weeping.*

The idea of making a *claim of [something]* as "*Not Good*"
or *making a forced sacrifice of one group* of *others* [in
order to benefit *another*], and calling it a *"Greater Good."*

Another **Dimensional Perspective** *of* **Construct** (SA →BK →T)

* (SA) *Thorn +* *"Wrath"* bi-directional *(protect from* and *harm)*

The idea of the *"Shield* and *Sword."*

Other variants or words built from (SA):

** סאון (SAVN) *<H5430>* as: *"a military boot"* *<protection from mud>* |
versus as: *"battle"* *<being in the mud>*

** סאן (SAN) *<H5431>* as: *a shoe, soldier shod <tread, tramp>* | *"warrior"*

→ (BK) *Plans + Flesh/body* *"Plans made Flesh"* = aka: *"Reality"*

The idea of *"Outcomes/Reality/Losses"* from *War.*

Other variants or words built from (BK):

** בכא (BKA) *<H1057>* as: *the weeping tree* | translated as:
balsam tree or *mulberry tree* [both *drips sap* when it is *cut*].

Note: Also words linking to the idea of being *"Young,"* as:
[firstborn, firstfruits, firstlings, birthright, earliest fruit, first-ripe]

The idea of *losing young men* in *war.*

Symbolically, the *dripping of blood when cut.*

→ (T) *weaving together* | The complexity of *war.*

In general terms, the interactions of/between
Nations, [internally and *externally]* <aka: *Politics*>.

> Concept of the *"Negative Reality"* of *War* [and *Politics*]

Another **Dimensional Construct** (SKA →BT)

* (SKA) **Note:** *Is not a biblical Hebrew word!?*

* סכ (SK) *<H5519>* as: *"a thicket of men, a crowd"*

* סכ (SK) *<H5520>* as: *"a hut, a lair"*

+ * (A) *"God's wrath"*

The idea of a *"wrathful"* lair or crowd.

Symbolically, as the *"depths of Hell."*

→ * (BT) <*H1323*> as: *"daughter"* <*emotional negotiation between people*>

> Symbolically, as *a young girl being surrounded by a crowd [negative=attacking or positive=protecting]*, and even like: *"Hell hath no fury, like a woman scorned."*

> Concept of *"overwhelming"* odds/danger/risk, and commonly with a type of *"violence."*

3 - Reflective Construct (AKTBS)

* (AK) <*H389*> as: *surely | indeed, howbeit | nevertheless | only*
Note: Most words built off this root go to a *sacrificial* condition.

+ * (TB) **Note:** *Is not a biblical Hebrew word!?*

Other variants or words built from (TB):

** (TBH) <*H8392*> as: *a box | ark [the vessel Noah built] | basket vessel [which baby Moses was placed].*
Note: Both have a connection to *"floating on water."*

+ * (S) *"Thorns"* <*Positive: "Good" or Negative: "Bad/Evil"*>

> Concept of a *"Jack in the Box"*

The Negative version = *"Pandora's Box"*

> Concept of being *"surprised by"* the *outcome.*

The idea of the *unintentional* acts, but from *giving [something] up.*

4 - Meaning Construct

> Concept of *forcibly taking action against another* or *others.*

Especially, with *intent of harming others*, and for *benefit of oneself.*

<**Examples:** *Lynching, <mob mentality>, theft, etc...*>

> 8) *Dante's Circles of Hell* — Idea of *Fraud*

9) *Dante's Circles of Hell* — Idea of *Treachery*

Cush's son #6

Nimrod, נמרד (NMRD) <H5248>

Seeds + Life/Truth + Mind of Man + Path

Genesis 10:9-10

English translation (King James Version)

9 He was a mighty hunter before the LORD: wherefore it is said, Even as Nimrod the mighty hunter before the LORD.

10 And the beginning of his kingdom was Babel, and Erech, and Accad, and Calneh, in the land of Shinar.

Babel (BBL)

(BBL) *[Plan + Plan + Learning/Lessons [Plan of Plans <bringing forth> Lessons]*

The Amorite king *Hammurabi* — founded the Old *Babylonian* Empire in the 18th century BC (1792-1750 BC) . <6th king of the First *Babylonian* Dynasty>

Erech (ARK)

(AR) *Mind of God + Mind of Man* + (K) *Flesh/Body* *["God to Man made Flesh"]*

Erech/Erek as *Uruk* was founded by the *Sumerian* king *Enmerkar*. He is credited in the Sumerian legend as the inventor of writing. *Uruk:* (played a leading role in the early urbanization of *Sumer* in the mid-4th millennium BC. It was also the *capital city of Gilgamesh* | [the *hero of the Epic of Gilgamesh,* and *Gilgamesh* builds the city wall around Uruk and is king of the city].

Accad (AKD)

(AKD) meaning: *"strengthen | fortress"*

(AK) *Mind of God + Flesh/Body* *["God made Flesh"]* + (D) *Path*

Sargon of *Akkad,* the first Empire builder <aka: *Akkadian* Empire (2334-2279 BC), and his grandson, who elevated himself as a *God-King* [title: *"God of Akkad"*].

Calneh (KLNH)

(KL) *every/all* + (NH) *lamentation | eminency, distinction | wailing*

Note: W.F. Albright (1944) stated that the word did not in origin refer to a city but has been corrupted from an expression meaning *"all of them."*

— Also identifying Calneh with the modern *Nippur,* a lofty mound of earth, and the *Sumerian "Holy City"* [and *temple*] *on a mound.*

[Land (BARTs) of] Shinar (ShNaR)

(ShN) *"Tooth"(Aspects of Creation/[Destructive]) + "Seed"(Potential)* + (aR) *Observation + Mind of Mind* = <translated as: *"Foe"*>

Symbolically, the *"biting truth"* of *observing* the *Minds of Mankind.*

1 - *Linear Construct* (NMR+D)

* נמר (NMR) <*H5246*> as: *leopard*

+ (D) *Path*

> Concept of "*The Way* or *Path of the Leopard*,"
> which seems to be a Title Name, rather than a Name.

The idea of a *spot* or *stain* from/by *dripping.*

Symbolically, as: *blood-stained* or *dripping* [from battle].

Other variants or words built from (NMR):

** נמרה (NMRH) <*H5247*> as: "*clear water*" | "*limpid or pure*"

> The idea of "*being transparent/pure.*"

Symbolically, what comes out of a *blood dripping sacrifice* is connected to being a *pure person,* and through *being transparent.*

The idea of "*being honest.*"

Other variants or words built from (NM):

** נמל (NML) <*H5243*> as: *to become clipped, circumcised*
— used in Gen 17:11 as (NMLTM) as: "*circumcised*"
— used in Job 14:2 as (VYML) as: "*and is cut down*"

> The idea of *removing* [as *something that is in the way*].

** נמלה (NMLH) <*H5244*> as: *an ant*

> Symbolically, the *cutting action* of ants as they *gather leaves* and then *carry them off* to the ant hill.
>
> Also, as a *leopard dragging* its prey by the neck.

> Concept of being "*forcefully*" taken away.

The idea of *being dragged off by one's neck.*

Another *Linear Construct* (NM+RD)

+ (NM) **Note:** *Is not a biblical Hebrew word!?* [see above]

+ (RD) **Note:** *Is not a biblical Hebrew word!?*

Other variants or words built from (RD):

** רדד (RDD) <*H7286*> as: *to beat down, to tread into pieces,*

> *conquer, overlay, subdue*

** רדה (RDH) *<H7287>* as: *to tread down, subjugate, crumble off*

** רדי (RDY) *<H7288>* as meaning: *"trampling"*

— *5th son of Jesse/brother to David*

The idea of *trampling over others* [as to be *"domineering"*].

Another *Linear Construct* (N+MR+D)

* **(N)** *"Seed"(Potential)*

+ ** מר (MR) *<H4751>* as: *bitter*

** מר (MR) *<H4752>* as: *a drop (a flowing down)*

** מר (MR) *<H4753>* as: *myrrh <like sap(gum) from a tree>*

+ **(D)** *Path*

> The idea of a *Path* coming from *bitterness*.
> Symbolically, like *the flowing of blood*.

2 - *Dimensional Construct* (ND →MR)

* נד (ND) *<H5067>* as: *a mound, wave | heap*

+ * מר (MR) *<H4751>* as: *bitter*

* מר (MR) *<H4752>* as: *a drop (a flowing down)*

* מר (MR) *<H4753>* as: *myrrh <like sap(gum) from a tree>*

> The idea of being *piled up* or *grouped together*,
> and *not being happy* or *pleased about it*.

> Concept of being *"Exiled."*

> Symbolically, this could represent being *"stereotyped,"*
> [as the *heap/mound*], which consequently could lead
> to one's *"progress slowed"* [like the *sap flowing*].

3 - *Reflective Construct* (DRMN)

* דר (DR) *<H1858>* as: *pearl, mother of pearl |* translated as: *white*
— used once in Esther 1:6 ... upon a pavement [mosaic] of red, and blue, and *white* (DR), and black marble.

* דר (DR) *<H1859>* as: *age, generation*
— used in two lines in Daniel 4:3 and 4:34 [both times the word was

linked together with itself [as: *"generation* to *generation"*].

Other variants or words built from (DR):

** דרכ (DRK) *<H1870>* as: *way, road, distance, journey, manner*
— used in Genesis 3:24 "So he drove out the man; and he placed at the east of the garden of Eden, Cherubim and a flaming sword which turned every way, to keep the *way* (DRK) of the tree of life."

The idea of *[something]* that makes it *possible*
to get from *one place to another.*

Symbolically, the (DR) is the [something] *"beautiful* [like: *pearlescent*] and *pure* [like: *white*]*"* and the (K) is the *Flesh/Body/(Physical)* = as the *"Way made Flesh"* [in this case: leading to the *"Tree of Life."*]

Concept of *[something]* being *"Secret"* or *"Hidden."*

Symbolically, as *"the Pearl"* is the hidden wealth deep within the clam, and additionally, to get to the clams, they too are *deep* within the *waters(seas).*

+ * מנ (MN) *<H4478>* as: *"Manna"* | Also translated as: *"What?"*
— *used in Exodus, Numbers, Deuteronomy, Joshua, Nehemiah, Psalm*

* מנ (MN) *<H4479>* as: *"Who?"* | Also translated as: *"What?"*
— *used in Ezra and Daniel*

* מנ (MN) *<H4480>* as: *"from, of, out, at, because"*
— *used over 1200 times in Genesis*

* מנ (MN) *<H4481>* as: *"from, of, I, soon/according, at, because"*
— *used in Ezra*

* מנ (MN) *<H4482>* as: *"stringed instrument," stringed* | *whereby*
— *used twice in Psalms 45:8 and 150:4*

Life/Truth + "Seed"(Potential) = "Watered Seed" = [the inspired potential]

The idea of *secrets extracted,* which *<brings*
forth> the *"Life Saving Nourishment."*

Symbolically, as *"Magically/Heavenly" Food.*

Note: Representing a portion of *life [mortal]* rather than *eternal life* versus the reflective nature of *"being in Exile,"* but then [out of it] becomes the *"What"* is/can be *extracted* [the *Secrets* or *Hidden*] within the *"Mortal"* Life.

4 - Meaning Construct

> Concept of *results* that led to being
> *"blood-stained"* after *efforts* of *battle/war.*

The idea of *the consequences* of *violent
acts* is to *have blood on one's hands.*

Symbolically, like *Pontius Pilate washing
hands* when *Jesus was sentenced to death.*

> 9) *Dante's Circles of Hell* — Idea of *Treachery*

Note: In Dante's Inferno, the *leopard* is one of three beasts that block
Dante's path in the dark forest. Dante uses the *Leopard* to represent
malicious or *fraudulent sins* [fraud, lust or malice], as well as two
other predator animals: the *Lion* [pride or violence] and the *She-Wolf*
[greed, avarice, or incontinence *"lack of control"*].

— Another more direct connection from Jeremiah 5:6, which warns of
a *lion* (from the forest will strike them down), *wolf* (from the desert
will ravage them), and *leopard* (will lie in wait near their cities).

Note: The traditional view is that Nimrod was the builder of the
Tower of Babel. [As mentioned earlier, the *City* symbolizes the *System*,
and the *Tower* represents the *Structure.*] Implying the idea of *Nimrod*,
as [a type of person] with *blood on his hands*, who built/builds a
Structure [aka: *Order* or *Control*].

Nimrod is listed in Genesis 10 along with genealogies of all three of
Noah's sons. Genesis 11 begins with the introduction to the *City* and
Tower of Babel, then relists the genealogy of Shem: this time to *Abram.*

(Genesis 12-15) → *Abram's* 1st Son: *Ishmael* (Genesis 16), Name
change to *Abraham* (Genesis 17) → 2nd Son: *Issac* (Genesis 21). Then
in (Genesis 25) *Issac* → 2 sons: *Esau & Jacob.*

Note: Due to the limited space available with this book, I need
to jump to the *final* (or *last*) grouping of names in Genesis.

Jacob(Israel) & Generations
"The 12 Sons"

The relationship between the Name grouping and the connection to a *"Path"* can be seen in Kabbalah, referred to as the *Twelve Paths*, based primarily on *Yaakov's* (Jacob's) blessings [Genesis 49:1-28].

1- Reuben – *The First*
2- Simeon – *The Aggressor*
3- Levi – *The Cleric*
4- Judah – *The Leader*
5- Dan – *The Judge*
6- Naphtali – *The Free Spirit*
7- Gad – *The Warrior*
8- Asher – *The Prosperous One*
9- Issachar – *The Scholar*
10- Zebulun – *The Businessperson*
11- Joseph – *The Sufferer*
    11a- Menashe(Manasseh) – *Reconnection*
    11b- Ephraim – *Transformation*
12- Benjamin – *The Ravenous Consumer*

Genesis 25:26
English translation (King James Version)
And after that came his brother out, and his hand took hold on *Esau's* heel; and his name was called *Jacob*...

Note: According to folk etymology, the name *Ya'aqōv [Jacob],* יעקב (YaQB) is derived from *'aqev,* עקב (aQB), as meaning *"heel."*

Describing the birth of Jacob as *grasping the heel* of his twin brother *Esau,* עשו (aShV) *Observations + Aspect(s) of Creation + <held back>.*

[*Esau* inferring a lesser understanding of the *patterns in creation,* and *Jacob* inferring the stage just after this perception].

Jacob, יעקב (YaQB) <H3290> *Ya'aqōv*
Efforts + Observations + Past/Ancient + Blueprint/Plan(s)

1 - Linear Construct (Ya+QB)

* יַע (Ya) <H3257> as: *a shovel*
— defined as: *to appoint, to designate, to meet, to assemble*]

The idea of *what comes out of [the event]* [as: *result of actions taken*].

+ * קַב (QB) <H6894> as: *a hollow, vessel | a dry measure*
<used to *measure* grains and other *dry commodities*>

Symbolically, *"scoop up a measure of grain,"* and as a larger
portion [with a shovel], versus a *"scoop in one's hand."*

> Concept of *having a potential value*
> *of worth more* or *getting more out of something*
> [from commonly *less* or in *smaller amounts*].

The idea that *God wanted to enter into a relationship with Jacob,*
but *Jacob needed to admit his weaknesses* before that could happen.

The connection to his Name meaning: *"Wrestling with God."*
— Inferring the idea that there's a *value to recognizing*
one's own weakness [to *gain value* and *success*].

Symbolically, it's *Jacob's inner struggle with*
himself, his faith, and *his relationship with God.*

2 - Dimensional Construct (YB →aQ)

* (YB) **Note:** *Is not a biblical Hebrew word!?*

The idea of a *"sadness/pain* [a type of *"suffering" | a "burden"*]

Other variants or words built from (YB):

** יְבֵב (YBB) <H2980> as: *to bawl, cry [shrilly] | wail, lament*
[that which comes from or leads to *"sadness/pain/suffering/burden"*]

The idea of *not handling one's burden(s).*

** יְבוּל (YBVL) <H2981> as: *produce, a crop, wealth*
[as <holding back> [that which leads to *"sadness/pain/suffering/*
burden"] and *learning* from it.

The idea of *handling one's burden leads to a crop/wealth.*

→ * (aQ) **Note:** *Is not a biblical Hebrew word!?* *Observation(s) + Past*

Other variants or words built from (aQ):

** עָקַב (aQB) <H6117> as: *to seize by the heel, to circumvent, to restrain*

The idea of *being pressured* or *leveraged* to do [something].

> ## Concept of *having to look within oneself*

The idea of *being out of necessity* [forced to] look into oneself.

Symbolically, *the idea of God's Plan* (AB) through *Jacob*
represents the struggle and overcoming of the human burdens,
and the realization of finding value in it.

3 - *Reflective Construct* (BQYa)

* בְּקִיעַ (BQYa) <H1233> as: *a fissure | cleaving, breaking, bursting*
— used in Isaiah 22:9 to describe (BQYaY) *breaching the walls* of the city
and in Amos 6:11 to describe *fragments/[into]pieces* (BQaYM)

Other variants or words built from (BQ+a):

** בָּקַע (BQa) <H1234> as: *to cleave, split, break open, divide, rip*
— used in Genesis, Exodus, Joshua, and more
— used in describing Moses *parting [were divided]* (VYBQaV) the waters

** בֶּקַע (BQa) <H1235> as: *a half-shekel | a section, division*

Note: The *half-shekel* is a biblical commandment to give a silver
coin as a form of *atonement for one's sins.*
— The annual contribution every Jew was required to give to
the Temple coffers [is equal to 160 grains of barley].

The idea of the *effort* within oneself to *give charity.*

Symbolically, is like the *parting of the sea* or *the breaching of a wall.*

Note: The concept of *charity* [*giving to others*] and the relationship to:
a person giving to help the *burdens of others* [group/others-help]
- versus -
one's own internal work, as a *struggle within.*

Another **Reflective Construct** (BQ+aY)

* (BQ)   **Note:** *Is not a biblical Hebrew word!?*

Other variants or words built from (BQ):

** בקבק (BQBQ) <H1229> as: *bottle/flask [to store liquids: water, wine, oil]*

** יבק (YBQ) <H3342> as: *a trough, a wine-vat*

The generalized idea of [something] that *holds* or *captures* a *limited amount of a liquid [fluid value].*

Note: The reflective (QB) is a *capturing* or *holding* of a *[dry measure].*

+ * עי (aY) <H5856> as: *ruins, heap of ruins (heaps)*

The idea of [something] that *is broken down into pieces.*

Symbolically, as *if you watch something long enough,*
it will eventually become a *ruin.*

Other variants or words built from (aY):

** עיט (aYTh) <H5861> as: *a hawk, other bird of prey, |"a swooper bird" ravenous (bird).*

Symbolically, as *if you watch something long enough,* it will →
<bring forth> the (Th) *"Container/Basket"* = "Snatching its prey."

> Concept of *"Self-preservation"*

The idea of the *internal struggle* with the
[primal] selfish need to *take for oneself.*

4 - Meaning Construct

> Concept of *"One's own internal work"*

The idea of *"Self-help,"* and the transition of *self-reflecting*
from *past motivations* to *moving on* (getting over the past).

Symbolically, the transition from *"Wrestling with God"*
represents not fully understanding God but attempting to...

Genesis 29:16-17
English translation (King James Version)

16 And Laban had two daughters: the name of the elder was *Leah*, and the name of the younger was *Rachel*.

17 *Leah* was tender eyed; but *Rachel* was beautiful and well favoured.

Note: Described as: *"Tender eyed"* = *And eyes [were]* (aYNY) + *delicate* (RKVT)

The use of the word *"eyes"* is עין (aYN) *<H5859>* → generally inferring how *someone* or *something* perceives *someone* or *something* else.

* עי (aYN) *<H5859>* translated as: *"a ruin"* [broken down into pieces]
  + * ני (NY) *<H5204>* translated as: *wailing*

The idea of *breaking down, making a snap judgment,* or *making an analysis* or *characterization* of *someone* or *something else.*

The use of the word *"delicate "* is רך (RK) *<H7390>* → generally inferring how *someone* carries or presents *themselves [to others].*

Mind of Man + Flesh/Body = "The Mind made Flesh"

* רך (RK) *<H7390>* translated as: *"tender, weak | delicate, frail"*
  + * ות (VT) *[held back] Interaction + Weaving together*

  ** אות (AVT) *<H225>* translated as: *to consent*

The idea of *not being weak* or *frail* [maybe *"strong-willed"*] yet *allowing oneself* to be *subservient* [maybe *"dutiful"*].

Wife of Jacob [1st Wife]

Leah, לאה (LAH) *<H3812>*

Learning/Teaching + Mind of God + Revealing

1 - *Linear Construct* (LA+H)

* לא (LA) <> as: *"Not/No"* Lacking [God's] Understanding *<God's Wrath>*

+ * ה (H) *Revealing/Revelations*

Lacking Understanding + Revelation (or *Lacking Wisdom*)

> Concept of *"no humbleness"* or *having a lack of humbleness* [*to* or *before* God].

273

The idea of *self-serving aspects* of human nature.
["*Me first" - feeling entitled*].

Symbolically, as *what is to "Give birth"* from
the *self-serving aspects of human nature.*

Another *Linear Construct* (L+AH)

* ל (L)   *Learning/Teaching*

+ * (AH)   **Note:** *Is not a biblical Hebrew word!?*   *Mind of God + Revealing*

The idea of *learning* to *<bring forward>* God's Revelations *comes out
of* or from experiencing others' *self-serving entitlements.*

3 - *Reflective Construct* (HAL)

* (H)   *Revealing/Revelation*

+ * אל (AL) *<H420>* as: *God   Mind of God + Learning/Teaching*

The idea of *Revelations <brings forth> God's Lessons.*

4 - *Meaning Construct*

> Concept of *"Self-Entitlement"*

Symbolically, *Leah* represents: the *Mother* of... feeling *"self-entitled."*

Note: As the oldest [1st born] daughter, she felt deserving of being
married off first. <Having the feeling that she *"paid her dues,"* being a
dutiful daughter, and *now wants what is owed* to her.

The union of *Jacob* ["*wrestling with God"*] and *Leah* [*self-entitlement*],
and what is *born from this* ["*the offspring"*] = "*Ruler(s)* or *Elite types."*

The next four offspring represent the *Pattern/process* of the *"Ruler types."*

Genesis 29:32
English translation (King James Version)
And *Leah* conceived, and bare a son, and she called his name *Reuben*:
for she said, Surely the LORD hath looked upon my affliction;
now therefore my husband will love me.

Reuben, ראובנ (RAVBN) <H7205>

Mind of Man + Mind of God + Interaction [held back] +
Blueprint(Plan) + Seed(Potential)

1 - *Linear Construct* (RAV+BN)

* רא (RA) + (V) *[held back]*

<see words like: *Bereshit="In the Beginning"* and *Bara="creates"* >

The generalized idea of (RA) is to elevate the *Human mind* to a *God mind* state, but as the (A) being in the suffix position which implies a *"wrath"* state. This could represent *"Mankind's wrath,"* or even *"a wrath against Mankind"* <for example: a ***"famine"***>.

+ * (V) *[held back]*   **Note:** The *"holding this back"* could represent a person with the capacity to *be wrathful*, but *suppressing/<holding back>* their *violent* nature in order to be a *leader* to the people.

+ * בנ (BN) <H1121> translated as: *Son [Offspring]*

Note: The *[holding back]* of (RA) to <bring forth> a *"Son"*
- versus -
the *"Son of RA"* [aka: The title of the Pharaoh]

Another *Linear Construct* (RA+V+BN)

* As the *interaction* (V) *between* the (RA) and (BN), or in other words, the *interaction(s)* with the *"Son of RA"* = [aka: a *"Pharaoh"*].

Examples [of interactions with the Pharaohs]:

Two examples are in Genesis

1) *Abram(Abraham)*: He sought refuge from **famine (in Canaan).** Additionally, the *"confusion"* with the Sarai [his wife and half-sister], and the Pharaoh wanting to marry her, which God brings plagues, then Pharaoh releases them and they return to Canaan.

2) *Joseph*: becomes *vizier* (the right hand man) to Pharaoh during a **famine (in Canaan)** and helps the people [crisis management and infrastructure oversight, which would have involved "water control"], and later allowed to bring his family to Egypt, which His father *[Jacob]* and his brothers *[sons of Jacob]* eventually return to Canaan.

One example is in Exodus

3) *Moses*: High official to the Pharaoh, Water connections, plagues and **famine**, Family connections, and eventually return to Canaan as *[the tribes of Jacob/Israel]*, and as escaping Pharaoh's oppression.

2 - *Dimensional Construct* (RN →AVB)

* רן (RN) <H7438> as: *a shout (of joy), ringing cry (singing)* | translated as: *Songs*

+ * אוב (AVB) <H178> definition: *Medium, necromancer, spiritualist, ghost, familiar spirit* | Meaning: *a mumble, a water skin, a necromancer*

As the *interaction within* (V) the (AB) = *Father*   -or-
the *Mind of God [held back]* + *<bringing forth> a Plan*

The idea of a *"joyous spirit."*

It could also symbolically represent the *"Song of the Necromancer."*

3 - *Reflective Construct* (NBVAR)

* בנ (NB) <H5011> as: *a high place*

-versus-

the *[held back] version*

* נבו (NBV) <H5015> as a Name: *Nebo* – is a name used in the Hebrew Bible, primarily referring to a location and a deity.

It is most commonly associated with *Mount Nebo*, a significant mountain in the biblical narrative, and with a Babylonian deity, *Nabu*, the god of *wisdom, writing,* and *prophecy.* This Babylonian deity presided over *learning* and *letters,* as well as corresponding to the Greek god *Hermes*, the Latin god *Mercury*, and the Egyptian god *Thoth.*

Word Origin: Derived from the root: נבא (NBA) <H5012>, meaning *"to prophesy"* or *"to speak by divine inspiration."*

+ * (AR)   **Note:** *Is not a biblical Hebrew word!?*

Other variants or words built from (aY):

** ארא (ARA) <H690> a Name meaning: *Lion*

— used once in 1 Chronicles 7:38 [describing the *"The Sons of Asher"* (one of Jacob's 12 sons/tribes) <as a generational offspring>.

** ארב (ARB) <H693> meaning as: *to lurk* | *to mix, to pledge, to exchange, to become surety* // translated as: *lies in wait, an ambush* — used in Deut., Joshua, Judges, Samuel, Chronicles

** ארבה (ARBH) <H697> as: *locusts* — used in Exodus, Leviticus, Deut., Judges, Kings, Chronicles, Job, Psalms, Proverbs, Jeremiah, Joel, etc..
[but with variants: (BARBH) (HARBH)(KARBH) (LARBH) (MARBH)

** ארי (ARY) <H738> as *"a lion"*

Note: Symbolically, as the proper direction of understanding (or a true understanding), the how or way God thinks (AR) as the *"Greater"* versus the reflective (RA) as a *"Lesser"* or mankind's version of understanding — [as in the BRAShYT)

* בָאר (BAR) <H874> as: *to dig, engrave, to explain*

* בְאר (BAR) <H875> as: *well, pit, spring*

* בְאר (BAR) <H876> as: *well <an oasis rest in desert during the Exodus>*

* בֹאר (BAR) <H877> as: *cistern, well, pit*

> Symbolically, linking imagery of a *Lion, Locusts,* and *Wells(Springs)* to ideas of *Wisdom, Writing,* and *Prophesy.*

4 - Meaning Construct

> Concept of *"Ruling by..." thinking of oneself as a god (or son of god) on Earth.*

The idea of a *"False"* God, and the fine line between a *"real"* or *"false"* Messiah or *Prophet.*

Kabbalah "12 Paths" = *Reuben* is labeled as: *"The First."*

> The concept of *thinking of oneself first.*

And the idea of *the source of one's motivation.*

Symbolically, this is adding the *fuel to a flame* [A small amount can run an engine for miles, but too much will explode like a bomb], and is the connection to understanding what is called the *"Ego."*

Blessings [from Israel]:

Genesis 49:3-4

3 *Reuben,* thou art my firstborn, my might, and the beginning of my strength, the excellency of dignity, and the excellency of power:

4 Uncontrolled as the waters, you will no longer excel, because you went up to your father's bed, onto my couch, and defiled it.

Genesis 29:33
English translation (King James Version)

And she conceived again, and bare a son; and said, Because the LORD hath
heard (ShMa) that I was *hated(unloved)* (ShNVAH),
he hath therefore given me this son also: and she called his name
Simeon (ShMaVN).

Simeon, שמעון (ShMaVN) <H8095>

*Aspect of Creation + Life/Truth + -> Observation [held back] +
interaction + -> Generations (Seed)*

1 - Linear Construct (ShMaVN)

* שם (ShM) <H8035> translated as: *name* | a Name: *Shem*
  — used in describing: *"who one is,"* not just a Name

+ * עון (aVN) <5770> as: *to watch* | *to eye, look at*

* עון (aVN) <5771> as: *perversity, depravity, iniquity, guilt,* or
punishment of iniquity

> Concept of *wanting what you see without restraint -
> lacking patience* [also: *envy*] — *"I want what I want."*

Another Linear Construct (ShMa+V+N)

* (ShMa) <H8085> as: *to hear, listen, obey*

+ (V) *[held back]* [as the *interaction* (V) *between]*

+ (N) *Seeds/Generations (Potential* from it)

> Concept of *intentionally not listening* or *obeying*

2 - Dimensional Construct (ShMN →aV)

* שמנ (ShMN) <H8080> as: *to be/become fat* | *grease, oil* | *rich/richness*

→ (aV)   *Observation + [held back] Interaction* with

The idea of *lacking observation* of *others* or *ignoring
others* [not just *putting oneself first,* but *only for oneself*].

Other variants or words built from (aV):

** עוב (aVB) <H5743> as: *to be dense, to cover with a cloud*

** עוד (aVD) <H5750> as: *to return, repeat,* or *do again*

** עוה (aVH) <H5753> as: *to crook, bend, twist, distort*
| *to do wrong, perverse, commit iniquity*

** עוה (aVH) <H5754> as: *a ruin, overturn, overthrow*

** עול (aVL) <H5763> as: *to suckle [give milk] | nursing [a baby]*

Another *Dimensional Construct* (ShN →MaV)

* שׁן (ShN) <H8127> as: *tooth, ivory*

> *Creation <bringing forth> the Seed (Potential)*

→ (Ma) **Note:** *Is not a biblical Hebrew word!?*   *Life/Truth + Observation*

There's a generalized idea of *individual actions,* and a
"focusing in on" [something] <*especially,* as *risky,*
dangerous, and *even morbid*>.

The combination of these two concepts <in the extreme
and morbid sense> is symbolically the *teeth biting* into
the *body* and *tearing at the insides* [like a *wild animal*].

+ (V) *[held back]*

> **Note:** The *"holding this back"* could represent: A person with
> the *capacity to be wrathful* and *suppressing,* but <*holding back*>
> their *violent* nature in order to be a *leader* to the people.

<As the idea of a *"Necessary Monster"*>

Concept of *not paying attention* to what you are *biting into.*

The idea of *looking for* [*danger* or *food*] in a *frenzy* or *frantic* way.

Symbolically, as the phrase *"A bull in a china shop."*

Concept of *not being observationally aware* of
one's surroundings [aka: not *"Reading the Room"*].

3 - *Reflective Construct* (NV+aM+Sh)

* (NV) **Note:** *not a biblical Hebrew word!?*

> (N) *Seeds [Potential] "Generations"* + (V) *[held back]*
> (as the generations yet to come)

> Concepts like: *having "No fountain" | "no ground"*
> or *"grounds for" |* [as: *no soil* to *plant the seed*]

The symbolic idea of a *pre-stage moment [before the purpose is revealed]* — an *earlier stage*, but *coming from a cycled event/process*.

Symbolically, as *waste/wasting* stage [pre-germinate = *"Fertilizer"*].

+ * עַם (aM) <H5971> as: *tribe, people, nation* *Observation + Life/Truth*

+ * (Sh) *Aspects of Creation*

> Concept of the *moments before*
> *coming together as a tribe/nation.*

Another *Reflective Construct* (NV+aMSh)

+ * עֲמֹשׂ (aMSh) <H6021-6022> as Names with a meaning of:
(aMShA) *burden* / (aMShY) *burdensome*

> The idea of *the stage prior* to the *Observation* of
> (MSh) or the *"coming of a Moses/Messiah-type."*

4 - *Meaning Construct*

> Concept of *"Ruling by..." being a Tyrant*

The idea of *invoking fear/terror/violence.*

> Kabbalah "12 Paths" = *Simeon* is labeled as: *"The Aggressor."*
>
> Symbolically, this is adding **too much** fuel to a flame, or as the
> *"exploding bomb."* In addition, there is the connection to the
> *"Inflated Ego,"* but also representing: the *burning up* or *burning
> out of it*, because it's also a *"fragile ego."*

Blessings [from Israel]:
Genesis 49:5-7

5 *Simeon* and *Levi* are brothers; their swords are weapons of violence.
6 May I never enter their council; may I never join their assembly.
For they kill men in their anger, and hamstring oxen on a whim.
7 Cursed be their anger, for it is strong, and their wrath, for it is cruel!
I will disperse them in Jacob and scatter them in Israel.

Genesis 29:34
English translation (King James Version)

And she conceived again, and bare a son; and said, Now this time will
my husband be joined unto me, because I have born him three sons:
therefore was his name called *Levi*.

Levi, לוי (LVY) <H3878>

Teach/Learning + [held back] Interaction + Efforts

1 - Linear Construct (LVY)

* לו (LV) <H3863> as: *Oh [that]* | *please* | *peradventure* | *If, If only*
[*perhaps/uncertainty* or *doubt* as to whether something is the case]

— used 22 times in multiple books

> Concept of *"lacking lessons learned"*

The idea of *learning [something]* or *not continuing to learn*
can lead to *"stubbornness"* [*ignorance/arrogance*].

** לוא (LVA) <H3863> as: *if, would that!*

— used in books of Samuel and Isaiah [as the [suffix] added
ending (A), which adds a concept of the *wrath of God* to it.

+ * (Y) *Efforts*

The idea of the *Efforts* coming from a place of *Lessons [held
back]* or as the *Interaction within* the actions from a set of
Lessons/Learning = such a state leads to *"Closed-mindedness."*

2 - *Dimensional Construct* (LY →V)

* (LY) **Note:** *not a biblical Hebrew word!?*

Other variants or words built from (LY):

** לילה (LYLH) <*H3915*> as: *"night"* | *a twist, adversity*

— used in Genesis 1:5 / inferring a symbolic relationship to *darkness,* as *"making it harder to see clearly,"* but heading in the right direction → towards the *light,* as *"looking at/to the stars."*

** ליה (LYH) <*H3914*> as: *a wreath*

** ליש (LYSh) <*H3918*> as: *a lion, [old] lion* | <*maybe the idea of a seasoned or experienced lion, rather than a younger, inexperienced one*>

The common connections with (LY+) infer ideas of *challenges* (especially, when *unseen*), so the addition of the →(V) as <*born within*> could infer the ideas like: *"taking the easy way"* | *"not taking (new) risks"* | *"falling into old habits* or *following the same routines."*

Symbolically, (LY) as: *Night Monster, Old Lion, Twisted Twig imagery* is connected to *mankind's challenges,* but also *being responsible for one's own actions.* The *restraint* or (V) *[held back]* is also connected to the *"Binding the Beast"* as both *[within oneself]* and *[in Book of Revelations =* <*symbolizing the collective behavior of human organizations/structure>]*.

3 - *Reflective Construct* (YVL)

+ * (YV) *effort* to make a *tethering* = <the attempt to *"Conceive"*>

-versus- (VY) *"Conception-Birthing"* = <the *"After Actions"*>

to initially get the *inspiration* for... + * (L) *Learning*

Concept of a *pre-learning state* or the <*holding back*> *Effort,* as the *attempt to learn*

-versus- * (YL) as the *[early] process* of *learning*

** ילד (YLD) <*H3205*> as: *to bear young, to begot/beget*

The idea of *just learning to walk [the path].*

Other variants or words built from (YL):

** ליל (LYL) <*H3915*> as: *a twist, night, adversity*

** לִילִית (LYLYT) *<H3917>* as the Name: *"Lilith"* <female goddess>

1) *"Lilith,"* the name of a female goddess known as a night demon who haunts the desolate places of Edom.

1a) might be a nocturnal animal that inhabits desolate places | AV translations: screech owl.

> **Note:** There is an inference of a very fine-line relationship between the reflective nature of this word/name, regarding which attribute is *[held back]* → *learning/teaching/lessons* or *efforts/actions.*

4 - Meaning Construct

> ### Concept of *"Ruling by..."* being a Priest/Holy Man
> (claiming authority in the name of *God/Divine*) [Agent of ...]

Note: This is not just an external influence but can be internalized (within one's own mind) as the idea of *"Being ruled by..."*.

"Learned behaviors" <born from the mother *"self-serving aspect"*>

> **Note:** The negative side of this is — as a *slave/servant* to one's *beliefs = "Blind Faith."* Also, *someone behaving* or *thinking themselves* as being *"Holier-than-thou"* [aka: *"Self-Righteous,"* which symbolically is another way to *"Flirt with the Beast"*].

Additionally, the idea of *counseling* is a *fine line* balance between *positive* and *negative.* The influence of *"selfish* or *self-serving"* traits and *"learned behaviors"* lingering with the *"selfless"* goal of *service* or *counsel* to *assist others* or *take care* of *oneself* is a delicate and hazardous mix.

> Kabbalah "12 Paths" = *Levi* is labeled as: *"The Cleric(Priest)."*
>
> Symbolically, this is the *blindness caused* by the *fueled flame* or *exploded bomb [of Simeon].* Additionally, this is the connection or outcome of having an *"Inflated Ego."*

Blessings [from Israel]:

Genesis 49:5-7

5 *Simeon* and *Levi* are brothers; their swords are weapons of violence.
6 May I never enter their council; may I never join their assembly.
For they kill men in their anger, and hamstring oxen on a whim.
7 Cursed be their anger, for it is strong, and their wrath, for it is cruel!
I will disperse them in Jacob and scatter them in Israel.

Genesis 29:35

English translation (King James Version)

Gen. 29:35 And she conceived again, and bare a son: and she said, Now will I praise the LORD: therefore she called his name Judah; and left bearing.

Judah, יהודה (YHVDH) <*H3063*>

Effort + Reveal + [held back] Interaction + Path + Revelation

(D) *"Path"* within (YHVH) or as a *leading* to (H) *"Revelation"*

1 - *Linear Construct* (YHVDH)

* (YHV) **Note:** *not a biblical Hebrew word!?*

Although not specifically as a biblical word/Name, it's still connected to the function and Name of (YHVH), (YH), or *Yah.* <see page 136>

---

* יהו (YHV) symbolizing the (V) *<hold backing>* as *restraining* the *"Negative"* conquest and war-like version of (YH) [aka: worship or serving the *"War god"*].

Also, the idea of *<holding back>* *growth* or *expansion* – as an *over-reaching* or *excessively growing crops* = the concept of *guiltily.*

+ *<bringing forth>* (H) *Revealing/Revelation* = (YHVH)

[as the *"Good"* or *"Good thing(s)"*] = the *"Positive"* way, as a concept of *having patience* and *reflecting on a decision [prior to taking action].*

+ * (DH) **Note:** *Is not a biblical Hebrew word!?*

Path + <brings forth/leads to> Revelation

The idea of the *hard/difficult way*, but leading to a *greater outcome* as well → is the *ideal/desired path* one can take.

Concept of the *path to finding wisdom* (or *within wisdom*)

The idea of *not taking the easy way*, but rather *the harder (more challenging) path*, which is usually the *wisest way (approach).*

{Aka: The *"Right/Righteous" Way*}

Other variants or words built from (DH):

** דהב (DHB) <H1722> as: *gold* — used in Ezra, Daniel

> The idea of the *desired path* [is like *the gold rush*]
> *"seeking the shiny valuable thing" / "digging for gold" /*
> *"panning [for gold] in the water (life/truth)"*

** דהם (DHM) <H1724> as: *dumb/dumbfounded | astonish/astound*
— used once in Jeremiah (NDHM)

> The idea of the *desired path one can take is the*
> *amazing things life provides / the miracle of life*

** דהר (DHR) <H1725> as: *to curvet, move irregularly | to rush, dash,*
gallop [a horse] — used once in Nahum (DHR)

> The idea of the *desired path one can take*
>
> The horse is symbolic of *"Ideas"* — the (R) is *Mind of Man*
> <as in having so many fast ideas like *galloping horses*>

** נדה (NDH) <H5078> as: *gifts | outcast, banished, driven away*
— used once in Ezekiel (NDH) as: *"make payments | give gifts [to harlots]"*

> The idea of *"Seeds(Potential)"* that lead to *the*
> *desired path* one can take are those that are
> *postponed, thrown out,* or *cast aside.*

2 - *Dimensional Construct* (YH →HVD)

* יה (YH) <H3050> *"Yah"* | also translated as: *"Lord"*

> The idea of *what will be revealed in time = outcome(s)*

+ * (HVD) <H1935> as: *grandeur | splendor | majesty | vigor*
— also translated as: *authority, thine honor*

> Concept of *Hard work will bring success* (or *rather it should*)

The idea of the fruits of one's labor will bring about grandeur.

> Symbolically, as the *"Lord" brings forth Majesty (Splendor).*
> {Aka: *"God is Great"*}

Another ***Dimensional Construct*** (YH+DH →V)

* (YH) + (DH) and the <born within> is (V)

> The ideas of the *harvest/conflict*, and *merging/union* with the *hard/difficult*, which leads to a *greater outcome* = The *ideal/desired* way of doing things, will then *give birth* to the (V) <holding back>.

> Symbolically, [War] *leads to Peace*, and [Harvest] *leads to Patience* [the *necessity to wait for the crops to grow mature* or *ripen*.

> Concept of *Difficult* or *Challenging Actions* will lead to [something] of *value* or *substance*."

Note: Once again, the idea of duality and of a fine line between the *negative* and *positive* or *good* and *bad/evil*, etc... At the core is the idea of *making a choice* or *choices*, and inferring the *right choice* is very close to the *wrong choice*. The *outcome of the choice* is not the value, but rather the *"wisdom" gained [is* or *should be]*.

3 - *Reflective Construct* (HDVHY)

* הד (HD) <H1906> as: *"a [joyful] shout, cheer"*

> *Revealing/Revelation* + <bringing forth> a Path

Note: This is a *Path* that can lead to *"Pride"* [Even to a *"Messiah complex"*]

> Concept of *self-aggrandizing joy/pride* [for/of *"Self"*]

Other variants or words built from (HD):

** הדכ (HDK) <H1915> as: *"to crush with foot"*
— used in Job 40:12 *"to put others down"* [to think *lesser* of them], because that person is thinking themselves to be *better* or *greater* than the other.

> <bring forth> Flesh/Body [physical/Earthly "form"] from the (HD)

** להד (LHD) <H3855> as a Name meaning: *"oppression"*
— as a *feeling of being weighed down in mind* or *body* | as *"a man of Judah"*

+ * (V) *[held back]*

+ * הי (HY) <H1658> as: *lamentation, wailing* | *"Woe"*

Other variants or words built from (HY):

** ויהי (VYHY) <H1961> as: *"And it will come to pass"*
— used in Genesis 1:3 translated as *"and there was..."*

4 - Meaning Construct

> Concept of *"Ruling by..."* being a King
> (modern terms: *President, Prime Minister*)

Symbolically, the (D) a *path within* (YHVH) is born from [Mother] of the *"Self serving [feeling entitled]* or having the *lack of humility* [for the role of *King*] is the *"Lesser"* {or *the "Earthly" version*} versus, the *"Greater"* {or *the "Heavenly/Divine" version*} which is the *"Path to Wisdom."*

> Kabbalah "12 Paths" = *Judah* is labeled as: *"The Leader(King)."*
>
> Symbolically, this is the *dangers (warnings) of the process leading* to *King/Leadership.* Additionally, the connection to the results or outcome of having an *"Inflated Ego"* versus *"Humility,"* which is a *difficult road* or *path to be on.*

Blessings [from Israel]:
Genesis 49:8-12

8 *Judah*, your brothers shall praise you. Your hand shall be on the necks of your enemies; your father's sons shall bow down to you.

9 Judah is a young lion: my son, you return from the prey. Like a lion, he crouches and lies down; like a lioness, who dares to rouse him?
10 The scepter will not depart from Judah, nor the staff from between his feet, until Shiloh comes and the allegiance of the nations is his.
11 He ties his donkey to the vine, his colt to the choicest branch. He washes his garments in wine, his robes in the blood of grapes.
12 His eyes are darker than wine, and his teeth are whiter than milk.

> **Note:** In addition to the idea of external leaders or leadership traits, these also apply to the internal traits within oneself, as *"Being ruled by..." [as the influence of thought within].*

Genesis 30:1-4
English translation (King James Version)

1 And when Rachel saw that she bare Jacob no children, Rachel envied her sister; and said unto Jacob, Give me children, or else I die.

2 And Jacob's anger was kindled against Rachel: and he said, Am I in God's stead, who hath withheld from thee the fruit of the womb?

3 And she said, Behold my maid *Bilhah*, go in unto her; and she shall bear upon my knees, that I may also have children by her.

4 And she gave him *Bilhah* her handmaid to wife: and Jacob went in unto her.

5 And *Bilhah* conceived, and bare Jacob a son.

Rachel's Servant, [1st Concubine]

Bilhah, בלהה (BLHH) <H1090>

Blueprint + Learn/Teach + Revelation of Revelations

1 - Linear Construct (BL+HH)

* בל (BL) <H1077> as: *a failure, nothing, not at all, lest*
 — used in 1 Chronicles 16:30, Job 41:23, Psalms

* בל (BL) <H1078> as: *lord, master* | [a chief Babylonian deity] = *Ba'al*
 — used in Isaiah 46:1, Jeremiah 50:2, 51:44

* בל (BL) <H1079> as: *anxiety, the heart(mind)* — used in Daniel 6:14

> Concept of *"being weighed down by time."*

+ * הה (HH) <H1929> as: *Alas!, Woe | ah!* [expressing *grief*]
 — used once in Ezekiel 30:2

> Concept of a *"Sigh"*
> *[of realization of being weighed down by time]*

The idea of the *last exhale after a challenging/stressful activity*
[as: the *relief* of...].

* בלה (BLH) <H1086> as: *to wear out, waste away, to decay*
 — used in Genesis 18:12 (BLTY) as: *"becoming old"*
 — used in Deuteronomy 8:4 (BLTH) as: *"wearing out/waxed [not old]*

* בלה (BLH) <H1087> as: *"worn-out"* — used in Joshua 9:4 (BLYM)

Another *Linear Construct* (B+LHH)

* (B) *Blueprint*

+ *להה (LHH) *<H3856>* as: *to be rabid, to languish, faint | to amaze, startle (as madman) | to be insane*

— only linked to two variants [neither is actually (LHH)]:

1) in Genesis 47:13 as: *languished* (TLH)
2) in Genesis 47:13 as: *languished* (KMTLHLH)

2 - *Dimensional Construct* (BH →LH)

* (BH) **Note:** *not a biblical Hebrew word!?*

The idea of *one's initial reaction* or *awareness* to the *"A-ha"* moment [the *moment things begin to become revealed...*].

---

* בהו (BHV) *<H922>* as: *emptiness, void, waste* — used in Genesis 1:2

The idea of the *blueprint/plan*, yet *revealed* or *origins*, not yet *observed*.

<"The how did things begin!">

+ * (LH) **Note:** *not a biblical Hebrew word!?*

Other variants or words built from (LH):

** להב (LHB) *<H3851>* as: *"flame, blade"*
[*flashing point of spear* or *blade of sword*] — used in Judges (HLHB)

** להב (LHBH) *<H3852>* as: *"a flame"*
— used in Numbers 21:28 (LHBH) as: *"head [of his spear]"*
— used in 1 Samuel 17:7 (LHBT)

** להט (LHTh) *<H3858>* as: *"the flaming sword"* — used in Gen. 3:24

Note: (LH) seems to be *"special lessons"* = *Learning/Teaching "Lessons"* that *<brings forth> Revealing/Revelation.* The reflective (HL) represents the concept of a *"departing from [to move/go away]."*

Concept of *what good can come from a bad situation*

The idea of *looking at the positive side of the negative experience.*

3 - *Reflective Construct* (HHLB)

* הה (HH) <H1929> as: *Alas!, Woe | ah!* [expressing *grief*]

— used once in Ezekiel 30:2

> ### Concept of a *"Sigh"*
> [of realization of being weighed down by time]

The idea of the *last exhale after a challenging/stressful activity* [as: the *relief* of...].

+ * לב (LB) <H3820> as: *the heart, the feelings, the will, the intellect, centre[center] | inner man, mind, soul, etc..*

Symbolically, it's referred to as *the caring, empathetic state* and perhaps even as the *increased beating heart.*

The idea of *having an emotional response* to a *challenging/stressful activity.*

Another **Dimensional (Reflective) Construct** (HB →LB)

* הב (HB) <H1890> as: *gift [precious stone/gem], [mine] offering | also: [holocaust]* — used once in Hosea 8:13 (HBHBY)

The idea of *[something]* providing a *"gift"* [afterwards].

→ <*born within*> * (HL)

> Concept of a *"departing from [to move/go away]"*

The idea of *"lashing out"* at others because of the *suffering* one has endured.

> Concept of *"Grief of the Heart"* [overwhelming sadness]

Note: ** הבל (HBL) <H1891> as: *to be vain, to lead astray | to act emptily*

4 - Meaning Construct

There is a generalized idea of what comes out of this state:

> Concept of *Self-Importance [self-worth]*

The idea of *what is to "give birth"* comes from the *self-importance* aspects of human nature.

Note: *Bilhah* was a *handmaid* of Rachel [or *concubine*]. She was given to *Jacob by Rachel* when *Rachel* was unable to have children. *Bilhah* bore two sons: *Dan* and *Naphtali,* who became the founders of two tribes [of Israel].

She was also involved in a scandal with *Reuben,* Jacob's eldest son, who slept with her. <Symbolically, *The Union of Self Interest + Self Importance*>. This resulted in Reuben losing his birthright to Joseph's sons <Genesis 35:22>.

Note: Perhaps the concept of *elevating initial revelations too high* can *lead to misguided truths.* <The worship of *Baal* (BaL), as: The need to *"own"* or *"possess,"* or the idea of *ownership grows to a selfish* [and *cruel behavior*]. <The *self-importance* aspects of human nature: *"I'm better"* or the *feeling superior* to *others.*

The union of *Jacob* [*"wrestling with God"*] and *Bilhah* [*Self-Importance*], then what is *born from this* [*"the offspring"*].

The next two offspring represent:
the ***Perspectives*** of the ***"Ruler(Elite) types."***

Genesis 30:6

English translation (King James Version)

And Rachel said, God hath judged me (DNNY), and hath also heard my voice, and hath given me a son: therefore called she his name *Dan*.

Note: * דנני (DNNY) <H1777> as: *"Judged me"* | *"has judged my case"*

* די (DY) <H1767> *enough, sufficiency | abundance*

→ <born within it> * (NN) *Potential* of *Potential*

Dan, דן (DN) <H1835>

Path + Generations [Seed] "Potentials"

1 - Linear Construct (DN)

The idea of (DN) *"Paths"* and *"Potentials"*

— as *many ways* to *go through life* and *many things* to *build off of* or *from*, then to choose (D) a *path* or direction to go.

> *"The two potentials"* - as the *fork in the road* and symbolically as an *unsprouted seed* (pre-branching) versus *a crossroads* versus *a two-way road.*

Note: Potentially the origin of the idea of *two witnesses,* and of the two choices of *Good versus Bad(Evil).*

Symbolic of the *Scale(s) [of Judgment]* = "The *Balance* of the *Scales.*"

> Concept of *"Pushing"* (as *"Directing"*) an *Intention* [or *even a "Narrative"*].

Note: Symbolically, as *two (2) brothers,* but also the *choosing of one.*

The idea of *others* will be *"judgmental"* about the *choices being made.* - opinionated (seeds) and motivations (paths) (as potential action), and additionally, the idea that *judging another* is and has the *potential* to be *"wrong".*

---

2 - Dimensional Construct (D_N)

Note: 2-letter words/roots can't have this function!?

Other variants or words built from (D_N):

** דִּין (DYN) *<H1777>* as: *a straight course, sail direct*
| *to judge, contend, plead*

** דְמַן (DMN) *<H1828>* as: *manure, dung*

Life/Truth <born within> the Judgment(s)

— used in 2 Kings 9:37 ...the corpse/carcass of Jezebel will be as *dung* [as *refuse*] (KDMN) on the surface of the field (HShDH)...

<Symbolically, describing as: *fertilizer* or *used as fertilizer*>

> **Note:** as: *Negative:* describing *people/person* <The modern concept: *"a piece of shit/crap"*]. As: *Positive:* as *Fertilizer* <using the by-product/decomposing of organic material to fertilize soil for seeds to sprout> [a *"cause"* for *development (of life to begin to grow)*].
>
> Maybe even a connection to *people/person* being as *"martyrs."*
> * דְם (DM) *<H1818>* as: *"blood"* + <brings forth> (N) *Seed/"Potential"*

3 - Reflective Construct (ND)

* נֵד (ND) *<H5067>* as: *a mound, wave* | *heap*

> Concept of *"slightly"* elevated

The idea of a *"Greater Good"* or *doing [some] good to help a limited number of people,* rather than *all* [or *everyone*].

> versus
>
> The idea of a *truly elevated* as: *a Mountain,* and the connection to being the *"Most high"* [*to God*].

Other variants or words built from (ND):

** נדב (NDB) *<H5068>* as: *to incite, to impel, make willing, to volunteer*
** נדב (NDB) *<H5069>* as: *be liberal, to volunteer, offer freely*
** נדד (NDD) *<H5074>* as: *fled, go from, thrust away, wanders abroad*
** נדד (NDD) *<H5076>* as: *tossed, a rolling* | *tossing (of sleeplessness)*

4 - Meaning Construct

> Concept of our *"Ways"* and *"What comes of it."*

The idea of *"Paths and Potentials"* is the *"Path" we take in life* and *the places it leads to* (what outcome come from it).

Note: There is also a connection to *Dan* to *Ships* and *Judgment* — this symbolically relates to terms like *Right-leaning/Conservative* or *Left-leaning/Liberal* = as being on a particular side of the boat.

Kabbalah "12 Paths" = *Dan* is labeled as: *"The Judge."*

Symbolically, it's the *"Perspective lens"* that people have going through life, and is both *internal* and *external*.
[as: *"Judgment"* of *others* and of *oneself*].

Blessings [from Israel]:
Genesis 49:16-18
16 *Dan* shall provide justice for his people as one of the tribes of Israel.
17 He will be a snake by the road, a viper in the path that bites the horse's heels so that its rider tumbles backward.
18 I await Your salvation, O LORD.

Genesis 30:7-8
English translation (King James Version)
7 And Bilhah Rachel's maid conceived again, and bare Jacob a second son.
8 And Rachel said, With great wrestlings have I wrestled with my sister, and I have prevailed: and she called his name *Naphtali*.

Note: Symbolically, *"wrestling with sister"* [The sister is *Leah*, representing: *The "self-serving" human nature [feeling entitled]*. *Rachel* means *"expanding the mind beyond selfish needs."*

Naphtali, נפתלי (NPTLY) <H5321>

Generations [Seed] "Potentials" + Spoken + Weaving together
+ Learning/Teaching/"Lessons" + Efforts

1 - *Linear Construct* (NPT+LY)

* נפת (NPT) <H5317> as: *a dipping(s) [of honey] | honeycomb*

   The idea of the *slow drip* of what is *anticipated to taste sweet* —
   or the *eagerness* to *want to hear words* that *sound good.*

   Symbolically, comparing a person to being a *"sweet talker"* or *"being charismatic"* — meaning their words sound *sweet* and *desirable.*

+ * (LY)   **Note:** *not a biblical Hebrew word!?*

   — connection to meanings as: *twisted, night monster.* <see page 282>

   The idea of *lacking lessons learned,* and as a pre-state condition
   of something that is a *challenge* or *challenging.*

   Symbolically, as *someone* [in a leadership position], who is *charming, charismatic* [talks *sweet* like *honey*], but the *outcome* of what they're *saying* is *lacking expected results* or *actions.* Additionally, may even have *"corrupt" intentions [twisted]* or *"unseen" consequences [night monster].*

Another *Linear Construct* (N+PTL+Y)

* (N) *"Seed"(Potential)*

+ * פתל (PTL) <H6617> as: *to wrestle | shew self unsavory*
   – *Struggling with oneself, regarding crookedness[cunningness].*

   + * (Y) *Efforts*

   The idea of *what a shrewd person's behavioral outcome produces.*

   In addition, these breakdowns suggest the idea of *"taking the easy way [in life],"* by focusing on what benefits oneself at the cost/loss of others.

2 - *Dimensional Construct* (NP+LY →T)

* (NP) <H5297> as a place Name: *Noph* | the city capital of Upper Egypt.
   Note: Associated with the meaning: *"presentability"* [defined as: *clean, well dressed,* or *decent enough to be seen in public.*]

Other variants or words built from (NP):

** נפג (NPG) <H5298> as a Name: *Nepheg* [as: *to spring forth, a sprout*]

** נפה (NPH) <H5299> as: *a lofty place, height | border, coast, region, sieve (winnowing implement →* Winnowing is a process by which chaff is separated from grain.*)*

** נפל (NPL) <H5307-8> as: *to fall, to lie, to be cast down*

** נפל (NPL) <H5309> as: *miscarriage, stillborn | untimely birth*

** נפש (NPSh) <H5315> as: *creature | a "breathing" creature, life, soul, self, person, heart, living being, animal of, vitality*

Seed"Potential" + Mouth + aspects of Creation

Potential [of a "Living, Breathing thing"] to breathe life into [something], which then becomes a part of Creation.

<**Note:** a visual image of *"blowing of a dandelion plant in the seed form* and *seeds flying off in the air, and eventually, potentially become a new plant."*>

Symbolically, as the *lacking* or *weak ability* of such creatures [including: Mankind] to *create,* in comparison to *God as the Creator* or to *Creation itself.*

The (NP) seems to relate to ideas like: *"weak, less forceful [efforts/actions], or something easier to do."*

+ * (LY)   **Note:** *not a biblical Hebrew word!?*
— connection to meanings as: *twisted, night monster.* <see page 282>

The idea of *lacking lessons learned,* and as a pre-state condition of something that is a *challenge* or *challenging.*

<born within> → * (T) *Weaving together*

The idea of ***scheming*** and inferring the *use* or the *power of speech* can bring this about.

> Concept of the *Great Speakers*

The idea of being in a [*pre-state* or *prior*], and *having lacked "lessons learned."*
<Inferring the idea of *inspirational speakers rising to power* via *speech.*>

Symbolically, there is a relationship and connection to the (NPLYM/NPYLYM) <H5303> *Nephlim [Giants] – Mighty men of old.*

Another ***Dimensional Construct*** (NY →PTL)

* יַ (NY) <H5204> as: *wailing*

+ * פתל (PTL) *<H6617>* as: *to wrestle | shew self unsavory*
  – *Struggling with oneself, in regard to crookedness[cunningness].*

The idea of *complaining/moaning* about
wanting to have things your way.

3 - Reflective Construct (YLTPN)

* (YL) *[early] process of learning [like: as a baby learns to walk]*

+ * (TP) *<H8596>* as: *a tambourine, trimbil [tabret]*

> Other variants or words built from (TP):
>
> ** (TPYNY) *<H8601>* as: *a cake, cookery | broken piece, baked
> pieces, pieces cooked*
>
> The idea of *prep cooking [meal prepping].*

+ * (N) *"Seed"/Potential*

The idea of *an instinctual/simple [experimental] learning process.*

> Concept of *testing the outcome*
> [as early stages of a *whole/larger end result*]

4 - Meaning Construct

> Concept of *having the "potential" to become
> [something], but also, "to go too far."*

The idea of *[something] sounds like a good idea,*
but then *falls short* or *over corrects.*

> Kabbalah "12 Paths" = *Naphtali* is labeled as: *"The Free Spirit."*

Blessings [from Israel]:

Genesis 49:21

21 Naphtali is a doe set free that bears beautiful fawns.

> *English translation (King James Version)*
> 21 Naphtali is a hind let loose: he giveth goodly words.

Genesis 30:9
English translation (King James Version)
When Leah saw that she had left bearing, she took *Zilpah* her maid,
and gave her Jacob to wife.

Leah's Servant, [2nd Concubine]

Zilpah, זלפה (ZLPH) <H2153>

Nourishing + Learning/Teaching + Spoken + Revealing

1 - Linear Construct (ZLPH)

* (ZL) **Note:** *not a biblical Hebrew word!?*

Other variants or words built from (ZL):

** זלזל (ZLZL) <H2150> as: *sprig* — used once in Isaiah 18:5

> **Sprig**: *a small stem with leaves on it from a plant* or
> *bush, used in cooking* or *as a decoration.*

The idea of a *small part* that has *value* and is
connected to a larger whole.

+ * פה (PH) <H6310> as: *mouth | edge, potion, side*

The idea of *[something] spoken.*

> Concept of *"Small piece* of the *whole conversion."*

The idea of an *opinion* or *idea* within the larger perspective.

2 - Dimensional Construct (ZH →LP)

* זה (ZH) <H2088> as: *this, these* [*something* that has *"come to be"*]

+ * (LP) **Note:** *not a biblical Hebrew word!?*

Other variants or words built from (LP):

** לפיד (LPYD) <H3940> as: *a flambeau, lamp, flame, torch | firebrand*

** אלף (ALP) <H502> as: *to learn*

** אלף (ALP) <H502> as: *to make thousandfold*

> **Note:** The *Aleph* is also the *First Letter* of the Alphabet, and the
> Glyph of the *Head of the Ox*, representing the *Mind of God.*

The idea of *what is to come to pass* is the everlasting *fire/flames* of *God*.

> Concept of the *Eternal Flame*

And the continuous sparks or sparking of God's flame/fire
[representing: *wisdom*] into the human mind.

3 - *Reflective Construct* (HPLZ)

* (HP) **Note:** *not a biblical Hebrew word!?*   *Revealing + "Mouth"/Speech*

Other variants or words built from (HP):

** הפגה (HPGH) *<H2014>* as: *stopping, intermission | interruption | relaxation* — used once in Lamentations 3:49 (implying eyes(crying) after enemies opened their mouths against [us])

** הפכ (HPK) *<H2015>* as: *to turn about, over, to change, overturn, return, pervert | overthrow*

+ * (LZ) **Note:** *not a biblical Hebrew word!?*   *Lessons + Nourishment*

Other variants or words built from (LZ):

** לזות (LZVT) *<H3891>* as: *deviation, perversity, crookedness* — used once in Proverbs 4:24 [in connection to lips and mouth]

** לוז (LVZ) *<H3868>* as: *to turn aside, to depart, be perverse* — used 5 times in Proverbs / actual variants as: (VNLVZIM), (YLZV), (NLVZ), (YLYZV), (VNLVZ) — used once in Isaiah 30:12 (VNLVZ)

** לוז (LVZ) *<H3869>* as: *almond | hazel* — used once in Genesis 30:37 (VLVZ) [referencing *types of trees*]

Note: Each word and variant all have the (V) *[held back].*

Symbolically, the relationship between a *nut* and *perverse/deviant* could be the lack of the *nut* becoming a *new tree*, either by *not falling/"departing" from the tree* [as, *not "leaving the nest"*] or *just not seeding in the ground* [as, *part of the process of life*].

> Concept of *Corruption*

The idea of *"to overturn/pervert" [something]* could be *beneficial*.

4 - *Meaning Construct*

> Concept of *attempting to get value [from learned/lessons]* and *spoken wisdom,* but as a servant to the *"self-serving."*

Genesis 30:10-11

English translation (King James Version)

10 And Zilpah Leah's maid bare Jacob a son.
11 And Leah said, A troop cometh [also translated as, What good fortune]: and she called his name *Gad*.

Note: The word name here is (ShMV) = Name + *[held back]*

Gad, גד (GD) <H1409>

Gathering + Path

1 - Linear Construct (GD)

* גד (GD) *<H1407>* as: *coriander [seed] | Fortune, troop*
  — used in Exodus 16:31 describing *Manna* (MN): like, *coriander* (GD) seed

* גד (GD) *<H1408>* as: *Fortune, luck*

* גד (GD) *<H1409>* as: *fortune/fortunate, troop*
  — used in Genesis 30:11 (BGD) (BA) (GD) = How fortunate and called his name (ShMV) Gad (GD) *<H1410>* as Name

  Other variants or words built from (GD):

** גדבר (GDBR) *<H1411>* as: *treasurer*
  — used in Daniel 3:2-3 (GDBRYA) <probably as the idea of the "*collector*" of *tax, debt,* or *money*>.

> **Note:** The idea that there is a *pressure/expectation,* which connects to the idea of (YA) as a suffix, as *the attempt to maintain a high standard,* or *that was set at a great level.*

** גדד (GDD) *<H1413>* as: *to crowd, to gash | to penetrate, cut, attack, invade | to cut oneself | to gather in troops or crowds*
  — used in Deut.14:1 (TTGDDDV)
  — used in Psalm 94:21 (YGVDV) *gather themselves together[against]*

** גדה (GDH) *<H1415>* as: *a river bank | a border of [a river]*
— used in Joshua, Chronicles, Isaiah | actually as (GDVTYV)

> **Note:** Interesting connection to *river banks* and to *"banks"* [*as a money gathering/gathered place*] — the attributes of the *river bank* are both the thing that *holds back* and is *slowly chewed away* [eroded] — as a fitting metaphor of the *interest one pays [losses]* on the *money loans* or a *tax* one has to pay...

** גדול (GDVL) <H1419> as: *great, large, important, mighty*
— used in Genesis 1:16 *made two great* (HGDLYM) lights, the *greater* (HGDL)...
— used in Genesis 4:13 My punishment is too *great* (GDVL) also: to bear [*greater* than I can bear]

** גדי (GDY) <H1423> as: *a young [male] goat, kid*

** גדל (GDL) <H1432> as: *becoming great, growing up*

** גדל (GDL) <H1433> as: *greatness, magnitude*

The idea of *simply having* [or *getting*] *things handed to you...*

Concept of *"Status given,* rather than *earned"*

2 - Dimensional Construct (G_D)

Note: *2-letter words/roots can't have this function!?*

Other variants or words built from (G_D):

** גמד (GMD) <H1574> as: *a span* | translated as: *a cubit*
— used once in Judges 3:16

** גמד (GMD) <H1575> as: *a warrior*

— used once in Ezekiel 27:11 and the *Gammadim* were in your towers also: and the [men] of *Gammadites* (VGMDYM) ... in your towers (BMGDLVTYK) — used with the "city and tower" [of Babel].

Note: * מד (MD) <H4055> translated as: *garment, robe [armor]* | also as: *extend, height, a measure* | *stature* [aka: "the *measure* of a man"].

The idea of (G) *Gathering* + (MD) *Life + Path* = as: *stature [power/strength]*, but also *garments [things carried/coverings]* | only relevant in *Life*, not in *Death* ["*can't take with you in death*"].

3 - Reflective Construct (DG)

* דג (DG) <H1709> as: *a fish*
— used in Genesis 9:2 ... and all the *fish* (DGY) in the sea

Path + Gathering

Symbolically, *a path* or *a way*, that brings a *gathering* | like: the gathering to the fish market, or *"followers of a way,"* | like: *a school of fish.*

Note: It also seems to imply a limitation to aspects of *being in a school of fish* — as: *catching many in a net* or *the ease of a predator to catch and eat [by targeting a school of fish]*.

The idea of *just going with the flow of how things are...*

Other variants or words built from (DG):

** דגל (DGL) *<H1713>* as: *to flaunt, raise a flag, to set up our banners, to be conspicuous | outstanding [among a group]*

The idea of *choosing a tribe, taking a stand, identifying one's group,* and *even "to raise the white flag" [to call a truce* or *to surrender]*.

4 - Meaning Construct

> Concept of *"Service to the Rule, Ruler, or Ruling..."*

The idea of *being a Soldier [of enforcement]* | <aka: Police>

Note: As just *having* or *getting* things handed to you....
{*"Status given,* rather than *earned."*}

Also, there's a connection to...

> Concept of having *"a one-track mind"*

the expectation of a constant level of *achievement/service/output/etc...*

The idea of *"being ruled"* by rules, procedure, policy, etc.
<as to *be blinded by them*>

This extends to the *obsessional needs* or *addiction behavior* [whether it's for *power, status,* or as a *coping mechanism*].

Kabbalah "12 Paths" = *Gad* is labeled as: *"The Warrior."*

Blessings [from Israel]:

Genesis 49:19
19 Gad will be attacked by raiders, but he will attack their heels.

Genesis 30:12-13

English translation (King James Version)

12 And Zilpah Leah's maid bare Jacob a second son.
13 And Leah said, *Happy* am I, for the daughters will call me *blessed*:
and she called his name *Asher.*

Note: There are three variants of the (AShR) word used in line 13:
Happy, blessed, and the *Name itself.*

---

* אָשֵׁר (AShR) *<H833>* as: *to be straight to go forward, be honest, make progress, proper, happiness*
Note: The Strong's number linked to 16 occurrences
— used in Genesis 30:13 ...[will call me] *blessed* (AShRVNY)

* אָשֵׁר (AShR) *<H837>* as: *Happy*
— used in Genesis 30:13 ...*Happy* am I -or- I am *happy* (BAShRY)

Asher, אָשֵׁר (AShR) *<H836>*

Mind of God + Aspect of Creation + Mind of Man

1 - Linear Construct (AShR)

* אָשֵׁר (AShR) *<H833>* as: *to be straight to go forward, be honest, make progress, proper, happiness*
Note: As stated above... as *"blessed"* – there are a variety of other variants connected to this Strong's number:
— used in Isaiah 9:16 uses the word (MAShRY) translated as: *"those who guide"* and also translated as: *"leaders."*

* אָשֵׁר (AShR) *<H834>* as: *which, whose, with, with which*
Note: The most common translation with over 5500 occurrences...
— used in Genesis 1:7 *<H834>* translated as: *"that [were],"* when describing the waters *that were* under the firmament (defined as: a vault or arch of the sky).
— used in Genesis 1:11 *<H834>* translated as: *"whose,"* when describing the fruit whose seed [is] in itself.
— used in Genesis 1:12 translated as: *"whose,"* when describing the tree [that] yields fruit whose seed [is] in itself.
Note: The connection to the *Fruit* (nourishment/food), but with a *seed* <to become [something] that potentially *sprouts* [a future]>.

* אֲשֵׁר (AShR) <H835> as: *blessed/blessedness | happiness*
  Note: Connected to 45 occurrences and is actually (AShRY)

* אֲשֵׁר (AShR) <H837> as: *Happy*
  — used once in Genesis 30:13 ...*Happy* am I -or- I am *happy* (BAShRY)

* אֲשֵׁר (AShR) <H838> as: *a step [his steps, my step, my goings]*
  Note: Connected to 9 occurrences and is also linked to (AShRY)

* אֲשֵׁר (AShR) <H835> as: *boxwood [the cedar tree, or some other light elastic wood]* | [of the Ashurites]
  — used once in Ezekiel 27:6 (AShRYM)

Another *Linear Construct* (A →ShR)

* (A) *Mind of God*

+ * שַׂר (ShR) <H8269> as: *head ruler, prince, chief, chief captain, commander, officials*

+ * שֹׁר (ShR) <H8270> as: *a string, umbilical cord, navel* | [as: *to your body/to thy naval*]

> The idea of *God* <*bringing forth*> *a ruler/prince*, and comparing it to a *"tethering"* or *"what is left over from it."*

Other variants or words built from (ShR):

** שָׂרָא (ShRA) <H8271> as: *to free, separate, to unravel, to loosen | begin, dissolve, dwell, loose*

The idea of a [*"God's wrath state"*] <*brought forth from*> *a ruler/ prince*, and comparing it to a *"tethering"* or *"what is left over from it."*

Another *Linear Construct* (ASh →R)

* אֵשׁ (ASh) <H784>, defined as *"a fire,"* but also translated as: *"blazing, burning, fiery, flaming, flashing."*

→ * (R) *Mind of Man*

> ### Concept of a *"Fire" Mind*

Symbolically, as the *"Mind on Fire."*

The idea of the *condition of the mind* as being on *fire*.

[to describe: *"Wisdom"* | as well as: *"Prophesy"*]

Note: Concept of *Fruit* (nourishment/food) but with a *seed within* (potential) {as to become [something] that potentially *sprouts* [a future]}.

Concept of a *Seer/Prophet*

Note: The connection to *Visions* is: *knowledge from God*, as a *gift* from *God*, and as being a *Benefactor of God's knowledge* [at least the perception of having or receiving it].

2 - *Dimensional Construct* (AR →Sh)

* אר‎ש (ARSh) <H781> as: *to engage [in matrimony]* | *betroth, engaged*

Other variants or words built from (AR):

** ארא (ARA) <H690> as Name meaning: *"lion"*

— from the * (ARY) <H738> as: *a lion*

** אראל (ARAL) <H691> as: *a hero, valiant one*

** אראלי (ARALY) <H692> as Name meaning: *"Lion of God"*

** אריאל (ARYAL) <H739> as Name meaning: *"Lion of God"* | *heroic*

** ארב (ARB) <H690> as: *to lurk* | *to lie in wait, ambush*

— as the attribute of being *hunted [by a lion]*.

3 - *Reflective Construct* (RSh+A)

* (RSh) **Note:** *not a biblical Hebrew word!?*

Mind of Man + aspects of Creation [Destruction]

Other variants or words built from (RSh):

** רשש (RShSh) <H7567> as: *to demolish* | *to beat down, shatter*

** רשף (RShP) <H7565> as: *plague, burning heat [fever], arrows (flaming, flashes), bolts of lightning/hot thunderbolts, flashes [of fire], a live coal (hot, burning heat).*

** רשעה (RShaH) <H7564> as: *wickedness, guilt, fault, wrong*

+ * (A) *Mind of God* **Note:** as a *"Wrathful"* state <brought forth>

Another *Linear Construct* (R+ShA)

* (R) *Mind of Man*

+ * (ShA) **Note:** *not a biblical Hebrew word!?*

> *aspects of Creation [Destruction] + Mind of God*
> **Note:** as a *"Wrathful"* state <*brought forth*>.

Other variants or words built from (ShA):

** שׁאמ (ShAM) <*H7589*> as: *contempt, despite*
** שׁאל (ShAL) <*H7592*> as: *to inquire, request, demand | borrow, beg*
** שׁאה (ShAH) <*H7582*> as: *to rush, to desolate, crash into ruins*

The idea of *affixing* or *stopping* the *movement of time.*

> Symbolically, the relationship to *flame* or *spark* from God
> — One way is a *benefit*, and the other is *harmful.*
> [The duality of *Creation* and *Destruction*]

4 - *Meaning Construct*

> Concept of *"Benefiting from the Rule, Ruler, or Ruling..."*

The idea of *being a Benefactor [of the system].*

Also, there's a connection to...

> Concept of being a *"Visionary-type"*

The idea of *taking advantage of a situation via the rules, procedures, policies, etc* <*to benefit oneself*>.

This extends to the *obsessional needs* or *addiction behavior (gluttony, greed, etc)* [whether it's for *power, status* or as a *coping mechanism*].

Kabbalah "12 Paths" = *Asher* is labeled as: *"The Prosperous One."*

Blessings [from Israel]:

Genesis 49:20
20 Asher's food will be rich; he shall provide royal delicacies.

> **Note:** Before the next son's births are described, there's a brief narration, referring back to *Reuben* and harvesting fields.

Genesis 30:14-16
English translation (King James Version)

14 And *Reuben* went in the days of wheat harvest, and found mandrakes in the field, and brought them unto his mother Leah.
Then Rachel said to Leah, Give me, I pray thee, of thy son's mandrakes.

15 And she said unto her, Is it a small matter that thou hast taken my husband? and wouldest thou take away my son's mandrakes also?
And Rachel said, Therefore he shall lie with thee to night for thy son's mandrakes.

16 And Jacob came out of the field in the evening, and Leah went out to meet him, and said, Thou must come in unto me; for surely I have hired thee with my son's mandrakes. And he lay with her that night.

Reuben, ראובן (RAVBN) <H7205>   <see page 275>

"Ruling by..." thinking of oneself as a god (or son of god) on Earth.

The concept of *thinking of oneself first*
(as *the source of one's motivation*)

<was *born* from *"Mother"* [Leah] = the Ideas/Thoughts of *Self Interest.*>

Note: Some key words:

Days, בימי (BYMY) <H3117>

(B) *Plan* + (YM) *Effort +Life/Truth* + (Y) *Effort*

Note: Not the יומ (YVM) as: *Day.* <The (V) *interaction within the* (YM) = *"Flowing River"* as the concept of *Time*>

The idea of the *plan* of *time* versus an *interaction within* **time.**

> Inferring the moment → When *farming wheat* was in the *early stages of development,* or rather, the early stages of *harvesting the wheat.*

Harvest, קציר (QTsYR) <H7105>

* (QT) **Note:** *not a biblical Hebrew word!?*   *Past + Weaving*
Symbolically, representing the *"End [times]"*

+ * (YR) **Note:** *not a biblical Hebrew word!?*   *Effort + Mind of Man*

Other variants or words built from (ShA):

** (YRA) <H3372-3> as: *to fear, revere awe [God]*

The idea of *How mankind will think* or *be thinking [in the "End times"].*

> **Note:** Also, the idea (or fact) that at the precipice we get our shit together and turn things around (make better).

Wheat, חטים (ChThYM)   [* חטה (ChThH) <H2406> as: *wheat*]

(ChTh) with (YM) *<the plural ending>*
versus
(ChTh) + (H) ending with *revealing/revelation*

Note: (Ch)+(Th) = *Branching off/(Diversity|Separating) + Containing/(Grouping)*

| Concept of *Separating into Groups* |

Other variants or words built from (ChTh):

** חטב (ChThB) <H2404> as: *to chop, carve wood*

** חטא (ChThA) <H2398-2403> as: *sin, 'missed the mark', offended*

Found, וימצא (VY+MTsA) <H4672> as: *"found, attain, acquire"*

* (VY) *"Conception-Birthing"* <to initially get the *inspiration* for... >

+ * מצ (MTs) <H4671> as: *chaff, threshed loose*

| Concept of *"Separating the Wheat from The Chaff"* |

> **Note:** When *separating the wheat from the chaff*, a method involves tossing it into the air, allowing the wind to blow the chaff away. Only the wheat grain would fall to the ground [as it was too heavy to be carried away by the wind].
>
> Symbolically, *[the grain]* is *"carrying a heavy burden,"* but in the end, *providing* or *having a responsibility of becoming the flour* that will then become the bread.

+ (A) *Mind of God* = *"God's wrath"*

The idea of *being aggressive* or *"wrathful" [in this action].*

The sequence of letters, as a word:

* מצא (MTsA) <H4672> as: *found, find, present, discover, come, caught, befall, be able, come forth (appear* or *exist).*

> Concept of *[What] was Learned from the Mistake*
> [*From a mistake that was: Bad, Evil, Painful, Awful, etc...*]

The idea of *getting [something] out of* or *exposing [something]*, as finding a value from it.

{Aka, the phase: *"Finding the Silver lining."*}

Mandrakes, דודים (DVDAYM) <H1736>

* דודי (DVDY) <H1736> as: *mandrake*

Other variants or words built from (DVD):
** דוד (DVD) <H1731> as the Name: *[King] David* <*"Beloved"*>
** דוד (DVD) <H1730> as: *to love (beloved)* | *uncle (father's brother)*

+ ** (AYM) <H> as: *"Frightful, Terrible, Dreadful"*

> Concept of *loving* (DVD) *intention*, but a *terrible* (AYM) outcome.

Field, (BShDH) <H7704>

* שדה (ShDH) <H7704> as: *field, country, land, soil, wild*

Other variants or words built from (BSh):
** (BShL) as: *to boil up, cooking (bake, roast), to ripen*
versus
** (ShD) = The idea of *"Taking the easy way out"*   <see page 148>

** שד (ShD) <H7699> as: *[female] "breasts"*
** שד (ShD) <H7700> as: *"demon"*

Other variants or words built from (ShD):
** שדי (ShDY) <H7706> translated as: *Almighty* | as: *field, land*

The idea of *the [wild] land* which *will be transformed into a "crop field"* [as both the *struggle* and *benefit*].

Note: The place where it's *needed to help reinforce the way things are* [or *need to be*], because of *"self-serving interests."* In addition, the necessity to teach the next generation(s) will [in theory] assist in this *enforcement* — Symbolically, as the preparation or condition of the soil for generations of farming [crop rotation for the continued health of the soil].

The idea of inferring a *shift* or *change* in thought, as from the *Ruler/Leadership* aspects of *guidance,* to *extracting what is positive from it.*

<Leah> *"self-serving"* aspects = as the *Beginning of the End* → leads to the *Revelation* of <**Rachel**> *"working together"* aspects.

{Symbolically, as the conversion Rachel spoke with Leah}

Rachel, רחל (RChL) *<H7354>*   <see page 321>

Concept of *"an open mind brings forth expanded potentials"*

The idea of *seeing the results*

Note: As multiple things are being *worked down (worked out),* and maybe even the under-pressure nature of this process [implying a strength of character — as someone *carrying a heavy burden* and *being worn down.*

Note: Back to **Leah** having sons being born again.

Genesis 30:17-18
English translation (King James Version)

17 And God hearkened unto Leah, and she conceived, and bare Jacob the fifth son. 18 And Leah said, God hath given me *my hire [wages],* because I have given my maiden to my husband: and she called his name *Issachar.*

Note: The word translated as: *"my hire [wages]"* = * שכרי (ShKRY) *<H7939>.*

Issachar, יששכר (YShShKR) *<H3485>*

Effort + Aspect of Creation + Aspect of Creation + Body/Flesh + Mind of Man
{*Man's knowledge,* as the *Lesser* versus the *Greater,* as *God's knowledge*}

1 - *Linear Construct* (YSh+ShK+R)

* יֵשׁ (YSh) <H3426> as: *there is, are | being, existence, substance*

Effort + [aspects of] Creation

<The *effects/outcomes* from the *process of Creation*>

The idea of the *unfolding of Earthly Creation* -or- the *patterns* of the *unfolding* of *Creation on Earth* [the *Lesser* versus *Greater*].

> Concept of *recognizing [observing] the "Patterns" of the world [in Nature] around them.*

+ * שַׂךְ (ShK) <H7899> as: *of them[shall be* or *will become] | as: pricks* [as: *a brier, thicket, lair, booth*]

— used once in Numbers 33:35, but actually is (LShKYM) plural version and the learning that brought forward [the concept of it] (ShK) — which could be/imply the idea of the pricked by thorns of the brier bush or as the scratches from pushing through a thicket of branches.

Aspect of Creation + Body/Flesh [made "Flesh"]

<The *creation of the flesh* to be *balanced* between the *just strong enough* [*to give some protection*] and *delicate* enough to also *teach life lessons* [especially when *"pushing through difficult times."*]>

+ * שֹׂךְ (ShK) <H7900> as: *tabernacle | a booth, pavilion | [thicket, hedge,* or *covering]*

— used once in Lamentations 2:6, actually as (ShKV) or (ShK) *[held back],* which could be/imply the idea of a *protected place [location].*

+ (R) *Mind of Man*   <How (mankind) process's experiences>

Another *Linear Construct* (YShSh+KR)

* יָשֵׁשׁ (YShSh) <H3486> as: *old man [gray-haired] | infirm [stooped of age]*
— also meaning: *"Blanch"*

Note: In cooking, [*to "blanch"*] refers to the process of briefly immersing food in boiling water, then quickly *plunging it into cold water* to *halt* the cooking process. It can also mean to *whiten* by *removing color* or to *bleach* something. Additionally, *"blanch"* can mean to *turn pale,* often due to *shock* or *fear.*

+ * כַּר (KR) <H3733> as: *Ram, lamb, a battering ram | a meadow, a pad, a camel's saddle*

— used once in Genesis 31:34 (BKR) *camel's saddle* — which could be/imply the idea of a *bumpy ride* or the *challenging aspect* of *staying on the seat [saddle] while riding.*

— used in Deuteronomy./1 Samuel, 2 Kings, Psalms, Ezekiel, Amos (KRYM) as: [of] *lambs | pastures | meadows* <which could be/imply the idea of *lambs bouncing [galloping, dancing, skipping] around* in a *pasture/meadow*>.

— used in Ezekiel (KRYM) as: *battering rams | captains* <which could be/imply the idea of *butting heads* [like: *rams* or the *young he-lamb* <as a *test/display of dominance*>].

+ * כר (KR) <*H3734*> as: *"kors" | a measure*

Also as: *"homer"* [*a deep round vessel, a cor, a dry measure*]

Note: In ancient Israel, the *"kor"* was a standard unit of measurement for agricultural produce, particularly grains, versus other dry measure words

What is the unit called a *"kor"*? An ancient Hebrew unit of *liquid capacity*, approx. 230 liters. It had the same volume as the *homer* [a dry measure].

> ## Concept of the *"Challenging aspects"*

The idea of the *straining* (or *taxing*) *effort of [something].*

Body/Flesh + Mind of Man

<The glyph version of [*Physical + Mental*] *existence*>

The idea of the *struggles of physical existence.*

{The *hardening oneself, mentally* — as *overcoming* the *mental* aspects of the *physical challenges.*}

2 - *Dimensional Construct* (YR →ShShK)

* (YR) **Note:** *not a biblical Hebrew word!?*

Other variants or words built from (YR):

** ירא (YRA) <*H3372*> as: *fear, to revere, to frighten, be afraid | to stand in awe.* [commonly used and various variants]

The idea of *"being in awe of..."* or *having an appreciation for...*

+ * ששך (ShShK) <*H8347*> as Location Name: *Sheshak*

— used in Jeremiah 25:26, 51:41

Note: It's believed to be a cryptogram/[*Atbash cipher*] for *"Babylon"* (בבל)

Other variants or words built from (ShSh):

** שֵׁשׁ (ShSh) <H8336> as: *bleached stuff, white linen "fine linen"* | *alabaster/marble.*

** שֵׁשׁ (ShSh) <H8337> as: *six, sixth*

> Concept of *the value [people] place/attach on [things]*
> {and based on the *efforts[actions]* one has taken to get it}

The idea of *"The finer things in life"/living extravagantly.*

3 - *Reflective Construct* (RKShShY)

* רַךְ (RK) <H7390-1> as: *tender, weak, soft, delicate* | *weak of heart, timid* | *soft (of words)*

Other variants or words built from (RK):

** רכב (RKB) <H7395> as: *charioteer, horsemen, driver*

** רכה (RKBH) <H7396> as: *a chariot* | *riding*

** רכוש (RKVSh) <H7399> as: *property, goods, riches, possessions* <general term for *all movable goods/livestock*]

** רכש (RKSh) <H7399> as: *the goods*

— used once in Genesis 14:11 ... And they took all the *goods* of Sodom and Gomorrah...

+ * שׁי (ShY) <H7862> as: *a gift, presents / a girt [offered as homage]*

(ShY) *Creation's Effort* = *Nature [Mother Nature or Laws of Nature]* [as: *"Creation's Laws"*] = The idea of *How things are.*

> Concept of *things given to you*
> [without having to work for it or earn it on one's own]

4 - *Meaning Construct*

> Concept of *"Maintaining the Rule, Ruler, or Ruling..."*

The idea of being a *Reinforcement of [the/a system].*

[aka: *"The Status Quo"*]

Additionally, ideas like: *seeing [only] what you want to see*, or *seeing [only] what gives you comfort*, or *the feeling of safety*.

[aka: *"Safe Spaces"*]

> Kabbalah "12 Paths" = *Issachar* is labeled as: *"The Scholar."*

Blessings [from Israel]:

Genesis 49:14-15

14 Issachar is a strong donkey, lying down between the sheepfolds. 15 He saw that his resting place was good and that his land was pleasant, so he bent his shoulder to the burden and submitted to labor as a servant.

Genesis 30:19-20
English translation (King James Version)

19 And Leah conceived again, and bare Jacob the sixth son. 20 And Leah said, God hath endued me with a good *dowry*; now will my husband *dwell with me*, because I have born him six sons: and she called his name *Zebulun*.

Note: The word translated as: *"dowry"* = * זבד (ZBD) <H2065>
The word translated as: *"dwell with me"* = * יזבלני (YZBLNY) <H2082>

Zebulun, זבלון (ZBLVN) <H2074>

Nourishment(Food) + Blueprint(Plan) + Learn/Teach + Interaction [held back] + Seeds [Generations]

1 - Linear Construct (ZB+LV+N)

* (ZB) *Nourishment/Food + Blueprint/Plan*

Other variants or words built from (ZB):

** זבד (ZBD) <H2064> as: *to endow, bestow, to confer*
— used once in Genesis 30:20 <actually (ZBDNY) ="has endowed">

** זבד (ZBD) <H2065> as: *a gift, endowment, dowry*
— used once in Genesis 30:20 <actually (ZBD) ="[with] endowment">

** זבד (ZBD) *<H2066>* a Name: *Zabad* [meaning: *he endows/giver*]
— used eight times in Chronicles and Ezra

Other variant words as: *<holding back>* (V) of the (ZB) = (ZBV)

** זבוב (ZBVB) *<H2070>* as: *a fly*
— used once in Ecclesiastes 10:1 and once in Isaiah 7:18

> **Note:** The Hebrew word *"zebub"* refers to a fly, specifically a type of flying insect. In the biblical context, it is often associated with pestilence and decay, symbolizing nuisance and corruption. The term is used metaphorically to describe the presence of evil or demonic influence, as seen in the name *"Beelzebub,"* which is translated as: *"lord of the flies."* [The name was used to refer to a Philistine god, later adopted in Jewish and Christian texts to denote a prince of demons.]
> In ancient Near Eastern cultures, flies were common pests, often associated with filth and disease. They were seen as carriers of decay and were sometimes linked to demonic activity.

** זבול (ZBVL) *<H2073>* as: *a residence | exalted, elevation, lofty abode, height, habitation, dwell, in, dwelling*

+ * (LV) *Learning/Teaching + [held back]* *"lacking lessons learned"*

+ * (N) *"Seed"/Potential* or the *potential* from *ignorance*

The idea of a *behavior* [or *situation*] *that may feel* [like *a gift*] and *as being justified [legally]*, but is still *ignorant, arrogant, unwise,* or just *having bad outcome for others.*

> Concept of [something] that's *established* as *being* *"one-sided"* or just *benefiting "one side."*

Another *Linear Construct* (Z+BLV+N)

* (Z) *Nourishment(Food)*

+ * בלו (BLV) *<H1093>* as: *excise | wearing out, decay, consumption | translated as: "tribute/custom"* — used in Ezra 4:13, 4:20, 7:24

Note: Also corresponds to a root word בלה (BLH) *<H1086>* as: *to become old, wear out* — used 17 times linked to various books from [Genesis, Deuteronomy, Joshua, Chronicles, Ezra, Nehemiah, Job, Psalms, Isaiah, Lamentations] with half of these actually being the (BLV).

Symbolically, the stage of "*Food*" is about *to turn [rotten* or *decaying].*

+ * (N) *"Seed"/Potential* or the *potential* from *worn-out [old] ways*

Symbolically, the (Z) is the "*Mattock*" Glyph [aka: a *hoe* or *hand* "*plow*"]. Ultimately, it's the *tool of the farmer,* then *ending* with the (N) "*Seed*" Glyph = The process of *Sowing(Planting) the Seed,* which infers the idea of *hard work that brings forth the crops[food].*

(Z) as the *Means of Production* — the *Worker*
+ (B) the "Blueprint"/*Plan*

versus

(V) *<holding back>* + (N) the "Seed"/*Potential*

The idea of the *Businessman* as: (V) *<holding back>* the *worker* and *<bringing forth>* the (N) *potential* — as the one who doesn't do the work (*planting* or *harvesting* crops), but *takes/possesses* the *Potential/* "*Seeds*".

Concept of *taking* or *getting [something]* by *not putting* in the *actual hard work.*

Note: Additionally, the (ZB) is *the hard work of the process of growing the food* and *establishing the plan for the continued process.* Then the (ZBL) is *the learning* or *improvements from* or *building off of the process.*

versus

(ZBLV) as *being [held back]* the idea of "*If it ain't broke, don't fix it*" and the "*Brother*" to the idea of *keeping* the "*Status Quo.*"

{A connection to the "*Existing state of Affairs.*"}

(ZBLVN) as the *potential* [from *how things have been*] or the *continuing cycle of what has always been,*

versus

Finding new ways or *practices to do [things],* which can include *making improvements.*

---

2 - *Dimensional Construct* (ZN →BLV)

* **ﬡﬨ (ZN)** <H2177> translated as: *nourished, sort, kind*
— used in 2 Chronicles 16:14, Psalm 144:13

* **ﬡﬨ (ZN)** <H2178> translated as: *nourished, sort, kind*
— used in Daniel 3:5,7,10,15 — actually (ZNY) and referring to: *music*

→ * בלו (BLV) <H1093> as: excise | wearing out, decay, consumption | translated as: "tribute/custom" — used in Ezra 4:13, 4:20, 7:24

Concept of *[something]* similar in kind *[like-minded]* and that *generates a tradition/custom*

The idea of *establishing* [or *doing*] a *routine.*
Additionally, as the idea of *"going through the motions."*

3 - *Reflective Construct* (NVLBZ)

* (NV) **Note:** *not a biblical Hebrew word!?*

(N) *"Seed"* + (V) *[held back]*

{As the stage before the *Seeds are ready [for planting]*}

Other variants or words built from (NV):

** נוב (NVB) <H5107-8> as: *"to bear fruit"*

** נוד (NVD) <H5110-3> as: *"to wander, wanderer"*

Symbolically, the pre-stage moment [before the *purpose is revealed* or the *destination is known*]

{An earlier stage, but *coming from a cycled event/process.*}

+ * לב (LB) <H3820-1> as: *the heart, the feelings* | *the will, the intellect* | *the "inner man"*

— used in Genesis 8:21 (LB) *"heart"* [of Mankind] and connected to the *wickedness* or *the "selfish"* behavior [of Mankind] -versus- the (LBV) *heart* [of (YHVH)'s], but as *[held back]* version.

+ * (Z) *Nourishment(Food)*

The idea of *what feeds or nourishes the <thoughts/ideas>* *connection to the desire of feelings [emotions].*

Symbolically, ideas like: *"Passions drive [us] to seek fulfillment"* or *"What the heart wants the heart wants."*

Note: A fine line between being a *positive* or *negative* *behavior* or *thought process.*

Concept of *[something] desired,* and *[a person's] willingness* to get it *["Intentionally"* versus *"Falling into a routine"].*

4 - Meaning Construct

Concept of *"Working within* the *Rule, Ruler, or Ruling..."*

The idea of being a *"servant of,"* and as *"clever benefiting."*

{or as *being a "Clever" Benefactor [of the system]*}

[Aka: as *"Finding a way to work the system"*]

Also, there's a connection to...

The idea of *Nobles of [a King]* | *"Elites,"* etc...

Concept of being a *"Puppet Master"*

Note: As the idea of a *Broker* [as: the *middle man*] rather than the *workers* themselves!!! Symbolically, *owning* the *Seeds,* rather than *working the land* or *sowing the seed* (in relation to *benefiting* from the *potential outcome* of the *planting, growing,* and *harvest* of them) — to take the *potential value* [as: *seed*] of something others will put in the effort.

Kabbalah "12 Paths" = *Zebulun* is labeled as: *"The Businessman."*

Blessings [from Israel]:

Genesis 49:13

13 Zebulun shall dwell by the seashore and become a harbor for ships; his border shall extend to Sidon.

Genesis 30:21

English translation (King James Version)

21 And afterwards she bare a daughter, and called her name *Dinah.*

Dinah, דינה (DYNH) <H1783>

Path + Effort + Seeds + Revealing

1 - Linear Construct (DYNH)

* די (DY) <H1767> as: *enough, sufficiency, according to the abundance of* — used in Exodus, Leviticus, and Deuteronomy

* **דִּי** (DY) *<H1767>* as: *that, of | forasmuch, who, now when, which*
— used in Ezra, Jeremiah, and Daniel

Other variants or words built from (DY):

** **דִּיג** (DYG) *<H1770>* as: *to fish, to catch fish*

** **דַּיָּג** (DYG) *<H1771>* as: *fisherman*

Path (or *direction*) + *Effort(s)* + [a person] *makes <brings forth> + Gathering*

The idea of *selecting (a set way)* within/from *limitless possibilities.*

— as related to *Dan,* * **דִּין** (DYN) *<H1777>* as: *a straight course, sail direct | to judge, contend, plead*

+ * **נֹה** (NH) *<H5089>* as: *lamentation | wailing, eminence* (of people), *famous* and *respected*, especially in a particular [profession], *distinction* | a position of *prominence* or *superiority*

Other variants or words built from (NH):

** **חנה** (ChNH) *<H2583>* as: *"to encamp, to pitch tents, to dwell, to rest"*

The ideas of *where one takes a stand, plants one's feet,* or *standing your ground,* etc…

> Concept of *the "settling" [of "self"]*

Symbolically, as: *"know thy self."*

Note: Essentially, it's asking an internal question like: *"What is enough?* [What will satisfy the *urges* or *desires* in *life* or *life's experiences*?].

The idea of *"when to stop"* [to *rest* or *rejuvenate*].

Symbolically, this represents the *"Sabbath" [Shabbat] = "The Day of Rest."*

2 - *Dimensional Construct* (DH →YN)

* (DH) **Note:** *not a biblical Hebrew word!?*   *Path + Revealing/Revelation*

Other variants or words built from (DH):

** **דהב** (DHB) *<H1722>* as: *"gold"*

Symbolically, as *"leading to [something] value* or *substance."*

The idea of *the hard/difficult/challenging [path]* brings about *greater outcome/value/worth.*

> ### Concept of *making a choice*
> [*Aiming* to make the *desired* or *ideal path* to take]

→ * יּנ (YN) *<H3238>* as: *to rage, be violent, to suppress, to maltreat*

> ### Concept of *"my way or the highway"*

The idea of *getting mad at/about others* **not**
doing things the same way as yourself.

3 - *Reflective Construct* (HNYD)

* הנ (HN) *<H2004>* as: *they* | translated as: *in which, therein, withal*
— used in Genesis, Exodus, Leviticus, Numbers, Jeremiah (B/M/K+HN)

* הנ (HN) *<H2005>* as: *lo!, Behold* | *even, good, here, if, look, see,*
since, though — used over 300 times in Genesis, Exodus, Leviticus,
Numbers, Deuteronomy, Joshua, Samuel, Kings, Chronicles, Ezra, Job as
(HN), (HNM), (HNNY), (HNNV), (HNV), (HNK), (HNKH)

* הנ (HN) *<H2006>* as, lo!, there, less, whether, but, if
— used in Ezra, Daniel as (HN), (LHN) / *[Aramaic]*

Revelation/Revealing + Seed[Potential] = "The *revealing* of the *potential*"

The idea of *"If"* or of a *"wishing/hoping of [something]."*

+ * יד (YD) *<H3027>* as: *a hand*
— used over 1600 times in Genesis, Exodus, Leviticus, Numbers,
Deuteronomy as: (YDN), (MYDK), (YDYNN), (BYDKM), (MYD),
(BYDK), (YDY), (YDV),

+ * יד (YD) *<H3028>* as: *a hand* | *attempts, hands, power*
— used in Ezra, Daniel as: (BYDHM), (BYD), (YDH), (BYDK),
(BYDYN), (YDY), (YDK), (BYDH) / *[Aramaic]*

Effort <brings forth> Path[Way]

The idea of *"How things are done"* or *"The way things are done"*
[by someone or *some group of people].*

> ### Concept of *"If"* + *"Way"*
> *"The How* or *Why"* things are being done

The idea of *questioning the way of things.*

> **Note:** An interesting line, which uses both of these words [separately].
>
> **Genesis 3:22**
>
> And the LORD God said, *Behold* (HN), the man is become as one of us, to know good and evil: and now, lest he put forth his *hand* (YDV), and take also of the tree of life, and eat, and live for ever.

4 - Meaning Construct

> Concept of *"what people will believe in"*
> [also as: *Hope(s)* and even *Dreams*]

Note: The concept of a *"Daughter"* is/has the *potential of Mother* (what will *potentially give birth* to *[unknown, as value* or *not value]* to come from it....)

Additionally, the 7th child [as: *daughter*] to *Leah* (self-serving), and representing: *The Faiths <of Man>* = *Religions*.

> **Note:** Connection to Genesis 6:1-3 with the Noah story, Men multiply on Earth, daughters are born, and the Sons of God take as wives, and the Lord said My spirit shall not always *strive* (YDVN) with man.
>
> As well as related to Rachel's son, *Dan* (DN) but as, an *Effort* (Y) born with the (DN) *<bringing forth>* (H) *Revelation/Revealing*.

> **Note:** The Greeks called them: *Fates*, or *Moirai* | The word: *Moirai*, also spelled *Moirae* or *Mœræ*, comes from Ancient Greek: μοῖρα, which means *"lots, destinies, apportioners."* It also means a *portion* or a *lot* of the whole. They were the *personifications of destiny*: three sisters, *Clotho, Lachesis,* and *Atropos*.
>
> Additionally, connected [other cultures and myths] to *Orion's belt* as three (3) sisters or three (3) kings versus the seven (7) sisters [both making up the constellation of *Orion* [7 stars], and also *Pleiades* [aka: the seven (7) sisters].

> **Note:** A connection to **"daughter(s)"** and **"seven"**.

Genesis 29:16-18
English translation (King James Version)

16 And Laban had two daughters: the name of the elder was *Leah*, and the name of the younger was *Rachel*.

17 *Leah* was tender eyed; but *Rachel* was beautiful and well favoured.

18 And Jacob loved Rachel; and said, I will serve thee *seven* years for Rachel thy younger daughter.

Note: Described as: *"beautiful"* (YPT) + *well favoured* (MRAH)

The Hebrew is יפה (YPT) *"beautiful"* + תאר (TAR) *"form"*
ריפה (V+YPT) *and "beautiful"* + מראה (MRAH) *"appearance"*

The use of the word *"beautiful"* (YPT) is * יפה <H3303> as: *fair, beautiful, pleasant, handsome, sleek, well, fitting, comely* → generally inferring how *someone* or *something* perceives *someone* or *something* else [in an *appealing* or *attractive way*].

The use of the word *"form"* (TAR) is * תאר <H8389> as: *form | outline (figure of appearance)* — used in Genesis, Judges, Samuel, Kings, Esther, Isaiah, Jeremiah, Lamentations // * תאר <H8388> as: *drawn, marked out, delineate, extend | curved* — used in Joshua, Isaiah

The use of the word *"appearance"* (MRAH) is * מראה <H4758> as: *sight, to look upon, appears, see/sight | face*

The idea of *having both a beautiful* and *pleasant figure* and *face*.

Symbolically, it could represent *the structure* and *expression* of *meaning* that is *beautiful* and *pleasant*. {*Meaning:* Inferring that being *"open-minded* and *the [outputs] coming out of it"* is *beautiful* and *pleasant*.}

Genesis 30:22
English translation (King James Version)
And God remembered *Rachel*, and God hearkened to her, and opened her *womb*.

Wife of Jacob [2nd Wife]
Rachel, רחל (RChL) <H7354>
Mind of man + Branching off (Diversity/Separating) + Learning/Teach

1 - Linear Construct (RChL)

* רחל (RChL) <H7353> as: *ewe/[female] sheep* {root meaning *to journey*} — used 4 times in Genesis 31:38 (RChLYK), 32:14 (RChLYM), Songs 6:6 (HRChLYM), Isaiah 53:7 (KRChL)   Word Origin: From an unused root meaning *to journey* [as *a ewe that is a good traveler*].

The idea of *sheep grazing,* and also *chewing down the grass across the plains/range* [as: *expanding the area as they graze*].

Another *Linear Construct* (RCh+L)

* (RCh) **Note:** *not a biblical Hebrew word!?*

> *Mind of man + Branching off (Diversity/Separating)*

Other variants or words built from (RCh):

** רחה (RChH) *<H7347>* as: *a mill-stone | hand-mill*
— used 5 times in Exodus (HRChYM), (BRChYM), (RChYM)

<Seems to be more directly referring to the bottom stone, which spreads out the materials as they are being ground down.>

Note: *Millstone:* [the stone tooling] used to grind down grains into flour [using stones to grind food is one of the oldest labors]. The practice had many uses: for grinding specific types of starchy nuts, ochres (earth-based pigments) for artwork, plant fibers for string, or plants for use in medicine.

The idea of *grinding a singular object down* and *across a broader/expanded area.*

Concept of *working out* (or *chipping away* and *grinding down*) *one thing* into a *useful another thing*

** רחב (RChB) *<H7337-41>* as: *to broaden | to be wide, to be spacious, to enlarge //* translated as: *has made room, enlarge/extends, speaks boldly.*

** רחם (RChM) *<H7355>* as: *to have compassion, to show mercy, to love deeply |* Meaning: *to fondle, to love, to be compassionate.*

** רחמה (RChMH) *<H7358>* "*womb*"

2 - *Dimensional Construct* (RL →Ch)

> *Mind of man + Learning/Lessons → gives birth to "Diversity/Branching"*

* (RL) **Note:** *not a biblical Hebrew word!?* {nor any words with RL+}

Other variants or words built from (R_L):

** רכל (RKL) *<H7402>* as: *to go about, to trade, to peddle, to slander | to travel (for trading) //* translated as: *merchants*

** רגל (RGL) *<H7270>* as: *to walk along, to go on foot | to spy | to be a tale-bearer | to slander*

** רעל (RaL) *<H7477>* as: *to reel, to brandish | to be made to quiver or shake [terribly shake]*

> **Note:** The (RL) infers *[things] with the capability of becoming harmful [to others]* or *lacking "divine" value.*

3 - *Reflective Construct* (LCh+R)

* לח (LCh) <H3892> as: *fresh, unused, undried | moist, green*

* לח (LCh) <H3893> as: *freshness, vigor | moisture* — translated as: *[his] natural force*

+ * (R) *Mind of man*

> Concept of *Fresh thoughts [New ideas]*

The idea of *"green grass" thinking,* or maybe leading to the phrase: *"the grass is always greener,"* [and even as the *fine line between the two ideas*].

4 - *Meaning Construct*

> Concept of *"an open mind brings forth expanded capabilities"*

The idea of *seeing the results [of others].*

... as multiple things are *being worked down (worked out) |* and maybe even the *process* or *condition of being under pressure* [implying a building of *strength of character* — as *someone carrying a heavy burden* and *being worn down.*

Symbolically, representing [Rachel] *expanding the mind beyond* [Leah] *selfish needs.* {*"wrestled with sister"* representing Leah's *"feeling entitled"*}

Genesis 30:23
English translation (King James Version)
And she conceived, and bare a son; and said, God hath *taken away* (ASP) my *reproach* (ChRPTY):

* אסף (ASP) <H622> as: *taken away | also means: "gathered"*

* חרפתי (ChRPTY) <H2781> as: *"reproach"*
— Definition of *"reproach"* (express *disapproval* or *disappointment*).

Note: (ChR) reflective (RCh) [from *Rachel*] and *Effort from,* rather than *Effort to bring* (PT) [from *Japheth* (YPT) as: *seduce/enlarge*]

The idea of *"what to take away [from the mistakes of the past* or *mistakes one makes] — learn from mistakes."*

Genesis 30:24

English translation (King James Version)

And she called his name *Joseph*; and said, The LORD shall add to me another son.

Joseph, יוסף (YVSP) <*H3130*>

Effort + [held back] Tethering (Interaction) +
Thorn (suffering-hate/protected) + Spoken

Meaning: *"He increases"*

1 - *Linear Construct* (YV+S+P)

* (YV) *Effort + Tethering* <See page 79-80 for full details>

— representing *[Effort to Conceive = The idea of Sexual Intercourse]*, as the *act* of <*bringing forth*> a *tethering* [as the *making* a *connection* to the *Earthly(Physical) realm]*.

> **Note:** Also, symbolic of the idea of *"influencing to grow,"* but capable of leading into [something] later | connecting to ideas like: *frustrations, stubbornness, ignorance, arrogance, etc...*

+ * (S) *The "Thorn"* + * (P) *The "Mouth"/[Speaking/Speech]*

> Concept of *thorny ("tough love") speech* or *speaking*

The introduction of *"New" ideas/beliefs* that are *hard to grasp.*

> **Note:** The key concepts are *"Communication"* and also *"Suffering."*
>
> The idea of *as a part of communication,* there's also *making sacrifices.*
>
> > Concept of *Negotiating*
>
> The idea of the *"Thorn"* [as a duality].
>
> *"Red" Rose* = a *bloody version*
> representing, *peace through/(after) conquering.*
>
> *"White" Lily* = a *pure/purity version*
> representing, *peace through/(after) negotiating.*
>
> **Note:** The idea of the *win-win* or *lose-lose* outcome; *simply finding a balance* that works where both parties are represented [getting a balanced outcome is very challenging: *"thorny aspect."*]

Another *Linear Construct* (Y+V+SP)

* **(Y)** *Effort* + **(V)** *[held back] Interaction with..*

+ * **סַ֫ף** (SP) <H5592> as: *a vestibule, a dish | threshold, door-frame, sill, basin, goblet //* translated as: *is in the basin/cups/bowls.*
— used in Exodus 12:22 (BSP) as: *basin/bowl*; Judges 19:27 (HSP) as: *on the threshold [of a doorway]*; 2 Samuel 17:28 (SPVT) as: *basins*; Kings 7:50 (HSPVT) as: *cups/bowls*.

> ### Concept of *Trying to Influence*
> *<Influencing/manipulating [something] that is in a bowl/cup>*

The idea of *influencing a particular idea, a way of doing something,* or *even the natural order/process.*

Note: The prefix (YV) is inferring the *"effortless" act of doing* or *convincing others to do [something].*

> Symbolically, this could imply the idea of a *cupbearer.*
>
> **Note:** Relates to a similar narrative/[pattern] to Sargon of Akkad, beginning as a cupbearer to the Ur-Zababa of Kish [Sumerian King].

2 - *Dimensional Construct* (YP →VS)

* **(YP)** *Effort + Mouth(speak)*

→ * **(V)** *[held back] Interaction "Tethered" to...*
+ **(S)** *The "Thorn" (*or *the risk of being either a soft/hard thorn)*

The idea of the *effort to speak out,* when there is *risk involved (looming).*

> Concept of *speaking out when it's risky to do so.*

Note: Also, maybe inferring the *effort to develop more advanced[complex] oral traditions.*

Another *Dimensional Construct* (YSP →V)

* **יֹסֶף** (YSP) <H3254-5> as: *to add, augment, increase, do again, to join*
+ but as... →**(V)** *Interaction within.*

The idea of an *interaction within [something* that *already repeats* or *is a common occurrence].*

3 - Reflective Construct (PSVY)

* כֶּ (PS) <H6446> as *a long and sleeved tunic | coat, piece, part*

— in Genesis 37:3 as (PSYM) translated as: *him a varicolored* or
(many) colors — as the *tunic worn* by *Joseph.*

+ * (VY) *"Conception-Birthing"* <See page 79-80 for full details>

— representing *[Conceived and Born]* = Symbolically, *"being Born"* or
"Giving Birth." The idea of *the initial moment of being inspired.*

Symbolically, the *clothes make the man* [*what one wears presents* or
reflects what one does] + (V) *[held back] Interaction* + (Y) *Effort.*

The idea of <*holding back*> *the vastness of abilities/efforts,* but
also implies *focusing on one of many.*

> Concept of *being* a *polymath* or a *Renaissance man*

4 - Meaning Construct

> Concept of *"born from an open mind"* is *new ideas/beliefs,*
> but this is also the *"Change is hard"* [as being like: *thorns*].

Note: The *origins* or *personification* of the *"Suffering Servant."*

While the *"**Suffering Servant** passage"* is commonly associated
with Isaiah 53 [actually begins at the end of Isaiah 52].

It's also the fourth time Isaiah speaks of a servant (see Isaiah 42,
49, and 50). {This passage is part of a larger whole.}

> Kabbalah "12 Paths" = *Joseph* is labeled as: *"The Sufferer."*

Blessings [from Israel]:
Genesis 49:22-26
22 Joseph is a fruitful vine — a fruitful vine by a spring, whose
branches scale the wall.
23 The archers attacked him with bitterness; they aimed at him in hostility.
24 Yet he steadied his bow, and his strong arms were tempered by the
hands of the Mighty One of Jacob, in the name of the Shepherd, the
Rock of Israel,

25 by the God of your father who helps you, and by the Almighty who blesses you, with blessings of the heavens above, with blessings of the depths below, with blessings of the breasts and womb.

26 The blessings of your father have surpassed the blessings of the ancient mountains and the bounty of the everlasting hills. May they rest on the head of Joseph, on the brow of the prince of his brothers.

Note: * (YV) as: *[something]* that was *birthed first* or *before conception* = The idea of *"being born of a virgin"* (reflected *birth* or to *set up bringing forth* rather than *giving birth*).

** *Jesus* ישוע (YShVa) | Symbolically, (Sh) *aspects of Creation* *<born within>* the (YV) {as: *"being born of a virgin"*}

* (YV) + * (S) *The "Thorn"*

Note: The crown of *"Thorns"* was placed on *Jesus's head* at the *crucifixion*.

Genesis 30:25
English translation (King James Version)

And it came to pass, when Rachel had born Joseph, that Jacob said unto Laban, Send me away, that I may go unto mine own place, and to my country.

And it came to pass, ויהי (VYHY) *<H1961>* Symbolically, represents: The idea of the *birth of realization* of an *[enlightened] understanding*. Symbolically, as: *"Let there be Light"* [from "in the beginning" section].

when, כאשר (K+AShR) *<H834>* Symbolically, represents: The idea of *"having a wisdom* [or *divine thought]."*

had borne, ילדה (YLDH) *<H3205>* Symbolically, represents: The idea of *"learning a way to do [something]."*

Rachel, רחל (RChL) *<H7354>* Symbolically, represents: The idea of *"expanding the mind."*

'ēt, את (AT) *<H853>* *Mind of God + Weaving together* [All is was/is/will be]

Joseph, יוסף (YVSP) *<H3130>* Symbolically, represents: The introduction of *"New"* ideas/beliefs.

> **Note:** Before the last son's birth is described, there's a lot of narration [Genesis 30-34], as well as Jacob getting a name change.

Genesis 35:10
English translation (King James Version)

And God said unto him, Thy name is Jacob: thy name shall not be called any more Jacob, but *Israel* shall be thy name: and he called his name *Israel*.

Israel, ישראל (YShRAL) *‹H›*

Efforts + Aspect of Creation + Mind of Man + Mind of God + Teachings

1 - Linear Construct (YShR+AL)

* ישר (YShR) *‹H3474-7›* as: *to be straight, right, level, upright, just, lawful, smoothed out*

+ * אל (AL) *‹H410›* "El" (singular) as: *"god, god-like one, mighty one"*
Mind of God + Learn/Teach = "Strong Understanding"

> Concept of *having "level"* or *"balanced" [strong] understanding*

The idea of *inferring a person* with *moral traits* will *promote [a higher, elevated, Godly] understanding.*

Another Linear Construct (YSh+R+AL)

* יש (YSh) *‹H3426›* as: *being, existence, substance | there is or are*
Efforts to ‹bring forth› the Creation.

The idea of *human behavior is reflected within Nature* [as the *cycling events* or *patterns of Creation*].
{*The How we are!*} [as the *ongoing movement of "Creation"*].

+ * (R) *Mind of Man [how mankind thinks]*

+ * (AL) *Mind of Man + Teaching/Learning = God's Lessons*

> Concept of *mankind's existence,* and *how the environment* we are in *affects* us.

2 - *Dimensional Construct* (YSh+AL →R)

Symbolically, this is like the *balance of nature,* but as the *balancing of man's mind* to *God's mind,* as the "*Advancing Understanding [God's Lessons],*" which also represents *moving from the old ways to new ways.*

> **Note:** The (YSh) represents the idea of "*Scientific proofs*" →
> The balancing of (R) *Mind of Man* ← the (AL) *God's Lessons*
> {*Strong Understanding* or "*Learning the Hard Way*"}
>
> Ultimately, this is the state of *being mentally aligned [balanced]* -or- "*one*" with God's Creation!

3 - *Reflective Construct* (LA+RSh+Y)

* לֹא (LA) <*H2524*> as: "*not, No*"

> The idea of *having a lack of understanding.*

+ * (RSh) **Note:** *not a biblical Hebrew word!?*

> *Mind of Man + aspects of Creation [Destruction]*

Other variants or words built from (RSh):

** רשׁשׁ (RShSh) <*H7567*> as: *to demolish | to beat down, shatter*

** רשׁף (RShP) <*H7565*> as: *plague, burning heat [fever], arrows (flaming, flashes), bolts of lightning/hot thunderbolts, flashes [of fire], a live coal (hot, burning heat).*

** רשׁעה (RShaH) <*H7564*> as: *wickedness, guilt, fault, wrong*

> The idea of *lacking the understanding of what doing the wrong thing really means,* or *not understanding the consequences of doing the wrong thing.*

4 - *Meaning Construct*

> Concept of *being "Honest* or *Truthful" [with oneself]*
> {Referring to *how mankind exists within Creation*
> and *how it affects everything else within it.*}

Note: The transition from [Jacob] ="*Wrestling with God*" as "*Not fully understanding God, but making the attempt to*" → to the alignment of [Enoch/Noah] "*Finding Balance*" = "*Walking with God,*" and leading to [Israel] = "*A proper way to understand God* [or *God's Lessons*]."

> **Note:** The first son after Jacob becomes Israel, which includes the mother [Rachel] dying during childbirth [Genesis 35:16-18].

Genesis 35:18
English translation (King James Version)

And it came to pass, as her soul was in departing, (for she died) that she called his name *Benoni*: but his father called him *Benjamin*.

Ben-oni, בֶּן־אוֹנִי (BN-AVNY) <H1126>

Blueprint(Plan) + Seed(Potential) →
Mind of God [held back] Seed(Potential) + Effort

Note: The mother's [Rachel's] name for him *<as she died in hard labor>* | Meaning: *"Son of my sorrow"*

Linear Construct (BN-AVNY)

* בֶּן (BN) <H1121> translated as: *Son [Offspring]*

  *"Plan" + "Potential" = **Planning** and **Potential** [as: Outcome/Actions]*

+ * אוֹנִי (AVNY) <H205> translated as: *"trouble, sorrow, affliction, misfortune,* and even as: *"iniquity, wickedness, wrongdoers"*

  The *<holding back>* the Mind of God (AV) = *"Godless Ways"*
  + will *<bring forth>* (NY) = *wailing/tears [of sadness]*

---

* אוֹ (AV) <H176> translated as: *"or"* | *at the least, whether* | *if, rather* — connected to: *desire* [and to **making a choice** or **option(s)**].

+ * נִי (NY) <H5204> translated as: *wailing* | *lamentation*.
  Also, connected to denote *"a river or a flowing body of water."*
  — although not actually used as a two-letter word, and is linked to (BNYHM) and used only once in Ezekiel 27:32 as: *[their] wailing.*

Another *Linear Construct* (AVN+Y)

* The (V) *interaction within* the (AN) as representing "Concept of Ancient Ways" | "Primal nature" or "Animal impulses," regarding Intentions [also as: "urges"]. <see page 208-209>

  + * (Y) as the *Efforts <brought forth>* from it

Note: The relationship to the (N) *"Seed"/Potential* from (BN) *Plan(s)* to the (NY) *"Seed's" Effort* [begins to *sprout*]. The representation of a transitional state.

Examples:

Symbolically, the connection of *Mental States:*
Mother/Eve [Emotional] to Father/Adam [Rational state].

Mother *gives birth [birthing pains]* {*"suffering" to birth forth a child*}, but then *spoils/protects* the *toddler;* then the Father *pushes/hardens their child* to *adulthood* [as: an introduction to the *"suffering"*].

Note: There are descriptions and comparisons to God's relationship to mankind in this way: Mankind becoming the *wife* to God; Daughters [of men] being *married* to Sons [of God]; and comparing the coming of the *Messianic times* as *birthing pains*, etc...

This transition is also like: *"Old ways"* to *"New ways"* | *"Old gods"* to *"New gods"* | *Polytheism* to *Monotheism* [*"Oneness of God"*] | and even the idea of *Conservative* or *Progressive/Liberal* as: [*Right* or *Left*].

Note: The father's [Israel's] name for him
| Meaning: *"Son of [the] Right hand"*

Benjamin, בנימיו (BNYMYV) <H1144>

Blueprint/Plan + Seed(Generations) + Effort + Life/Truth + Effort + [held back]

1 - Linear Construct (BN+YMYV)

* בנ (BN) <H1121> translated as: *Son [Offspring]*

+ * (YMY)   **Note:** *not a biblical Hebrew word!?*
The idea of the *right hand* = [the *greatness/strength/power* of...]

+ * (V) *[held back]*

Other variants or words built from (YMY):

** ימימה (YMYMH) <H3224> Name: *Jemimah* // derived from the root (YMYN) <H3225> meaning: *right hand* or *south* | often associated with *direction* or *favor*.

** יָמִין (YMYN) <H3225> as: *right hand* or *south*

— used in Genesis 48:13 And Joseph took them both, Ephraim in his *right hand* (BYMYNV) towards Israel's left hand, and Manasseh in his left hand toward Israel's *right hand* (MYMYN), and brought them near unto him. 14 And Israel stretched out his *right hand* (YMYNV), and laid it upon Ephraim's head, who was the younger, and his left hand upon Manasseh's head, guiding his hands wittingly; for Manasseh was the firstborn. [also as: (HYMYN),(MYMYN),(YMYNK)]

Note: The use of the (V) as a suffix or as to hold back — in this case, as the right (which is the hand that strikes with a *weapon* or *violence in general*) is used <u>not</u> in a *violent way* or as *being [held back].*

Symbolically, the * (YM) *Effort + Life/Truth = The "Flowing River"* or *"The ebb and flow of the waves"* = Concept of *Time*

+ * (MY) *Life/Truth + Effort = The Path of Life* or *moments of Time.*

= * (YMY) as the visual imagery of: *the waves crashing into the shore* or *on the rocks [at the cliff edge]* or *the eroding of the river bank.*

— *but then* (V) *[held back]* or (YV) as: Trying to *Force/Manipulate - Influence [natural order/process].*

---

2 - *Dimensional Construct* (BN+YV →YM)

* (BN) *Plan + Potential*

+ * (YV) Trying to *Force/Manipulate - Influence [natural order/process]*

→ (YM) *The "Flowing River"* = Concept of *Time*

This could infer the idea of *attempting to force events* or *manipulate outcomes* [within *the "Flowing River" = "Time"*].

Another *Dimensional Construct* (B+V →NYMY)

* (B) *Plan* + (V) *[held back]*

+ * נִי (NY) <H5204> translated as: *wailing | lamentation.*

+ * (MY) *The Path of Life* or *moments of Time.*

This could infer the idea that *not making* [or *having*] *a plan* can bring a *wailing/lamentations* within moments of time [in ones life].

3 - Reflective Construct (VYMYNB)

* (VY) *"Conception-Birthing"* <to initially get the *inspiration* for... >

  + * (MY) *Life/Truth* + *<bringing forth>* + *Effort*

    + * נב (NB) *<H5011>* as: *a high place*

    Other variants or words built from (NB):

** נבו (NBV) *<H5015>* as a Name: *Nebo*

— primarily referring to a location associated with *Mount Nebo*, a significant mountain in the biblical narrative.

> **Note:** The name Nebo is also associated with a Babylonian god, *Nabu*, who was linked to *wisdom, writing,* and *prophecy*. A Babylonian deity who presided over learning and letters; corresponds to Greek *Hermes*, Latin *Mercury*, and Egyptian *Thoth*.

Word Origin: Derived from the root: * נבא (NBA) *<H5012-3>* "naba" | meaning: *"to prophesy"* or *"to speak by divine inspiration."*

The idea of the *<conception/birth>* of *living* by *being in a "high place."* [*Elevated/higher morals, etc.*] versus *The reflective: the threat of force*].

4 - Meaning Construct

> Concept of *Moments of Life* getting in the way to *Future planning [preparing for the future]*

The idea of *Planning for the future* is *not being/getting done* because of *Life* or *Living in the moment*.

Additionally, as the idea of *doing wrong* [i.e., *not planning ahead*] for the *sake of living in the present* [which isn't *necessarily bad*].

Kabbalah "12 Paths" = *Benjamin* is labeled as: *"The Ravenous Consumer."*

Blessings [from Israel]:

Genesis 49:27

27 Benjamin is a ravenous wolf; in the morning he devours the prey, in the evening he divides the plunder."

28 These are the tribes of Israel, twelve in all, and this was what their father said to them. He blessed them, and he blessed each one with a suitable blessing.

> **Note:** Joseph's inheritance [from Jacob] is split between his sons.

The Sons of Joseph

Genesis 41:50-52
English translation (King James Version)

50 And unto Joseph were born two sons before the years of famine came, which *Asenath* the daughter of Potipherah priest of On bare unto him.

51 And Joseph called the name of the firstborn *Manasseh*: For God, said he, hath made me forget all my toil, and all my father's house.

52 And the name of the second called he *Ephraim*: For God hath caused me to be fruitful in the land of my affliction.

Joseph's Wife

Asenath, אסנת (ASNT) <H621>

Mind of God + Thorns + Seeds[Potential] + Weaving together

1 - Linear Construct (AS+NT)

* (AS) **Note:** *not a biblical Hebrew word!?*   *Mind of God + Thorns*

The idea of the "*action of thorns*" as the "*protection to the plant*" or the "*harm to others*" [as: both *positive* and *negative* results].

Other variants or words built from (AS):

** אסא (ASA) <H609> as a Name: *Asa* [meaning: *healer* or *injurious*]
Note: The connection to plants is both *medicine* and *poison*.

** אסוכ (ASVK) <H610> as: *anointed* | *an oil-flask*
— used once in 2 Kings 4:2 ...hath not any thing in the house, save a *pot/jar* (ASVK) of oil.

** אסונ (ASVN) <H611> as: *harm, mischief, calamity, disaster*
— used 5 times in Genesis (x3) | Exodus (x2) **Note:** The term is often associated with situations that result in *death* or *serious injury*.

** אסור (ASVR) <H612> as: *bonds, imprisonment, fetter* | translated as: *bonds, chains, bands, prison*
Note: The (ASV) = the negative *result/benefit* of ... "*the idea of hard work will yield a good return [for others by others]*."

** אסים (ASYP) <H614> as: *gathering, harvest, ingathering* | *gathered, a gathering in of crops*

Note: The (AS) = the positive *result/benefit of* … *"the idea of hard work will yield a good return"* — *"fruits of the labor"*

— used 5 times in Exodus 23:16, 34:22 …the Feast *of the Ingathering* (HASP) — describes the Feast after the final (end of the season cycle) "harvest" versus the "first fruits" of the planting season…

— used Exodus 23:16 And the feast of harvest, the firstfruits of thy labours, which thou hast sown in the field: and the feast *of ingathering* (HASYP), which is in the end of the year, when thou hast gathered in thy labours out of the field. — as [something] one has no choice but to do = is the need to eat to survive

** אסף (ASP) *<H622>* as: *to gather, collect, assemble, remove, take away | received, brought //* [as: *the idea of the harvested*]
— used over 200 times in Genesis, Exodus, Leviticus, Numbers, Deuteronomy, Joshua, Judges, Samuel, Kings, Chronicles, Ezra, Job, Isaiah, Jeremiah, Ezekiel, and others.

** אסיר (ASYR) *<H615>* as: *prisoner, captive | bound*
Note: as [something] *one has no choice but to do* = like the *eating/feeding* of the mind, or the idea that *if imprisoned,* the only thing of value to do is to *"think."*

** אסם (ASM) *<H618>* as: *barn, storehouse, granary*
Note: as the place where the *harvested [crops/grains]* are placed to help *"extend"* life/living needs to food, but also the *storage* *["imprisoned"] of "fruits of the labor [or harvest]."*

Generalized idea of *making sacrifices* or *"putting in time* and *making an effort."*

Concept of *"No Pain, No Gain"*

+ * (NT) **Note:** *not a biblical Hebrew word!?* Potential + Weaving together

The idea of the *stitching/weaving together* to eventually have a *"finished"* basket/net/etc…

Other variants or words built from (NT):

** נתח (NTCh) *<H5408>* as: *to dismember, cut [up]/[in pieces], divide*

** נתיב (NTYB) *<H5410>* as: *a track, to trodden with feet, path*

** נתך (NTK) *<H5413>* as: *to flow forth, to liquefy | to pour out* or *forth, drop (or rain), to be melted* or *molten.*

** נתן (NTN) *<H5414>* as: *to give, bestow, grant, permit, to employ, give wages.*

> Concept of the *potential of a step-by-step process,* which
> will eventually *produce a functional object.*

{as the *moment-to-moment* [actions] to *achieve a result*}

2 - *Dimensional Construct* (AT →SN)

* את (AT) <H853> *Mind of God + Weaving together* [All is was/is/will be]

→ * (SN) **Note:** *not a biblical Hebrew word!?* *"Thorny"* + *"Seeds"/Potentials*

Other variants or words built from (SN):

** סנה (SNH) <H5572> as: *a bramble | a bush, thorny bush*

Note: [the "Burning Bush" of Moses] as the (H) *revelation* from
putting in hard work, and (*burning/flame* is the *wisdom* from it).

** סנור (SNVR) <H5575> as *blindness, sudden blindness*

> **Note:** If there is a *weaving together* (T) *born within* this (SN)
> idea, it becomes the word: * סטן (STN) as: *"Satan."*

The idea of a *fine line between* the *function* or *benefit* of *hard
work* and *hard labor* [or *doing hard time* {aka: *prison*}].

3 - *Reflective Construct* (TN+SA)

* תן (TN) <H8565> as a *monster, sea-serpent* [*whale* or *maybe the
extinct dinosaur (the plesiosaurus)*], *a jackal | dragon*

> **Note:** Symbolically, a similar description to the *Chaos "god" [tiamat].*
> Additionally, the suffix (S) + (TN) = (STN) *"Satan"* or *"Thorny Monster,
> Thorny Sea-Serpent, Thorny Dragon, etc."* [And making a connection
> from *Thorn* to *Horn* = creates a visual of the *"horned devil imagery"*].

Other variants or words built from (TN):

** תנה (TNH) <H8566> as: *to present, bargain with, | to hire*

The idea of *bargaining* with the aspect of a *chaos monster*
to *make a deal, especially in employer/employee cases.*

** תנה (TNH) <H8568> as: *a female jackal | dragon*

+ * (SA) **Note:** *not a biblical Hebrew word!?* *"Thorny"* + *[Wrath]*

Other variants or words built from (SA):

** מאה (SAH) <H5429> as: *a seah, certain measure [of grain, flour]*
— probably equal to 1/3 *ephah* {**Note:** maybe a connection to the tradition inferring to: *"a third (1/3) of the angels had fallen"* – and to *flour* and to *bread falling[collapsing]* as a *failure* in the *yeast rising*}.

** סאון (SAVN) <H5430> as: *a military boot, sandal [as protection from mud] | battle*

** סאן (SAN) <H5431> as: *to shoe, a soldier shod | to tread, tramp / warrior*

The idea of *"measured"* or *"limited,"* but with a *"strong"* *motivation/urge* to bring about a *battle* or the *warrior attitude.*
[as a *belligerent, aggressive* type of *demeanor.*]

> Concept of *"Destructive"* without the *"Creation"*

4 - Meaning Construct

> Concept of *putting in challenging efforts* to eventually get a *"positive" result* or *outcome*
> — like: *"putting together a puzzle."*

In addition, the idea of *stored anger,* and the *negative actions* that are influenced by it.
— like: being *"conniving"* [devious/scheming/plotting].

> Symbolically, the *"Mother"* [*as the challenges in life*]
> + the *"Father"* [*as the suffering in(from) life*]
> = the *"Offspring"* [2 sons] representing:
> *"How people react to their suffering."*

Joseph's 1st Son

Manasseh, מנשה (MNShH) <H4519>

Life/Truth + "Seeds"[Potential] + aspects of Creations + Revealing/Revelations

1 - Linear Construct (MNShH)

* מן (MN) <H4478> translated as: *"Manna"* | *a what-ness* — *[the watered seed — as the inspired potential]*

+ * שׂה (ShH) <H7716> as: *member of the flock | lamb, sheep, goat, young sheep, young goat*

> Manna [inspired potentials] + the members of a flock | lamb

Symbolically, the like the *Manna* [that which *falls from Heaven*], will *<bring forth>* the *Lamb* {a connection to the *"Sacrificial Lamb"* tradition}.

> Concept of the *Lamb [of God]*

The idea of *people* who *bring inspiration [inspired" people].*

Other variants or words built from (ShH):

** שׂהד (ShHD) as: *witness*

> *Lamb* (ShH) that *<brings forth>* the (D) *Path* or *the way*
>
> Symbolically, as *Jesus's Path* or *Way*

> **Note:** The *two witnesses* narrative found in Revelation 11:3-12.
> Symbolically, representing these *two brothers* as:
> *Lamb [of God]* and *Lion [of God]*

> Concept of *[something] that will bring inspiration*
> [within the group/tribe/nation]

2 - Dimensional Construct (MH →NSh)

* (MH) <H4100-4101> translated as: *what?* [as a questioning]

> *Life/Truth + Revealing/Revelation*

The idea of *"What Life or Truth can Reveal."*

+ * (NSh) **Note:** *not a biblical Hebrew word!?*

"Seeds"/[Potential] + aspects of Creations

Infers a general idea of *"Force,"* but also as the *balance of "the pressure"* or [the *balance of nature*].

{From *God* (as *Creator*) | The *potential* of *"Forces of Creation/[Nature]"*}

Other variants or words built from (NSh):

** נשא (NShA) *<H5375>* as: *to lift, bear up, carry, take | to be lifted up, carried away*

— used in Genesis 4:13 And Cain said unto the LORD, My punishment is greater than I can *bear* (MNShA).

— used in Genesis 13:6 And the land was not able to *bear* (NShA) them, that they might dwell together: for their substance was great, so that they could not dwell together. [Referring to the combination of Lot's *flocks, herds,* and *tents* being added in with Abram's *animals* and *people.*

The idea that the *balance* between *mankind/animals* and the *land* was *off balance,* or the land was *too pressured* [as: *not enough natural resources to sustain*].

The general idea of *"Force"* that *<brings forth>* the (A) {usually as a negative effect of meaning [as: *wrath*]}.

Symbolically, as the *"Pressure"* or as both *carrying a heavy weight* or the *burden of it.*

** נשב (NShB) *<H5380>* as: *to blow, disperse*

The idea of *"Force"* that *<brings forth>* the (B) *Plan*

Symbolically, as the *Wind/Air* or as *God's Breath.*

Note: The connection to the *mouth,* and as the idea of *"Speaking Creation into existence"*) = the *Force [of God's "Plan" of Creation/Creation].*

** נשג (NShG) *<H5381>* as: *to reach, overtake, take hold upon*

3 - *Reflective Construct* (HShNM)

* (HSh) **Note:** *not a biblical Hebrew word!?*   *Revealing + Creation*

{The prefix to words like: *Hashem, Heaven,* the *Sixth* [day]}

+ * (NM) **Note:** *not a biblical Hebrew word!?* *"Seeds"[Potential] + Life/Truth*

Other variants or words built from (NSh):

** נמל (NML) *<H5243>* as: *to become clipped, circumcised*

Symbolically, as a *pre-stage* (or *preparation*) is to be *circumcised.*

The idea of *what one sacrifices* or *doing without*
[*living modestly* or *being modest*]

> Concept of *being* [or rather the *preparation of*] humble
> *(before God, God's Creation, or the Forces of God/Creation/Nature)*

4 - Meaning Construct

> Concept of *"Being Wise"*

The idea of *gaining* from *one's suffering*, and *moving forward.*
{as *[something]* that will *bring inspiration*}

> Kabbalah "12 Paths" = *Menashe* is labeled as: *"The Reconnection."*

Joseph's 2nd Son

Ephraim, אפרים (APRYM) <H669>

Mind of God + Spoken + Mind of Man + Effort + Life/Truth

1 - Linear Construct (AP+RY+M)

* אף (AP) <H637> as: *indeed, yea, also, even* | *furthermore, also*
(denoting *addition*, especially: *of something greater*)

Note: Linked to a meaning of *Accession,* defined as: *the attainment* or
acquisition of a position of rank or *power*, typically that of *monarch* or
president. In addition, connected to the idea of doing so *adversatively*
— *expressing opposition* or *antithesis.*

The idea of *being put into power without the desire to have it* or
without seeking it [positive version] -versus *taking power
when others didn't want them to have it* [negative version].

* אף (AP) <H638-9> as: *the nose, nostril, "anger," the face*

+ * רי (RY) <H7377> as: *moisture/irrigation, shower*
Symbolically, as a *"runny nose [from crying/anger]"* | *"tears of angry/frustration."*

+ (M) *The "Water" Glyph = Life/Truth*

Another *Linear Construct* (A+PR+YM)

* **א** (A) *Mind of God*

(P) *Mouth/Speak* + (R) *Mind of Man* = *"Speaking your Mind"*

+ * **פר** (PR) <H6499> as: *you bull, a bullock*

+ * **מי** (YM) as plural ending = *the bulls* or *young bulls*

Symbolically, the visual image of the *bull's nostrils and snorting.*

The idea of *when people are at the point
of getting angry with a situation.*

Concept of *"Enough is Enough"*

2 - *Dimensional Construct* (AM →PRY)

* **אמ** (AM) <H517> translated as: *"Mother"*

→ * **פרי** (PRY) <H6529> translated as: *fruit, produce | offspring*

The idea of that which *gives birth* the *fruit* [as the *"sweet"
nourishment of mankind*) or *taste sweet(sugary)* – a sensory effect.

Symbolically, as Adam's wife [Eve] *eating the fruit*
(MPRY) from the *Tree of Knowledge of good and evil.*
— used in Genesis 3:2

Other variants or words built from (PR/PRY):

** **יפריא** (YPRYA) <H6500> as: *is fruitful*

** **פרה** (PRH) <H6509> as: *be fruitful* [having success in/on the land]
— used in Genesis 1:22 actually **פרו** (PRV)
— used in Genesis 41:52 For God *hath caused me to be fruitful* (HPRYM)
in the land of my affliction.

The idea of the (Y) *Efforts* to *gain* from (PR) = *"ill-gotten gains"*
versus (PRV) *holding back* from *"ill-gotten gains."*

3 - *Reflective Construct* (MYRPA)

* **מי** (MY) <H4310> translated as: *Who?*   *Life/Truth + Effort*
Note: as in the *"Moment to/by moment"*
The idea of *life's efforts* [as to do *"something"*].

+ * **רפא** (RPA) <H7495> as: *to mend, to cure*
The idea of *making the effort to mend* [wounds of life].

4 - Meaning Construct

Concept of *"Frustration [Bitterness]"*

Symbolically, like: *"many young bulls snorting."*
[as when people are *annoyed, aggravated, frustrated, etc...*]

The idea is <u>not</u> *the best way to make things better,* but
unfortunately, being *"triggered"* will lead to a *cause for change.*

Negative version → *reaction to suffering*
* (APRYM) process (as a path) to *anger → vengeance*

versus

Positive version → *response to suffering*
* (ALHYM) process (as a path) to *wisdom → enlightenment*

Kabbalah "12 Paths" = *Ephraim* is labeled as: *"The Transformation."*

Blessings [from Israel]:
Genesis 48:13
English translation (King James Version)

13 And Joseph took them both, Ephraim in his right hand (BYMYNV)
towards Israel's left hand, and Manasseh in his left hand toward Israel's
right hand (MYMYN), and brought them near unto him.

14 And Israel stretched out his right hand (YMYNV), and laid it upon
Ephraim's head, who was the younger, and his left hand upon Manasseh's
head, guiding[crossed] his hands wittingly; for Manasseh was the firstborn.

Note: Joseph tried to guide his father's choice of blessing as...

{The blessing of Israel's right hand was greater than the left hand.}

The Right-hand Blessing [of *Power/Strength/Greatness*], and is
normally considered the *"Birthright of the Firstborn."*

---

17 When Joseph saw that his father laid his right hand on Ephraim's head, it
displeased him; and he grasped his father's hand to remove it from Ephraim's
head to Manasseh's head.

18 Joseph said to his father, "Not so, my father, for this one is the firstborn.
Place your right hand on his head."

19 But his father refused and said, "I know, my son, I know; he also will
become a people and he also will be great. However, his younger brother shall
be greater than he, and his descendants shall become a multitude of nations."

The Symbolism of the Right and Left Hands

Traditionally, the *right hand*, in particular, is frequently associated with *power*, *blessing*, and *honor*, while the *left hand* can symbolize *secondary status* or, in some contexts, *judgment* and *misfortune*.

Judgment for those on the *left* of Christ, *salvation* is on his *right*.

Matthew 25:33, 41, "and He will put the sheep on His right, and the goats on the left. 41 Then He will also say to those on His left, 'Depart from Me, accursed ones, into the eternal fire which has been prepared for the devil and his angels."

Ecclesiastes 10:2, "A *wise* man's heart directs him toward the *right*, but the *foolish [stupid]* man's heart directs him toward the *left*."

Joseph wanted Israel's right hand on *Manasseh* → "Wise people" or [*wisdom* within people]

and Israel's left hand | *Ephraim* → "Frustrated people" or [*bitterness* within people]

...but the *blessing* was reversed giving the power to the *frustration(bitterness)* rather than *wisdom*. → this infers that people's go-to is to default to *frustration(bitterness)* rather than *wisdom*.

...because Joseph learned to value his *suffering* and *elevate wisdom* over *frustration(bitterness)*.

Note: There is also an interesting connection to this two brother concept, which is in the book of Exodus [*Moses* and *Aharon/Aaron*].

Moses (MShH) connection to *Manasseh* (MNShH) <as a *Positive* reaction to *Suffering*> is (MShH →N) or the (N) "*Seed*"(as "*Potential*," rather than "*Offspring/Child*") *within* (MShH) "*Moses*."

Aharon/Aaron (AHRVN) <H175> actually (AHRN) in Exodus | the elder brother of *Moses* [and was a *high priest*]. His connection to the making of the *golden calf [idolatry]*, and the *iniquity of Ephraim* [in the book of Hosea], which is linked to *idolatry* and *apostasy*.

> **Note:** This section covers concept(s) of "Name(s)," and began with *"HaShem"* (HShM), so it seems appropriate to end it with the *reflected* version of it = (MShH).

Moses, משׁה (MShH) <H4872>

Life/Truth + Aspect of Creation <brings forth> → Revealing/Revelation

1 - Linear Construct (MShH)

* משׁה (MShH) <H4872 > as a Name: *Moses* — used in Exodus 2:10

* משׁ (MSh) <H4851> meaning: *"drawn out"*

The idea of *"What we can draw from"*
["*making conclusions from* or *connections to*"]

as the "*what*" we can get out of *Revelation*
[or that which is *Revealed*].

Another *Linear Construct* (M+ShH)

* (M) *Life/Truth*

+ * (ShH) <H7716> as: *"the member of the flock, sheep, goat, lamb*

The idea of *the true nature of life* and our role in
it [is a *member of the flock* grazing in *creation*].

> Concept of *"Living Life"*
> {as Life's role to continue the Creation process}

2 - Dimensional Construct (MH→Sh)

* מה (MH) <H4100> as: *"what?"* [of *what kind?*]

The idea of *what will life/truth reveal?*

> Concept of [one's own] *Perception*

+ * (Sh) *Aspect of Creation*

The idea of *"What something or someone is,"*
as part of the *birth of Creation"* or *"What is,"* as *"what's meant to be."*

3 - *Reflective Construct* (HShM)

* השם (HShM) <*H2044*> translated as: *"the Name."*   <see page 130>

> **Note:** The reflected relationship is The *"Give* and *Take"* (ShM–MSh).
>
> {The *What* is *"Given/Taken"* in relation to *What we can Draw from* its *Revelation/Revealing* (H) as going from *understanding* to *wisdom.*}

4 - *Meaning Construct*

> Concept of *"What we can get out of living our life,"*
> as: *"Life experiences"* will define *who we are to be,*
> but also as the concept of *"eventually knowing."*

The idea of *when* there is a *benefit,* and when it's *no longer the case* [the *time to move on,* and as the *hardship* and *difficulties* of change].

Furthermore, the idea of the *old ways* evolving from what once was working to something that is no longer, and the effort to make new [*new ways*], but by re-analyzing and returning to what was older.

> The concept of *re-birth/born again*
> as, "The *same,* but *different.*"

> Of course, then there's the relationship between these letters and the word *Messiah* and the Jewish word: *Mashiach/Moshiach.*

Messiah, משיה (MShYH)   *Note: not a biblical Hebrew word!?*

Life/Truth + God/Creation Aspect + Effort + Reveal

Symbolically, the representation of adding *Effort* within *Moses,* as well as the *Effort* to <*bring forth*> the *Revealing/Revelation.*

Linear Construct (MShY+H)

* משי (MShY) <*H4897*> as: *silk (costly material for garments)* | perhaps *silk (*also: as *drawn from a cocoon)*

— used twice in Ezekiel 16:10, 16:13

<Note: The *"nature's thread"* used to *weave a fabric,* like the symbolic *"fabric of the universe"* or the idea of *reflecting it.*>

+ * (H) *Revealing/Revelation*

The idea of *"what comes from...the "Silk,* and *leading to Revealing/Revelation.*

> Concept of *"The Silky Revelation"*

Mashiach, מש״יח (MShYCh) <*H4899*> as: *"anointed"*
— used in Leviticus, Samuel, Chronicles, and Psalm 2:2

Linear Construct (MShY+Ch)

The idea of *"what comes from...the "Silk,* and *leading to branching/generations(diversity).*

> Concepts of *"The Silky Generations,"*
> *"The Silky Branches,"* or *"The Silky Diversity."*

Reflective Construct (Ch+ShM)

* חשׁמ (ChShM) <*H2828*> as: *wealthy, rich*
— variant (ChShML) as: *[something]* like *"glowing metal" [polished spectrum metal],* of *Amber [Bronze],* and *Electrum [natural alleys of gold and silver].*

Other variants or words built from (ChShM):
** חשׁמנ (ChShMN) <*H2831*> as: *Envoys, Princes [Noble, nobleman]*
— which is connected to the idea of *wealthy, rich.*

Meaning

There seems to be an inference of *multiple "messiah-types,"* as a notion of a *diversity* of them [or just *many attributes* associated with the *idea* of one].

As a way to go *back to the beginning* and reference the symbolism of the *Seeds [plant-life]* and concepts like the *Tree of Life,* it would seem fitting to compare this concept to the *"buds"* on a tree/plant. A *bud* is a *crucial part* of a *tree's growth cycle.* There are different types: *lateral buds widens* or *branches* out the tree, whereas the **terminal bud** halts the *widening/branching,* and *extends* the *elongation of the stem* and also *promotes* the *production* of **new** *leaves* and *flowers* [which become *"fruit"*] → a relevant comparison to the *"End of Days" Messiah/Mashiach,* as: **elevating** the *growth of humanity* [the stem] and **new** *inspirations* and *outcomes* [*leaves* and *flowers/fruit*].

www.ingramcontent.com/pod-product-compliance
Lightning Source LLC
Chambersburg PA
CBHW060242100426
42742CB00011B/1617